CW00552829

Marriage
— and —
Property
— Women and —
Marital Customs
— in History —

edited by
Elizabeth Craik

ABERDEEN UNIVERSITY PRESS

First published 1984
This edition published 1991
Aberdeen University Press

© Editor and Contributors 1984

British Library Cataloguing in Publication Data
Marriage and property
  1. Community property—History
  2. Separate property—History
  3. Sociological jurisprudence
  I. Craik, Elizabeth M.
  342.64   K690

ISBN 0-08-041205-X

PRINTED IN GREAT BRITAIN
THE UNIVERSITY PRESS
ABERDEEN

Foreword

J. Steven Watson

*Principal and Vice-Chancellor
University of St. Andrews*

Historians, at least those whose main interest is in the eighteenth century, can still be usefully advised when in difficulty, doubt, or even downright despair, to 'go and see what you can find in Pargellis and Medley'. I had better explain (because I do not know whether Mrs. Craik and the publisher are going to allow one in this text to skate on over discreet footnotes) that I am talking about the bibliography which the Oxford Press produced for the Historical Associations some thirty years ago and which has not really been replaced since then. Consultation of Pargellis and Medley reveals, I must confess, that they cater for political historians or at most for those social historians who flourished before the school of Paris encouraged 'total recall' in the pages of Annales.

Under social history, I find my own well-thumbed copy of the bibliography has a promising heading, 'Domestic Life'. Alas, that is no pathway to matrimonial issues: the sub-heads are such things as 'Cookery', 'Tea', 'Tobacco', 'Servants'. Closely following Domestic Life comes a section on sports and amusements (Angling, Falconry and so to Cricket and Football) that, in mounting despair, I found myself exploring. In this whole social survey the nearest I could come to the subject which I had heard Mrs. Craik's learned friends discussing in seminar, was a mention of Burns' study of parsons and marriage keepers operating from the Fleet Prison along with Martin Maddon's 'Thelyphthora—a treatise on female ruin . . . considered on the basis of divine law'.

It was a long way from *Marriage and Property*. As I rapidly turned pages, it was with a new inspiration. It was perhaps in the entries on legal history that I would find what I was looking for in this field. But there was no entry on matrimonial causes and even under Wills only a general list of laws relating to testaments and last wills. This was disappointing. I thought of the speculative lists Lord Glenbervice made in George III's reign about who really begat who. Why no entry under 'Illegitimacy, its effects upon the aristocracy'? Even the general index failed to suggest sources.

The results of this little exploration I offer to other readers as proof of the importance and courage of the present enterprise. 'Les livres', said Molière, 'cadrent mal avec le marriage.' It seems to me that books hardly touch it historically. But—you will say—he meant no more than that the married state was bad for reading in bed (notably untrue) and that his comment was as superficial as Mr. Shandy's summing up Uncle Toby's fate—'He will never lie diagonally in his bed again as long as he lives.' In the past Marriage has been too often considered cynically or tragically or in terms of psychology but rarely until the last few years in terms of historical patterns.

Marriage, however, is the area where the deepest feelings of men and women, their most intimate, private, and self-distinguishing feelings come into contact with the needs of society and with the future of the community. It is the point of intersection of the poetry of young people and the power struggles of classes, of physical satisfaction and political strategy, of property management and personal status.

Any study of a subject so central to our historical development must be extremely difficult to conduct. We can no longer be satisfied, like Rousseau and the Encyclopaedists, to start from imaginary states of nature or preconceived ideas of the origins of the family, or of its operation. The difficulties have become apparent in the controversies which have accompanied the stimulating work of Professor Lawrence Stone. The evidence is at once voluminous enough for a computer but scattered and various so as to require fine judgement in its pursuit. Mrs. Craik and her eight companions have been trained in different ways of thought. They look at different epochs. Yet certain themes recur. It seems to me that the reader cannot but become wiser as he compares these essays one with another and makes his own generalisations about the way in which our institutions have been affected by contracts which are the basis of the family and of so much more.

Contents

Preface

This book originates from a series of extra-mural lectures on the general theme of *Women through the Ages*, conducted under the auspices of the Adult Education Department of the University of St. Andrews. Several contributors to the series have developed their lectures into chapters for the book, with its more sharply focused theme, and other authors have been recruited to give it a more complete chronological spread. Our thanks are due to all who participated in the original series; also to those who attended our *Marriage* seminar in St. John's House when the book was in embryonic form.

At all stages of the book's production, it has been a genuine pleasure to deal with Aberdeen University Press. To them, especially to Mr. Colin MacLean and Miss Marjorie Leith, go our warmest thanks.

I

Introduction

Elizabeth M. Craik

Department of Greek, University of St. Andrews

Marriage as a social institution regulates the sexual relationships of individual men and women, and imposes on these a superficially uniform pattern. It has an intimate private importance to the individuals who contract it, as well as being of public concern to the state. The history of marriage is the history of society itself. While the institution is of little interest to political or military historians (who will merely offer *en passant* footnotes on sexual proclivities or marital status), it is of fundamental importance in sociological, economic and legal studies—fields where specialisation is of more recent origin. Marriage, with the family, has been claimed also as an aspect of that still more recent and rather struggling field, 'women's history'.[1] But as marriage of its very essence involves men and women, together, in a human situation, the history of marriage can scarcely be regarded as the prerogative of one sex. (Of course, men could write 'women's history' or—to use a less emotive phrase—study women in society, but few choose to do so. Perhaps this is a pity: it is as if ecclesiastical history were abandoned to Churchmen—Churchpeople?—or, indeed, the history of men's activities to men.)

Like all social institutions, marriage has a levelling effect: but—unlike many—it does not suppress individuality. In every society, there are marriages exceptional by the current standards and it can be misleading, though it is often tempting, to focus on those. And from one society to another there are vast differences in the degree of influence or interference exercised on marital conduct by the authorities of state or of Church; and in the extent to which personal inclinations are circumscribed by social pressures. In a particular marriage, as well as within a particular society, different aspects may be of greater or lesser importance at different times: sexual and emotional, economic and contractual, familial and parental, religious or ideological. To establish the norm, it is necessary to look at the normal, and ask some simple questions (which do not always have simple answers).

Who marries—i.e. what proportion of the population, male and female? When do people marry—i.e. at what stage in their other activities? Why do people marry—e.g. for economic reasons, to continue the family, for support and companionship, for love or romantic attachment? Whom do people marry—i.e. to what extent is choice limited by blood relationships, parental arrangement etc.? How do people marry—with civil ceremony, religious rites or simply by consent? On what grounds, if at all, can marriage be dissolved? Do marriages last—i.e., what is the incidence of divorce, separation and desertion? What is the attitude to widowhood? To remarriage? To homosexuality? To prostitution? How many children do couples have, and at what point in the marriage are they born? What is known of premarital sex and marital infidelity?

The secondary theme of property runs through all the chapters of this book. Dowry and bride-price are its most obvious expression: the main questions relate to the property brought into the marriage at its inception. However, testamentary provisions and prohibitions are important also, as is the question of work and wages. Legal concern with marriage relates primarily to the disposal of property. The more 'patriarchal' the society, the more important such questions become.

This book is concerned with the history of monogamy, 'the only true type of marriage'.[2] In practice, polygamous marriage, polygyny more commonly than polyandry, has of course existed; and indeed continues sporadically to exist. In theory, on the evolutionary view of such pioneer anthropologists as Morgan, the primeval practice was group-marriage based on the sharing of partners and children within a group, and allied with original ignorance of the facts of paternity; later, this gave way to a matriarchal, or at least matrilocal, monogamous system and ultimately to a patriarchal one. Bronislaw Malinowski originally embraced, but later rejected, the evolutionary view.[3]

Current ideas on marriage are influenced more or less directly by the iconoclastic work of Marx on property (relevant to marriage in society) and of Freud on sex (relevant to the individual marriage). Engels' work on the family borrowed heavily from Darwinian evolutionary theory and from the anthropological researches of Morgan: it differed radically in suggesting that a primitive *modus vivendi* might be better than a developed one. The idea that society was once arranged differently, and therefore might be arranged differently again, has had a great appeal for many feminists. An alternative society, in which the unity of the family would be fragmented, and 'oppression of women' come to an end is fondly envisaged. But doctrinaire Marxism tends to over-simplify and over-schematise the hypothetical future, as much as the past and the present. One is left with a much clearer picture of what will not be the case in this brave new world than with any positive aspects. In particular, the place of children and their relationship with adults (a matter of concern to most people, including many feminists) is left vague.

On another level, much of the more popular writing about the 'oppression of women' is middle-class in origin.[4] In attaching so much importance to 'work'—paid employment outside the home—as an emancipating benefit, many middle-class women lose sight of the fact that their lives are relatively comfortable, and that most working-class women, like many working-class men, would, with good reason, prefer not to have to work at all. It is easy, but simplistic, to regard wives, debarred by convention from all means of production, as 'oppressed' or 'exploited' in a Marxist sense. Within any society different men have different attitudes— e.g. grudging or generous—to 'keeping' women; and different women have different attitudes—e.g. grateful or grasping—to being 'kept'. There is not necessarily resentment on either side, though there may be resentment on one or other or both.

The importance of property in marital relationships was perceived by John Stuart Mill, far ahead of his time in his championship of equality for women, not only in educational, economic and political opportunities, but also within marriage. Mill's belief was that potential earning power, secured by education, would be enough to satisfy women, and that most wives would, in fact, continue to choose the traditional sphere of household superintendence and upbringing of children, and would not actually support themselves. Victorian romanticism is not after all far away: 'The great occupation of woman should be to beautify life . . . to diffuse beauty elegance, and grace everywhere' and sex is dismissed as an 'animal function'.[5]

Freud's exploration of human sexuality engendered a furore of incredulous criticism, as well as much emulative adulation. While empirical psychoanalysis has tended to follow Freud's lead, relegating women to a subordinate, dependent and above all passive role, psychological study of sex-roles or gender, in terms of historical and cultural evolution and of social expectations, has done much to revolutionise twentieth-century marriage. Subsequent studies of sexual response and of sexual behaviour are stimulated by Freud's monumental example.[6] Even if Freud was mistaken in many of his assertions—as, for instance, on the nature of woman's orgasm and sexual satisfaction (a matter peripheral to his main theories, but one which has aroused particularly violent reactions), his views undoubtedly led to more realism in attitudes to women and to marriage. Change has come, though more slowly than might have been expected.[7]

In writing about marriage—in historical terms as well as on the philosophical plane—one is affected indirectly but inevitably by one's own experience of it in the lives of others, particularly parents and immediate family, and of oneself. It is not easy to view the topic dispassionately and objectively, without importing any personal attitudes and without reflecting or reacting against current views. Deep-seated, often irrational, preconceptions and prejudices can engender irrelevant or anachronistic value-judgements. Perhaps this is why some scholars are attracted to 'modelling' theories, following an illusorily safe and seemingly objective structuralist approach. This book, however, is concerned with particular societies, not with theories about society. The evidence is left to speak for itself. The book aims to fill a gap: for, although there is a constant proliferation of works on the psychology, physiology and sociology of marriage and of manuals instructing in its techniques or purporting to predict its future as an institution, there is a shortage of serious works on the history of marriage, and especially of writing which is academic rather than activist. Throughout, we concentrate on marriage, a recognisable concept, rather than on 'the position of women', a vague idea embodied in a vague and rather tendentious phrase.

The studies here presented are based primarily on the evidence of life, not of literature: on records, testaments and letters, not on poems, plays and novels. Certain non-fictional literary genres—biography, essays, speeches—provide useful adjuncts to the more austere and bald documentary evidence; but the common presence of polemic or apologetic as a conscious aim, in addition to the inevitable presence of some subconscious bias, makes caution imperative in the handling of this material. Fiction is even more complex as a historical source: the timeless ideals of fantasy and wish fulfilment are fused with the reality of contemporary experience in such a way that the two can rarely be disentangled. Sometimes a writer seems to transcend his own age and to anticipate intuitively the ideas of a later era. It is, however, always dangerous to stress the presence of any elements of which an author cannot have had a developed conscious awareness.[8]

Literary criticism has been used extensively and effectively in the analysis of heterosexual relationships by feminist writers, notably Simone de Beavoir, first in the new wave, and Kate Millett, perhaps most influential.[9] For the sociologist or the psychologist, this is a legitimate technique. For the historian, the task of relating the subjective world of literature to the objectively attested material is more complex and challenging. One important point—which should be stressed—is that until very recently European literature has been almost entirely the work of men. The evidence for women's viewpoint on marriage, that perennial literary theme, is sadly deficient over the centuries.

The evidence available varies from one era to another, and the specialist interests of the contributors are not completely uniform. Two are primarily legal in approach, three take account of literary sources and the others are 'straight' historians. Each contributor is a specialist in the period discussed; each contribution is based on original research, combining a review of the evidence available, a synthesis (with brief bibliography) of current scholarship and an independent analysis of some documentary material. In the 2500 years separating Ancient Greece (Chapter II) from nineteenth-century Britain and America (Chapters IX and X), much happened in terms of invasions, revolutions, wars, dynasties—historical 'events'. By contrast, the domestic and social scene seems, at first sight, static. The transition in Eastern Europe from Hellenism to Roman rule, the advent of the new world religion Christianity, the long interaction between Church and State, demographic change in mediaeval Europe, the French revolution and subsequent democratic movements: the impact of all these, and much else, on marital customs is described and discussed in the following pages.

NOTES

1. Carl N. Degler, 'Is there a History of Women?' Inaugural lecture, Oxford 1974 (O.U.P. 1975). Sheila Ryan Johansson, ' "Herstory" as History: a New Field or Another Fad?' in Berenice A. Carroll (ed.), *Liberating Women's History* (Chicago and London 1976), pp. 400–30.

2. So *Encyclopaedia Britannica*, 1929 edn and repr.

3. Lewis H. Morgan, *Ancient Society* (New York 1877). Bronislaw Malinowski, *The Sexual Life of Savages*, 3rd edn (London 1932), 'special foreword', pp. xxii–xxiii.

4. Betty Friedan, *The Feminine Mystique* (New York 1963).

5. Alice S. Rossi (ed.), John Stuart Mill and Harriet Taylor Mill, *Essays on Sex Equality* (Chicago 1970), pp. 104, 160. See also John Stuart Mill, 'The Subjection of Women' (London 1869), repr. in *Three Essays by J. S. Mill*, World's Classics Series (London 1966).

6. Marie Stopes, *Married Love* (London 1918). Alfred C. Kinsey, Wardell B. Pomeroy and Clyde E. Martin, *Sexual Behaviour in the Human Male* (Philadelphia and London 1953)—and P. H. Gebhard, *Sexual Behaviour in the Human Female* (Philadelphia and London 1953).

7. See Bertrand Russell, *Marriage and Morals* (first publ. London 1929) for expectations still only very partially fulfilled.

8. Robert Seidenberg, *Marriage in Life and Literature* (N.Y. 1970)—the work of a practising psychiatrist and psychoanalyst—contains many insights into contemporary fiction, but becomes unacceptably speculative in finding, p. 81, 'oedipal struggle', complete with 'phallic oedipal mother' in Sophocles' *Ajax*.

9. Simone de Beauvoir, *The Second Sex* (trans. and ed. H. M. Parshley) (N.Y. 1953), pp. 199–252. Kate Millett, *Sexual Politics* (N.Y. 1970), pp. 237–363.

Marriage in Ancient Greece

Elizabeth M. Craik

Department of Greek, University of St. Andrews

Review of secondary literature

In this field, scholarship reflects society. Writers attempt to 'come unbiassed to the task' (Donaldson 1907, pp. 2–3), but all are inexorably 'the victims of their own times and social backgrounds' (Pomeroy 1975, p. 59). When Victorian and Edwardian gentlemen, whose own wives, mothers and daughters led sheltered and dependent lives, were prompted by debate on the 'woman question' to examine ancient society, they remarked on differences not always easy for today's reader to perceive between their England and Ancient Greece: '. . . we are struck . . . by a divergence from the modern point of view . . . eminently prosaic way of conceiving the marriage relation . . . the position of the wife in ancient Greece was simply that of the domestic drudge . . .' (Lowes Dickinson 1896, pp. 172, 173, 177. The same writer omits 'homosexuality' from his index and deals with this topic under the coy heading of 'friendship', pp. 184–201; with this may be contrasted the robust modern treatment of Dover 1978, where—and this is not a metaphor—no holds are barred.)

It was 'romance' that Lowes Dickinson missed in Greek marriage (p. 175). In the more realistic social climate after the first world war, it was argued in an influential article that Athenian society was not, after all, so very different from modern European society: that women were neither secluded nor despised (Gomme 1925). This carries little conviction now; one critic has dismissed Gomme's position as 'a simplistic fantasy' (Gould 1980, p. 42). A contemporary of Gomme argued similarly, on the evidence of inscriptions, that there was 'much to render the lot of Athenian women comparatively happy and *normal*' and that 'there must have been women who inherited the qualities of their *fathers*' (McClees 1920, pp. 2, 3; the words in [my] italics are revealing). Later, it was widely urged that, while women were indeed secluded in antiquity, this was a good and positive state, for their safeguard and protection (Kitto 1951, ch. 12; Seltman 1957, p. 94; Lacey 1968, *passim*).

Writers of the present time tend to be polemical if female, apologetic if male. Historians writing generally often prefer—circumspect or craven—to skirt the topic. Contributors to the Fontana History of the Ancient World are typical: J. K. Davies in *Democracy and Classical Greece* (London 1980), despite a chapter on 'Athenian society in the fifth century' and F. W.

Walbank in *The Hellenistic World* (1981), despite a chapter on 'Social and economic trends', find no space for marriage, or women; Oswyn Murray in *Early Greece* (1980) gives them only a few pages.

Since the rise of the feminist movement, one general study of women in antiquity has appeared (Pomeroy 1975). Some attempt to correlate different types of evidence, combined with an awareness of the difficulties inherent in this, is found there and elsewhere (Gould 1980); but the tendency is to more specialised studies. Many articles have appeared on individual authors, particular works or special topics (*see* e.g. *Arethusa* 6 (1973) and 11 (1978)). Certain regions of unusual interest have been studied in depth—notably Sparta, long conventionally regarded as different from Athens (Cartledge 1981) and Crete, another Dorian state where detail of social organisation is documented in the Law Code of Gortyn (Willetts 1967). The economic and legal position of married women has been much clarified by work on the law of Athens (Harrison 1968; MacDowell 1978) and, more specifically, by investigation of women's property rights (de Ste Croix 1970; Karnezis 1972; Schaps 1979). The nature of family relationships has been explored (Lacey 1968, 1980), as has the practice of contracting marriage within the family, and the permitted degrees of kinship (Thompson 1967, 1972). Conventional Greek attitudes to women (Dover 1974; den Boer 1979) and to sexual relationships (Dover 1973, 1978) have been probed.

Some attempt has been made by writers with anthropological or sociological interests to bridge disciplines and bring structuralist methods to bear on the classics. (In this Vernant, especially 1974 trans. 1980, has been influential; *see Arethusa* 15 (1982), American Classical Studies in honor of Jean-Pierre Vernant. Humphreys 1978 provides a useful summary and valuable critique.) Similarly, imaginative attempts have been made to approach Greek authors and analyse Greek attitudes in terms of modern psychoanalytical ideas. (*See Arethusa* 7 (1974); Devereux 1976; Simon 1978.) Such bridge methods are potentially illuminating, but demand of their practitioners great restraint and sensitivity; unfortunately the common absence of these qualities has rather detracted from their utility.

Review of primary sources

There is little documentary evidence for Greek social history. Epigraphical records, inscribed on stone, are sketchy, late, formulaic and fragmentary; further, those which have survived the ravages of time and the elements are not necessarily representative in content. Such material is unamenable to methods demanding firm data or statistics. Epitaphs do, however, provide some information about family relationships—evidently often affectionate (Lattimore 1943). Vase-paintings and sculpture (though here it is rarely possible to identify figures conclusively as marriage partners) give the same impression of domestic harmony. Source material from wills, biographies and letters is relatively scanty and unhelpful. Biographies of prominent people were written in the Hellenistic era, but little credence can be placed in them: they were short sketches with bald statements of 'fact' padded out by colourful anecdotal matter. Typically, they contain statements about the subjects' parentage and marriage, allegations or innuendoes about their sexual proclivities; but very little of wider relevance. Those letters which have survived from the classical period are for the most part specimens written as rhetorical exercises for imaginary situations; later, Plutarch's correspondence comes in a self-conscious form, worked up for publication. Some wills have survived, but in many cases authenticity is suspect.

The literary evidence is copious and complex. One problem—often rehearsed yet easily forgotten—is that it is 'male-dominated'. Men tell men what real or imaginary women did or said (very rarely what they felt or thought), or what they should do or say. Without supposing that there was a corporate feminine point of view—for surely there was not, any more than there is today—one must wish for an occasional female voice (and a strongly heterosexual one would be particularly welcome). The evidence is also, at least for the classical era, Athens-dominated and pervaded by a degree of chauvinism which inhibits our perception of the practices not only of foreigners at home, but even of foreigners in Athens. Much of Greek literature has a public, even civic, character, being written for a state occasion, or commissioned by powerful and wealthy public figures. Further, the writers are the relatively leisured, rich and educated members of an Athenian urban élite in a peasant Attic society; and they are middle-aged—or, rather, surviving works tend to come from mature or late work. There is inevitably a degree of bias in this material.

Certain difficulties arise from the nature of the subject. Marriage, with the relationship between the sexes, is a question of universal and perennial interest: many views expressed by Greeks are human, or masculine, in tenor rather than specifically Greek. A stereotyped perception of the tensions and divisions potentially arising in the marital relationship will be seen to characterise Greek myth, and to colour various literary genres—most obviously drama. In comedy, relationships are simplified; in tragedy, the paradigmatic lies beyond the specific.

There are difficulties too in using literature as a historical source. With all creative literature, it is hard to define the boundaries between the world presented and the world experienced by the writer. This problem is intensified when the subject is distant in time and place from the writer's environment, as in the case of Greek epic and tragedy. The writer may be depicting conditions of his own society (deliberately, or in unconscious anachronism); he may be depicting another society (faithfully, or without achieving verisimilitude); he may simply be inventing his material; or finally, and perhaps most probably, he may be combining all three approaches, in an amalgam of realism, history and fantasy. Prose fiction of a type resembling the modern novel was a new creation in late antiquity.

Can we look to non-fiction for help? Aristotle's generalisation, 'Creative writing (*poiesis*), then, is more philosophical and more worthwhile than history (*historia*); for it tells of the general, while history tells of the particular' (Arist. *Po.* 1451b5–7) offers some hope; but—as will be seen—*historia*, especially the history of Herodotos, is open to the same objections as *poiesis*. Fourth-century forensic oratory is to some extent exempt from these limitations. The speeches cannot be regarded as transcripts of court proceedings, as they have been written up—and, probably, in some cases, extensively changed—for publication, with the aim of boosting the speech-writer's reputation. Nor are they necessarily, or even probably, an accurate record of events leading up to the case: allowance must be made for mendacity, selectivity and skewing of emphasis on the part of a litigant aiming to persuade a large all-male jury. But here at least we are in the real world. It is recognisably the same world as that of tragedy; both are concerned with relationships, especially family relationships, in conditions of stress and breakdown, with all its consequent bitterness, resentment and misery. In the articulation of this, the same terminological patterns are used to express recurrent attitudes and expectations.

It is not always easy to reconcile the real world of the orators with the imaginary world of the poets, or the ideal world of the philosophers; but if we do not try to do so our picture must be partial and may be distorted. Similarly, to understand fifth- and fourth-century Athens, it is necessary to range further afield—to Homer, a powerful influence in formal and informal education, and to the following centuries, influenced in their turn by classical Athens. Within genres, as well as between them, there are often unrealised conflicts, and theory does not necessarily square with practice. Thus, medical theory was hostile to women, but medical practice was humanitarian. And philosophers, writing as individuals with different personal experience, offer different slants on their own society: while Plato's social Utopia is an imaginative reshaping of the contemporary Cretan blueprint, Aristotle's consists rather of an intellectualisation and schematisation of popular views of the day. The treatises on household management by Aristotle the contemplative researcher and by Xenophon the military man turned country squire have many points of contact.

In the past, certain types of evidence have been over-exploited, to the neglect of others; and a few sayings, notably passages of Thucydides, Xenophon and Demosthenes, discussed later in this chapter, have acquired an exaggerated notoriety which has to be combated (Th.2.45, [D.]59.122, X.*Oec.*3). 'Quotable quotes' make good anthologies, but bad history; isolated sentences are not necessarily an accurate reflection of an author's point of view, far less of the corporate point of view of the society to which he belongs. This caveat may seem obvious, but it is often forgotten by critics who would not dream of dissecting modern society with such a blunt instrument. The dangers of the method will be readily evident to anyone who cares to dip into Stobaios' moral manual of maxims on miscellaneous subjects. Stobaios compiling an anthology in the fifth century A.D. quotes from works which have survived in entirety and from works now lost, and cases of the former where the excerpt is misleading or atypical in tenor ought to warn against the use of the latter—or any—aphorisms wrested from context. Stobaios' selection of views on marriage conveys the—not very surprising—information that marriage is, and marriages are, sometimes good but sometimes bad. Perusal of Athenaios *Deipnosophistai* 13, a miscellany of citations assembled around A.D. 200 on the same subject, with a wealth of detail on names and activities of *hetairai*, leaves a similar impression.

It is the modest aim of the following discussion to integrate the various types of evidence, and to present Greek views throughout in their immediate Greek context and against their wider Greek background. A discussion of the terminology used of marriage and the family, with particular reference to one play of Euripides, provides a specific illustration of these general views. The evidence for Greek society is such that the historian cannot afford to be insensitive to literary criticism or heedless of linguistic expression.

Discussion

Myth
Whatever theoretical view we choose to adopt on the nature of myth in general, the pragmatic Greek view—which has been much disregarded of late—is more helpful for understanding Greek myths, in the context of Greek society. The Greeks saw their myths as representing and reinterpreting early history—though often (they realised) in a blatantly invented or grossly distorted fashion—and as providing a pattern for creative literature and an influence in education (see Craik 1980, pp. 149–52).

In mythical representation of early history, which was characterised by constant warfare, women are commonly cast as links between warring men: objects of seduction or abduction, who can be persuaded or forced to abandon husband or father in favour of a newcomer offering a temporary or permanent sexual alliance: Jason and Medea, Theseus and Ariadne, Paris and Helen are perhaps the best-known of many examples.[1] In such myths, women are not just 'spoils of war', but often exercise a choice, and this is not merely whether or not to capitulate to male overtures: they take the initiative, voluntarily offering active assistance (of strategy, not force) to their new partners, in preference to furthering the local cause. Fears of the divided loyalties of women in marriage—to their own original family and to their husband's—are here evident, as are fears about alienation of affection.

It is not necessary to have recourse to anthropological modelling or psychological analysis to labour the point that in the formation of myth such deep-seated irrational fears and hopes find expression; and that these relate particularly to sex and the sexes. In many myths—Greek as other—men see women ambivalently as essential but dangerous companions, embodying simultaneously nurturing security and threatening, potentially subversive, sexuality (cf. Slater 1974; Segal 1978; Gould 1980). But this is not remarkable: it is the universal dual stereotype which finds expression in the human (especially male) imagination in literature and the visual arts, as well as in myth as such.[2] The ambivalence is encapsulated in the figure of Pandora, or of Kalypso. It appears in the Oidipous myth, which combines the irreconcilable, mother and wife, primal nurture and ultimate sex; and—with a similar fear of forbidden carnal relationships—in the story of Phaidra's passion for her stepson Hippolytos (a story which in its outcome resembles the Biblical tale of Joseph and Potiphar's wife). Marriages in myth are seldom happy, and in them can be seen writ large the paradigms of lesser human miseries.

Homer

The position of women in Homeric society has been described as entirely different from, and happier than, that which prevailed in classical times (by Gomme 1925, p. 1 and others). It is true that in the epics bride-price (paid by the husband to his wife's family) is in some cases found, rather than dowry (paid by the latter to the former); and this suggests a preferential status for the woman (or, perhaps, an imbalance of the sexes in the population); but the two systems apparently coexisted, and the legal picture is blurred. The poems purport to describe events of the distant past (of some four centuries before 'Homer') and they incorporate material accumulated over centuries of oral transmission as well as material relating to the era of the main composer. This cultural amalgam accounts for many discrepancies (Snodgrass 1974).

The conduct of marriage is variously depicted also. Alkinoos and Arete, rulers of the peaceful Phaiacians, rule on equal terms (*Od*.6); Hektor and Andromache, in war-torn Troy, though emotionally close, have distinct roles. Hektor dismisses Andromache's advice on defence: 'All these matters are my affair' (*Il*.6.441), also, 'Go into the house and see to your own tasks, loom and distaff, and tell the servants to go about their business. War will be the affair of all the men, and especially of me, the men who live in the city' (*Il*.6.490–3). The same formula for the separation of roles is used in Telemachos' snub to Penelope in Ithaca: 'Go into the house and see to your own tasks. . . . Speaking will be the affair of all the men and especially of me; for I have mastery in the house' (*Od*.1.356–9). Conversational ripostes are probably (as similes are recognised to be) late poetic invention in the compilation of epic material; but the formulaic format is early, and the attitudes, while foreshadowing the indoor–outdoor view of the sexes which prevailed in later Greek society, have a universally conventional flavour.

As in classical society, conditions of war and civil strife sharpened the divisions between the sexes. This accounts, in part, for the differences between the Phaiacians and other peoples. Some believe that the epics show a transition from matriarchal to patriarchal practices (bibliography, Pomeroy 1973, p. 573). They may, rather, show the intrusion of some Minoan practices—among the peace-loving Phaiacians—alongside a preponderance of Mycenaean ones and, as already noted, elements from dark age and archaic society.[3]

In the marriage of Odysseus and Penelope, a model of conjugal fidelity and felicity, both partners submit to certain restraints. Penelope can keep her suitors waiting so long as she gives hope to all, but commitment to none. Odysseus is permitted his liaisons with the powerful and supernatural Kirke and Kalypso, but must be circumspect with the young princess Nausikaa, stopping short (just) of proposition or proposal. Long after Homer, it remained conventional to praise the sterling qualities of Odysseus and Penelope: Aristotle contrasts the Odysseus–Nausikaa relationship with the Agamemnon–Chryseis one, to Agamemnon's detriment (Arist.*Oec*.3.3), while Plutarch finds Odysseus 'sensible' and Penelope 'restrained' by contrast with the 'pleasure-seeking' Paris and 'mercenary' Helen (Plu.*Mor*.140–1).

Hesiod and Semonides

From Homer's sprightly story-telling, the dour didacticism of Hesiod is a world apart in spirit and in location (from Ionia to mainland Boiotia), though not far removed in time. Quoted in isolation (as they often are), Hesiod's strictures on women and marriage seem to express a crude misogyny—and he has been treated as the influential originator of misogynistic traditions in the Western world (Arthur 1973). But in the context of his poems and against a background of a starkly impoverished rural society—the society of isolated communities struggling to emerge from the dark age—they convey a degree of pessimistic realism. Gone is the heroic aristocratic society which so valued prowess.

Hesiod glumly opines that while men work, women are parasitical on their labours—a variant on the indoor–outdoor theme. 'Women consort well with Plenty, but ill with Poverty' (*Th*.593); they are like drones in society's beehive (*Th*.594–602; cf. Sussman 1978). The male dilemma is trenchantly put: 'Refuse to marry and you'll have no one to inherit; get married and you'll have either bad and good fortune (if you have a good wife) or all bad (if you have a bad one)' (*Th*.603–12). Elsewhere, Hesoid relents somewhat: 'A man can get nothing better than a good wife, nothing worse than a bad one' (*Th*.703–4, the bad one is specified as a glutton).

Semonides, writing an inventory of female types in the latter half of the eighth century, echoes the content and at times the phraseology of Hesiod; of the good wife it is said, 'Possessions flourish and find increase in her hands; she grows old in affection for and from her husband, having borne a good and glorious family' (85, 87; see Lloyd-Jones 1975). Here, as in Hesiod, production of heirs is the immediate and preservation of property the ultimate purpose of marriage. And here too expression of misogyny must be seen in the context of genre (with humorous intent) and of the poem as a whole (there being, at least, one virtuous type). It may be added that the fourth-century writer Theophrastos is not generally regarded as a misanthrope because of his portrayal in *The Characters* of unpleasant male types.

Tragedy
Drama developed rapidly from rudimentary beginnings to a fully realised art form in Athens of the early classical period. Paradoxically, in a society where women were in political terms ciphers, in economic and legal terms seriously disadvantaged and in social terms subject to many restraints, drama presents strong heroines. The paradox is partly, though not entirely, accountable to conventions of the genre. Tragedy must be understood on two levels, not readily separable: the plane of the heroic age, where characters and action are set, and the plane of fifth-century Athens, where and for which the works were performed. The marriages of Aischylos show more of the former, but, with an innovatory realism which was to shape the development of drama in the following century (and, indeed, the ensuing dramatic traditions of western Europe) Euripides often highlights the latter.

It is hard to imagine that any women watching the Oresteia in 458 B.C. (and that women did attend the dramatic festivals is probable, though not certain) would 'identify' with Aischylos' Klytaimestra, wife of Agamemnon and mistress of Aigisthos. Io, reluctant bedfellow of Zeus in *Prometheus Bound* and Queen Atossa in *Persians* are equally remote. Perhaps the plight in *Suppliants* of the Danaid girls, forced into marriage with their cousins, would strike a chord of response in a society where intra-familial marriage was common, and in certain cases obligatory, but that there are fifty of them mutes the effect. When a man died leaving a daughter but no sons, the nearest male relative was obliged to marry the girl *epikleros*, 'heiress', or to find her a suitable husband; the expectation was that the couple would have children to inherit the estate (see Schaps 1979; and, on attitudes to marriage in the play and among the audience, A. F. Garvie, *Aeschylus' Supplices: Play and Trilogy* (Cambridge 1969), esp. pp. 211–24).

Sophokles composed one play without any part at all for a woman (*Philoktetes*), as did Aischylos (*Seven against Thebes*, which does however have a female chorus, castigated during the siege of Thebes in terms echoing Hektor's dismissal of Andromache, *Th*.200–1). Sophokles portrays two marital situations (in addition to the exceptional case of Oidipous and Iokaste): in *Ajax* that of Ajax and Tekmessa and in *Women of Trachis* that of Herakles and Deianeira. In both plays, an ordinary woman has a superhuman partner, whom she fails to influence—perhaps an extrapolation of the inequalities inherent in fifth-century marriage. Neither play can be securely dated, but on miscellaneous cumulative criteria (the most telling of which are language and structure) *Ajax* can be placed early in Sophokles' extant output, probably in the decade 450–440 B.C., and *Women of Trachis* somewhat later.

In 451/0, a law was passed, re-enacted 403/2, restricting citizenship to those born of citizen parents on both sides: the effect, and probably the intention, was to prevent Athenian aristocrats from contracting marriages with foreigners, as had been a very widespread practice (MacDowell 1978, pp. 67, 87; Humphreys 1974). Against this background, Sophokles' *Ajax* may have a more specific contemporary relevance: Tekmessa, a foreign slave, but of royal birth and dignified character, is treated by Ajax, and respected by his men, as his wife, and their son is regarded as his legitimate heir.

According to late, but probably reliable sources, it was subsequently decreed that an Athenian citizen could 'marry one citizen woman and procreate children also from another' (Ath.556a etc.; see MacDowell 1978, p. 90). This decree must have exacerbated domestic tensions in many households, and it may be that the situation of Deianeira, contemplating a *ménage à trois*, has this contemporary analogue. Deianeira is as hard to assess as any of Sophokles' characters, variously seen as laudable or as reprehensible. As often, Sophokles seems to be posing, rather than answering questions; in this play, questions relating to marital commitment and compatibility.

It is generally agreed that Deianeira has affinities with Euripidean heroines. The different preoccupations of the dramatists are evident in their plays on the theme of Antigone. In Sophokles', the impending marriage of Antigone to her cousin Haimon is an element, but not a dominant one; in Euripides' (known in fragments) it is central. It is evident from his surviving plays that Euripides' interest is not in the 'ordinary' woman or the ordinary marriage; but in the unusual—in morbid, excessive or deviant sexuality. He brings on a 'wife' whose husband respects her superior social position too much to sleep with her (*Elektra*), a wife willing to die in her husband's place (*Alkestis*), a woman so devoured by sexual jealousy as to kill her own children in revenge for her partner's disloyalty (*Medea*), a woman passionately enamoured of her own stepson (*Hippolytos*): none—save possibly the last—reflect situations likely to have obtained often in Athenian society.[4]

Euripides is bold in treating relationships between women, linked in piquant fashion by their relationships with men: Hekabe and Helen, mother and mistress of Paris in *Trojan Women*, Andromache and Hermione, concubine and wife of Neoptolemos in *Andromache*, Klytaimestra and Elektra, widow and daughter of Agamemnon in *Elektra*. Isolated quotations from Euripides have often been used as evidence of Euripidean, and even of Greek, misogyny (and Aristophanes' burlesque shows he had a reputation for hating women); but the characters shown and the actions performed by his female characters give a totally different impression. Comments hostile to women must, in any case, be viewed in dramatic context: how seriously are we to take criticism of women by women (as *Andr*.944–53) or the fulminations of the blinkered Hippolytos (616–68)? Iphigeneia in *Iphigeneia at Aulis* has, for all her youth, strength of character, purpose and principle by contrast with the timid Agamemnon and blustering Menelaus; Alkestis in *Alkestis* is altruistic and brave when her husband Admetos is selfish and cowardly, and Herakles shallow and sensual; Medea's triumph over Jason is, in part, one of the strong over the weak (cf. Vellacott 1975, pp. 82–126). The terminology used in *Andromache* of relationships between individuals and families allied in marriage is discussed at the end of this chapter.

Comedy

The plays of Aristophanes are set in Athens, but are inconsequential caricatures of Athenian society. Certain marriages have an air of being true to life—e.g. the relationship between the rustic Strepsiades and his pretentious wife (who does not appear) in *Clouds*, the earthy cooperation of Dikaiopolis with his wife and daughter in celebrating the rural Dionysia in *Acharnians* and the sexual teasing by Myrrhine of her husband Kinesias in *Lysistrata*. And certain deductions about attitudes to marriage may be made from plot construction: in *Lysistrata*, the effectiveness of a sex-strike on the part of wives to pressurise husbands to accede to their wishes presupposes that the husbands will care enough to comply (Dover 1973, p. 71; see, more generally, Ehrenberg 1951).

Meander's comedy of situation and intrigue owes much, as has long been recognised, both in content and technique, to Euripides' stretching of tragic convention and bold crossing of the frontiers between the genres. Seduction (or, more commonly, rape), exposure of an unwanted child, mistaken identity with ultimate recognition, marriage settlements and family squabbles are standard themes—all already present in Euripides, most markedly in *Ion*. Like Euripides, Menander is a fertile source for anthologists and is well represented in Stobaios' sections on marriage by generalisations on the conduct to be expected of a wife, and on the related questions of dowry and property. As in the case of Euripides, such truncated quotations give a misleading impression of the tenor of his plays, which are not hostile to women (cf. Fantham 1975, pp. 45–6), and which show sensitivity and insight in exploring marriage relationships. For instance, in *Epitrepontes* we see a husband who expects his own sexual adventures to be condoned, but fails to accord the same latitude to his wife; the novelty is that Menander's husband comes to perceive the unfairness of this dual standard.

Menander affords an insight not only into ephemeral social attitudes and prejudices, but into Attic law, their more solid underpinning. In many cases he corroborates—and in some even supplements—information available from other sources about legal provisions and juridical practice. (On marriage in Menander, see A. W. Gomme and F. H. Sandbach, *Menander A Commentary* (Oxford 1973) pp. 28–35; on Menander and the law, see MacDowell 1982.)

Menander was writing in a time of military upheaval, political uncertainty and social mobility. With Alexander's meteoric career of conquest (which lasted from his accession in 336 to his death in 323), new regions were opened up and Greece was no longer an amalgam of relatively isolated city-states. Some of Menander's plays, the first of which was staged in 321, have a non-Attic setting and many of his characters are non-

Athenians. In the ensuing years, the intermingling of ideas and influences continued, concentrated in the new urban centre, both administrative and cultural, of Alexandria.

Against this background, Herodas presents in his *Mimes* vignettes of women's activities which draw on a long comic tradition, but which are new—and startlingly frank—in detail. Semonides had set up the stereotypes of libidinous, bibulous, gossiping women; Aristophanes and Menander had portrayed such characters; Herodas introduces us to the intimate conversations in their boudoirs. Sexual experiment, marital infidelity and masturbation with dildoes are the supposed preoccupations of these leisured women.

Verse: Comment
The mimes are not indicative of a bouleversement of moral values, or of a new freedom for women; as always in comedy, attitudes are exaggerated and actions burlesqued. In addition, it must be remembered that, as laughter is a means of relieving tension and exorcising apprehension, comedy can afford a glimpse of society's shadowy fears—taking us back to the undertow of myth. In the classical era, it was the obligation of the adult male to take up arms to protect his city; in the Hellenistic era, state boundaries and allegiances were fluid and, also, professional armies and mercenary soldiers had changed the face of warfare. The physical strength of the ordinary adult male was no longer of paramount importance for the survival of his family and for the security of society. As will be seen in discussion of Plato and Aristotle, the innate difference between the sexes was viewed in terms of man's relative strength, and specifically strength for battle. It may be that the new conditions of leisured Hellenistic society brought to the surface a deep-seated fear, earlier submerged: the male fear of female self-sufficiency. This fear underlies the myth of the Amazons, fighting women who had no need of men for protection, and only a brief need of them for impregnation.[5]

Much of Greek verse may be interpreted in terms of a meeting between the tidal flow of myth and the directional current of society. Much of Greek prose, being, or purporting to be, non-fictional, can be related more narrowly and specifically to society. Early Greek prose is characterised as *historia*, 'enquiry', a blanket term applied to researches in many subjects— historical, philosophical, scientific—not at first differentiated. In such researches, some degree of conscious rationalisation—but often a very limited one—is present.

Herodotos
Herodotos, 'father of history' in Cicero's much quoted phrase, accords women a prominent place in his narrative, where they are often ingeniously resourceful and expediently seductive, in conformity with mythical stereotype. Such women influence events: men may dominate women, but women manipulate men. Examples will illustrate. When King Gyges, in

ANCIENT GREECE 17

uxorious pride, insinuates his servant Kandaules into the matrimonial bedroom to view his wife's bodily charms, the queen feigns ignorance, but forces Kandaules into a plot to assassinate Gyges (the alternative being execution for himself) and so to become simultaneously king and her husband (1.9–12). Humbler in origins, but equally in command of the situation is a Koan girl who escapes from the Persian camp after the Greek victory of Plataia, explaining her presence there with the story that she had been forcibly carried off to be mistress of the nephew of the Persian king: the defection is well-timed, with a shrewd assessment of military realities, and earns her safe conduct to Aigina (9.76).

Herodotos' remark that women are not abducted unless they want to be (1.4.2) sums up his attitude to relations between the sexes;[6] this is part of a debate on the degree of choice exercised by women such as Helen. It is in terms of a series of abductions that Herodotos begins his account of the distant causes of conflict between East and West, Persia and Greece; although he is dismissive of such events.

Thucydides

Thucydides, whose aim is narrow in comparison with Herodotos' sweeping embrace of subjects which would now be categorised as anthropological, ethnological, sociological rather than historical, accords women little place in his narrative; this is the inevitable consequence of their low political status. But he wrote one sentence—allegedly spoken by Perikles in a funeral oration—often held to epitomise Greek views: 'If I am to make some mention of womanly virtue for those of you who will now experience widowhood, I shall outline the whole matter in a brief counsel: there will be great credit for you in not falling short of your innate nature, and glory for the woman least discussed by men in praise or censure' (Th.2.45).

The degree of credence to be placed in Thucydides' accuracy in recording or paraphrasing actual speeches is debatable; in this case, it is arguably just as improbable that Perikles, who led a mildly scandalous private life, would have ventured such a remark in public, as that Thucydides would have attributed it to him had he not done so. Perikles' personal life had two facets: a conventional marriage to a relative, by whom he had sons—a marriage of duty, followed by divorce by mutual consent and the remarriage of the woman; and then an unconventional liaison with the foreigner Aspasia, by whom he had another son, later legitimised by special decree (Plu.Per.34; Perikles' sons who, like their father, died in the plague of 429 B.C. are mentioned Pl.Prt.315a and the association with Aspasia is lampooned by Aristophanes, esp.Ach.527). Both facets suggest a respect for women, in the family and as individuals. And it is not often remembered that the advice is directed at widows, not at women generally.

Consideration of the literary context, as well as the social, further defuses this celebrated remark. In epideictic oratory, its immediate context, the bromide is calculated to win sage nods of approval. On a wider view, it is surely a contribution to an ongoing rhetorical debate. The evidence is

clear: Plutarch expresses his disagreement with the Thucydidean sentiments and a preference for the injunction of the rhetorician Gorgias, 'that a
woman's reputation, though not her form, should be familiar to many men'
(*Mor*.242e).[7] The literary context may be extended to embrace theoretical
views on the institution of marriage, views which did not always square
with the practice of the theorists themselves, far less that of their
contemporaries.

Oratory
Family disputes reaching litigation are often sad and sordid; sex, children
and property are the main issues. The speeches of Isaios, who specialised in
cases of disputed inheritance, tell much about the Attic laws of succession;
two speeches of more general interest, one of Demosthenes (or, rather, one
preserved in the Demosthenic corpus) and one of Lysias are here discussed.
The pseudo-Demosthenic speech against Neaira contains one much-
quoted sentence: 'We have *hetairai* for pleasure, *pallakai* to look after our
personal everyday needs, wives in order to have legitimate children and to
have a reliable custodian of our household' ([D.]59.122, an arresting
passage already quoted in late antiquity, Ath.13.573d).

The *hetaira* needs little introduction or explication. Usually a foreigner,
often educated, she was dependent on a clientèle—or in some cases one
man—who slept with her and provided direct or indirect financial support.
The word *pallake* is generally translated 'concubine'; but 'common-law
wife' is often in context nearer the mark (Harrison 1968, p. 15 n. 1 and den
Boer, p. 255). Most women in this position were foreigners, that is non-
Athenian, not necessarily non-Greek; some were also slaves. As already
noted, legal constraints debarring the children of the union from citizenship militated against marriage with foreigners; but there was no social
stigma attached to a citizen living on a long-term basis with a foreign
pallake. Demosthenes' expression of the wifely role, with stress on children
and property, is, in Greek terms, a commonplace.

The three categories *hetaira, pallake* and wife are not mutually exclusive;
subtle gradation from one to another was entirely possible, as the Neaira
case demonstrates. It is not implied that all men have all categories of
relationship (as, 'Every man, said the orator Demosthenes, requires besides
his wife at least two mistresses . . .' (Lowes Dickinson 1896, p. 183)).

The case of Neaira is a complex tale of passion and family intrigue.
Neaira, originally a slave *hetaira* at Corinth, bought her freedom with the
help of lovers' largesse, lived for a time in Athens with one of them,
Phrynion, returned to prostitution at Megara, then again came to Athens,
this time with one Stephanos. A dispute between Phrynion and Stephanos
for Neaira, whose status was now confused, was resolved by arbitration:
Neaira was to live alternately with the two men, in freedom and regarded as
a *hetaira*.

The irregularities of Neaira's position continued in the next generation.
An Athenian, Phrastor, was duped into marrying Neaira's daughter, in the

belief that she was of citizen parentage, daughter of Stephanos by a previous marriage (51); on discovering his error, he divorced her within the year—although she was by then pregnant. A dispute ensued between Phrastor and Stephanos—the latter demanding restoration of the dowry and alimony for the girl, the former demanding stringent penalties for the misrepresentation of her status (52–3)—and this was resolved privately, without recourse to the courts (54).

Subsequently, Phrastor fell ill and was nursed back to health by Neaira and her daughter (55–6; the term used for nursing is that for 'look after' in the comment on a *pallake*; cf.47.62, 67 of a doctor). Softened by this, Phrastor decided to recognise the baby boy; his motives were 'so that his relatives would not get his estate and he would not die childless' (57); he was 'forced by his illness, his childlessness and his bad feeling towards his relatives, wishing to prevent their inheriting his estate if anything happened to him' (58). The recognition procedure fell through: Phrastor was challenged and in the event would not swear that he believed the child to be his son, 'born of a citizen woman betrothed to him in accordance with the law' (59–61), Phrastor did not effect a reconciliation with his ex-wife, but married another woman, a citizen this time (58, 63). Then Neaira's daughter, under a changed name (50, 121 from Strybele to Phano) was insinuated into the highest échelons of Athenian society.

Neaira's status evidently remained ambivalent for many years. It seems that Stephanos intended to claim in court that he had kept her as a *hetaira*; but he might have alleged she was a *pallake*, or attempted to pass her off as of citizen birth and his legitimate wife (118–19). The distinction was important for the transmission of property to legitimate heirs and for the safeguarding of the jealously guarded privilege of full citizenship. It is the existence of children which raises these questions. The offence of Stephanos and others like him lay in marriage *and* procreation (94); the fear of the precedent is that citizen women will act like *hetairai* and 'bear children just as they please' (113). In a different context, foreigners becoming phil-Hellenes are said to 'have children, taking wives from our number' (Isoc.*Eu*.50): procreation rather than marriage is the accolade.[8]

An unusually intimate glimpse of the private life of an Athenian married couple comes in Lysias 1, a speech delivered by a man who has killed his wife's lover. Many details reveal the wife's ascendancy over her ingenuous husband, whom she disarms by teasing flattery (12). In this particular marriage can be seen universal features in practice and attitudes: division of responsibility (wife at home, husband in the fields), importance of children (after their child is born, the husband trusts his wife implicitly, 6) and fear of adultery (pernicious because it casts doubts on the true paternity of children, 33). From the speech, it transpires that penalties for seduction are steeper than penalties for rape, and that a man had the right of summary execution over the seducer of his wife, *pallake* or female relative (31). An affair of this kind between a married woman and a younger man is unlikely to have been an isolated occurrence; predisposing conditions are discrepancy in age between a teenage wife and her husband and late marriage for men. This affair began when the wife was seen at a funeral; other contacts were made at festivals. Opportunity, though limited, did exist.

Plato

Plato, himself a bachelor, made utopian provisions for the marriage of the citizens in his *Republic*.[9] His radical ideas—regimentation of sexual relationships with a view to eugenics and elimination of private property for the welfare of the state—were much modified by the time he came to write *Laws*. Here, the views put forward are much more conventional: property and procreation are brought back into the individual's purview. Monogamous marriage is now enjoined. The emphasis placed on property in marriage settlements is recognised, but disparaged: in choosing a marriage partner, one should neither shun poverty nor seek wealth (773a). Marriage is above all for the procreation of children (772d, 776b, 779d–e) and both partners should pay attention to the best conditions for this (783b, d); divorce should follow in the case of ten years of childlessness.

Plato still seems to hanker after certain elements of communal living. He recommends *syssitia* (communal eating arrangements) as in theory a good idea, but ruefully asserts that, in practice, women themselves, accustomed to living in seclusion (781c) and in temperament inclined to seek privacy (781a) would resist. Men like women would be subject to penalties for adultery (784e).

Aristotle

Aristotle, originally a pupil of Plato, spent a lifetime reacting against him. Much of his writing is imbued with criticism—sometimes overt and clearly aware, sometimes oblique and perhaps unconscious—of Plato's ideas. Aristotle's method is descriptive rather than prescriptive: his forte, far removed from the imaginative range of Plato, is classification. There is a full and direct critique of *Republic* in *Politics* 2, where attention is drawn to Plato's disregard of the need for population control and property regulations (1265a–b). Plato had made the state his starting point; Aristotle argues that the household, *oikia*, precedes the *polis* (*Pol.*1252b) and that personal relationships are more readily formed than political (*EN* 8.12.7). Aristotle is strongly critical of the idea of political equality for women (*Pol.*1269b) and has uncompromising views on women's place in marriage.

The husband should 'rule' but not over-rule (nor should the wife if she has the power, as happens occasionally, for example in the case of an *epikleros*, heiress (*EN* 8.10.4; *EE* 1241b)). The husband has 'political' control over his wife, 'regal' control over his children; such analogies are recurrent (*Pol.*1259a). The husband has more power, but not more advantage (*EN* 8.11.4; cf. *EE* 1238b and 1241a where the husband is described as the benefactor and where Aristotle makes the acute psychological observation that benefactors are more prone to like their beneficiaries than vice-versa). Men and women need one another (*Pol.*1252a) and the sexes have complementary roles (*EE* 1242a)—viz. the conventional outdoors and indoors (*Oec.*1343b10–14)—and it is desirable that women stay indoors (*Pol.*1300a). They come together to have children, who cement a relationship (*EN* 8.12.7), but also for companionship (*Oec.*1343b10–14). Like Plato, Aristotle enjoins fidelity on both partners (*ibid.*). The same injunction is found in Isokrates (*Nikokles* 36–42) and later in Plutarch; it seems to have become a rhetorical commonplace.

Xenophon

Xenophon's treatise on household management expounds and explores the proper relationship between husband and wife. Sentiments expressed by the young husband, Ischomachos, are often quoted as evidence of 'male chauvinism' and wifely subservience; but, overall the treatise is more balanced than such excerpts would imply. The indoor-outdoor division of responsibilities is clearly and explicitly laid down (X.*Oec.*7.3, 3.22), and justified on the grounds that men and women have a different physique (23–5). It is remarked that the psychological qualities of recollection, responsibility and self-control (dear to Xenophon) may be possessed by either sex (3.26). The girl's mother had instructed her to be *sophron* (prudent, self-controlled) in her new role; Ischomachos' father had given him the same advice (3.14). A marriage partner is chosen with a view to harmony in household and parenthood; in this, a wife's contribution, though different from a husband's, is equally valuable (7.11–12). In short, the partnership of marriage and the complementarity of the sexes are constantly stressed (3.15, 18, 30, 39–40).

Xenophon's attitudes are very similar to those seen in Plutarch's letters, precepts on marriage addressed to young newly-weds. Here too, marriage is seen as a partnership, demanding mutual consideration and understanding. Plutarch leaves us in no doubt that the husband is (not that he ought to be: he simply is) the dominant partner; but stresses that the husband should act 'not as a master with a possession' but 'giving his wife pleasure and being agreeable to her'. The letter of consolation to his wife, on the death of their two-year-old daughter, is on a stock rhetorical theme, but the stereotyped philosophical *sententiae* do not mask personal emotion and affection.

By contrast with Aristotle and Xenophon, who stolidly subscribe to the status quo, the ideas of Plato on social organisation are radical and visionary. These ideas were shaped by his familiarity with, and admiration for, practices in Crete (Morrow 1960) and, perhaps, somewhat conditioned by his private life and sexual proclivities (Wender 1973 interestingly—but rather speculatively—contrasts Plato and Xenophon in this respect). Aristotle, rather like the sophists of the fifth century, travelled widely, conducting teaching and research in different regions: Macedon, where he was tutor of Alexander; Athens, where he was pupil of Plato; Asia Minor, where he opened a school after Plato's death and Euboia, where he died.

The will of Aristotle, generally believed to be an authentic record, allows us to compare the practice of his personal life with the theory of his writings (Chroust 1973, vol. I, pp. 183–220). The document is informed with generosity and humanity. Aristotle evidently took seriously his obligations to the women in his life: to his wife Pythias, by whose side (at her request) he was buried and to his mistress Herpyllis, with whom he cohabited after his wife's death, and who nursed him during his last illness; he made provisions for the welfare of their son.

Prose: Comment

The inherent difference between the sexes is seen by both Aristotle and Xenophon in terms of strength and stamina, synonymous with fighting capacity (Arist.*Oec.*1343b, X.*Oec.*23–25). Plato's remark that woman is *weaker* carries the same implication (*R.*455e, cf. note 9). The assumption that frequent and bloody warfare is an inevitable part of human life underlies the assumption that the roles of the sexes are fixed. An indoor-outdoor pattern readily follows, especially in a society which places emphasis on the continuation of the family through children.[10] When Euripides makes his Medea claim, 'I would rather stand in the battle-line three times than bear one child' (E.*Med.*250–1) he is making a fundamental point about the relations between men and women in his society: both battle and childbirth involved danger, possibly death, and both men and women might feel the other sex had a better deal.

Ancient warfare demanded strength and stamina. Soldiers had to endure the rigours of long marches overland (the only transport being horse, and cavalry service a prerogative reserved for the wealthy) and sailors of long stints at the oars of their warships (which they rowed themselves) and then be ready to join battle with good morale and unflagging physical strength. The harsh realities of fighting can be seen from the Hippokratic treatise *On Head Wounds.* Apparently a manual for army surgeons, it gives an insight into the appalling wounds inflicted in hand-to-hand conflict. In such fighting, sheer brute force is the crucial determining factor. It is not surprising that women subject to unpredictable biological demands and undeniably less strong (average for average) than men, were seen as debarred by their nature (*physis*, the same word is used for 'sex') rather than by convention (*nomos*) from such activities. It is the more remarkable that Plato enlisted women as guardians. To Plato's scheme, Aristotle's reply is devastatingly simple—'It is an absurdity for Sokrates to draw his analogy from animals, in arguing that women should have the same occupations as men, since animals have no households to manage' (*Pol.*1264b).

Terminology

While attitudes are reflected in language, there is—of course—no one-to-one correspondence between lexical units and social phenomena. 'The joining together of husband and wife has no name' remarks Aristotle, using the expression *koinonia gamike* or *teknopoietike* (*Pol*.1253b). Similarly, Plato uses the term *koinonia* of *gamoi* in this sense (*Lg*.721a).

Gamos is the marriage ceremony and the verb *gamein* (active, of the man), *gameisthai* (middle, of the woman) is 'get married'[11] while *koinonos* is used of any partner, and *koinonia* of any partnership the root being *koinos* 'common' and the implication of sharing (verb *koinonein*), for example in politics, business or religion (Pl.*Grg*.507e, D.56.1.5; Arist.*EE* 1241b).

Koinonia is used of the union of marriage, both in the abstract, contract (Arist.*EE* 1242a) and in the concrete, sexual intercourse (Arist.*Pol*.1334b33, E.*Ba*.1276). The double usage is evident in Xenophon's treatise, which makes constant use of *koinonia* terms (*Oec*.3.15, 18, 30, 42–3; 7.11–12; 10.4). The legal formula of betrothal (known only from Menander) contained a reference to 'the begetting (*arotos* or *spora*) of legitimate children' (see Gomme and Sandbach commentary p. 531 on *Perikeiromene* 1010). It may be that a legal formula underlies expressions relating to *koinonia* and the birth of children. Certainly, such phrases recur (E.*Ph*.16, request of an oracle for '*koinonia* resulting in sons'; Pl.*Lg*.772, purpose of marriage '*koinonia* with the birth of children' and similarly, Musonius cited Stob.90, to the effect that the purpose of marriage is '*koinonia* in life and in the birth of children' (cf. note 8).

Marriage centres on the *oikia*, house, the main component of one's *oikos*, estate or *oikeia* (neuter plural adjective) property. One's *oikeioi* (masculine plural adjective) are relatives, whether or not actually living under the same roof (D.59.58) or very close friends (Pl.*Phd*.89e). *Oikeiotes* is the bond between a couple, physical (Isoc.10.42, Paris' desire for *oikeiotes* with Helen) or emotional (Lys.1.6, the birth of a son the greatest *oikeiotes* between Euphiletos and his wife). The verb *synoikein*, cohabit, is commonly used of the marital relationship, while *synoikizein*, cause to cohabit, is used of giving a woman in marriage (Pl.*R*.546d).

The *oikia* is synonymous with indoors, the woman's area and responsibility, and *oikonomia* is management of a household, especially as practised by a wife; hence the title of the treatises discussed. The adjective *oikouros*, guarding or watching the house, with the abstract *oikouria*, concrete *oikourema* and verb *oikourein*, is used more generally of a wife's role, often simply descriptive (D.59.86), but sometimes dismissive (E.*Or*.928) or complimentary (Ph.2.431); of a man, the term is derogatory, with the implication of inertia (Plu.*Per*.34), cowardice (A.*Ag*.1225, E.*Heracl*.700) or unnatural reversal of roles (S.*OC* 343).

The term *syngeneis* is used of blood relatives, properly not including one's children, who are born *ek*-, of, not *syn*-, with, one (cf.Is.8.30, 33), nor one's in-laws, who, joined by a *kedos*, marriage bond, are collectively *kedestai* (cf.X.*HG* 2.4.21, separate abstracts *syngeneia* and *kedestia*), with the singular *kedestes* used of various marriage connections (cf. Willetts 1972). However, with common intra-familial marriage, the distinction could readily become blurred: thus, a man who marries his brother's daughter has his own brother as *kedestes* (Lys.32.5); and a man who marries his sister's daughter has a *kedestes* simultaneously brother-in-law and father-in-law (D.59.1–2). *Gambros*, like *kedestes*, is used for various connections by marriage, and shows the same complexities.

Anankaioi, adjective from *ananke*, 'necessity'—cf. Latin *necessarius*—is a term used of family relations, especially in cases where the tie is a basic and ineluctable one (Pl.*R*.574b, a new association with a *hetaira* not *anankaios*, in contrast with the truly *anankaios* relationship with parents). As such, it imposes obligations on oneself or others (D.19.290; 44.26; Lys.32.5; Antipho 1.4 etc.).

Philoi, adjective 'dear' is used, especially in verse, of family as well as friends. To Aristotle, the arch-classifier, there are three types of *philia*: family relationships, relationships between friends and political alliances (*EE* 1242a); in family life, he viewed the *oikia* as a sort of *philia* and the *philia* of husband and wife as a *koinonia* (*EN* 8.9.1). Relationships between *philoi* are the stock-in-trade of tragedy (cf.Arist.*Po*.1453b20), and a complex terminological situation arises when family *philoi* are not *philoi*, friendly. (For the history of the concept, see Snell 1961 and on usage cf. Dover 1974, pp. 273–8.)

A brief analysis of Euripides' *Andromache* will draw together the threads of this excursus on terminology: Euripides' characters use language which subtly indicates the interplay of family tensions and divided loyalties. The dramatic situation has a certain piquancy. Andromache, widow of Hektor, Trojan booty of Achilles' son Neoptolemos, had borne Neoptolemos a son before he married Hermione, daughter of Menelaos and Helen. In the play's somewhat episodic action, Hermione, childless and resentful, plots to kill Andromache and her son; she is aided and abetted in this by her father Menelaus, but thwarted by Neoptolemos' grandfather Peleus; she is rescued from the consequences of her actions by Orestes, her cousin (son of Agamemnon, Menelaus' brother and Neoptolemos' enemy); news comes of the death of Neoptolemos; Peleus, destitute, is comforted by the divine Thetis. Here there are two 'triangular' situations: Hermione-Neoptolemos-Andromache (with the dead Hektor in the background) and Neoptolemos-Hermione-Orestes. Personalities are involved, but also principles: Hermione's ambivalent loyalties to kin and husband, Andromache's to past husband and present master.

The scene of the play is the house, *oikia* or *domos*, of Neoptolemos (21, 24 etc.) and Peleus (581); the action revolves round relationships within it, and in particular round Hermione's allegation that Andromache wishes to supplant her (34, 156, 198). *Philos* words dominate the play. While the adjective may mean simply 'friendly' (426, cf.734–5) or 'dear' (1260), or describe a group of friends—particular (1068, 1272) or in generalisations (376, cf.585)—it is pervasively used rather of the family, where obligation and not affection is the constant element (and cf. usage of servants, in relation to their masters, 87, 802, 816, 818–19). There is evidently no connotation of affection in Hermione's statement that among barbarians *hoi philtatoi* (superlative, the closest relatives) murder one another (175–6). Because of his matricide, Orestes may marry one of his *philoi*, but not readily outwith that group (974–5); he remarks that, 'Kinship (*to syngenes*) is a strange thing and in time of misfortune there is nothing better than an *oikeios philos*' (985–6). Hermione is to Orestes *syngenes* (887) and *phile* (890), the latter term perhaps a double entendre. Ties of blood, affection and prospective marriage make Hermione and Orestes truly and triply *philoi*.

By contrast, Hermione and her father have no affectionate *philia* for Neoptolemos, though they are subject to the claims of family *philia*. Menelaus rhetorically asks Peleus if he is treating his *anankaioi philoi* so badly for the sake of a foreign woman (670–1): here *anankaioi* suggests reproach, conveying a reminder of obligations. The non-committal *gambros* is elsewhere used of the relationship between the two men, tacitly leaving the question of *philia*, with its double connotation, aside (359, 739). Hermione and Neoptolemos are bound by a *kedos* (620, 648, 869) or their shared *lechos*, bed (371, 905, 909); he is in many cases called her *posis* (869, 990 etc.) or *aner* (228, 902), husband, by herself and others. The neutral terms used of the relationship between Hermione and Neoptolemos show that the *philia* which should exist between them is precarious and threatened with extinction.

Andromache's case is different. While Andromache affectionately apostrophises her dead husband Hektor as *philtate*, 'dearest' (222) and it is elsewhere implied that her *philoi* are bound up with Troy (138, cf.203 and— if addressed to Andromache—1042), her present ties of *philia* centre on Neoptolemos, as his slave and mother of his child. In Neoptolemos' absence, Andromache is without *philoi* (78, 138; for her reliance on and answerability to Neoptolemos cf.49–50, 75–6, 255, 268, 359, 568–70). Andromache's son appeals to the absent Neoptolemos as *philos* (509), as does Andromache to Peleus (574). Significantly, a similar appeal by the child to Menelaus is brusquely repudiated with the words, 'I have no *philtron* (tie of *philia*) with you' (540, cf.724). Menelaus as Hermione's father is subject to ties with her husband, but will not countenance a claim from that husband's concubine's son. (Menelaus' claim to be *kyrios* of Andromache is not take seriously, nor intended to be so (580, cf.558).)

Peleus at the end of the play is destitute of *philoi* (1179–80), perhaps the ultimate personal tragedy. In so far as Peleus points a 'moral' in the last speech of the play—where it is reasonable to look for some conclusion—it is on the need to choose one's marriage partner wisely, with regard to character and not to worldly goods (1279–83; cf.622–3 and 639–41—the statement that it is better to have a good poor than a bad rich *gambros* and *philos*, probably a hendiadys, 'relation by marriage' rather than two ideas, 'relative *or* marriage connection'). It is true that, '. . . it was not the dowry, lineage, or character of his bride that led to his death, but the ill-will of the injured Orestes' (P. T. Stevens, *Euripides' Andromache* (Oxford 1971) *ad loc.).* Pelus however in his desolation feels that the marriage of his grandson to Hermione was crucial in precipitating the disaster, and he is surely right on this general point.

The birth of a child constitutes a strong bond in marriage: Andromache's motherhood is stressed not only in relation to Neoptolemos, but also to Hektor (4, 'wife to bear his children') and Hermione's childlessness is equally stressed (33, 360, 663, 709). Andromache informs Hermione smugly that good conduct is a more effective *philtron* than good looks (207). In leaving Menelaus, Helen left his Zeus Philios (603). In marital trouble, a wife's affairs rest with her parents and *philoi* (676)—that is, with her original family. It is evident that the *philia* between husband and wife is more precarious than the old kinship *philia*, and it may be either maintained or disrupted. The presence or absence of *philia* terms describing relationships in *Andromache* quietly reinforces what the plot tells us of the contracting and conducting of marriage. And the attitudes of the play are in conformity with those seen to prevail in society. Significantly, Stobaios has a great many excerpts from *Andromache* in his sections on marriage (cf. citation Plutarch, in his precepts on marriage, 143f, of *Andr.*930).

Terminology: Conclusion

From this kaleidoscopic survey of a thousand years of Greek literature, from Homer to Plutarch, it is apparent that attitudes to the conduct and purpose of marriage remained remarkably consistent. In simple terms, the roles of the sexes were fixed in an outdoor–indoor pattern, with male physical strength a prerequisite for outdoor activities. Marriage ensured the continuation of the family through legitimate children, and the preservation of its property through proper inheritance procedures. In Greek terms, the family was the extended family, within which one might find a marriage partner; property was not money in the bank and rarely earned (most Greeks being self-employed), but land and tangible goods kept in the home. One's family were *philoi, syngeneis* or *anankaioi*, to whom one was bound by mutual obligation; *eros*, sexual love had no necessary connection with *philia*, but rather with sexual outlets outwith marriage. The family was an aggregate of individuals, with collective obligations to the family; the state was an aggregate of families with collective obligations to the state. Partnership in marriage is a microcosm of cooperation in society: one Greek word, *koinonia*, significantly does duty for both concepts, 'marriage' and 'society'.

NOTES

1. The ambivalent representation of Helen—as culprit or as victim—indicates the range of views held about sexuality and the emotions: overwhelming ineluctable force of Aphrodite or Eros, an agency external to human will, or desires of internal origin open to resistance (cf. *Od.*3.272 *sqq.*). Until late antiquity, there was no romantic view of erotic and emotional stirrings.

2. It is telling that a contemporary novelist, describing her characters, expresses herself in these terms: 'Half of the woman is sexual and rapacious, but the other half is committed to the prodigious effort of childbearing' (Edna O'Brien, *Scotsman*, October 1978).

3. Arete is Alkinoos' niece, according to the explicit genealogy, *Od*.7.61–6, or his daughter according to clear implication, 7.54–5. This ruling duo of close relatives recalls Egypt, from which the story may have come via Crete; other features too suggest a Minoan background.

4. The confined living conditions, where a woman was on familiar terms with her own male relatives, but with no other men, combined with the acceptance of marriage within close degrees of kinship, were liable to engender and foster such incestuous or para-incestuous yearnings. Kimon, a leading general and politician, allegedly had a long-term incestuous relationship with his half-sister Elpinike, presumably his mother's daughter, as by Greek law, stepbrother and sister could marry if born of the same father, though not if born of the same mother (cf. D.57.20).

5. Perhaps science fiction is today's expression of mythology: in *The Day of the Triffids* it is recognised that survival depends on the number of women (not of men) in the population.

6. The translation 'abduct' is close to the meaning of *harpazo* ('seize', carry off'); the mistranslation 'rape' is common and can lead to serious misinterpretation. Thus, with the translation 'rape', Herodotos' remark—which is, in Greek terms, a bland, or merely wry, commonplace—is mistakenly treated by Walcot 1978, as an expression of the 'male myth' that women want to be raped and enjoy sex spiced with violence. (Greek for 'rape' is *bia*, verb *biazomai* (Lys.1.32, Ar.*Pl*.1092)— literally, 'force' often opposed to 'persuasion', i.e. seduction (e.g. X.*Cyr*.6.1.34).)

7. The conventional nature of epideictic oratory lends itself to the expression of stock themes, evident from comparison of extant specimens of the genre. For a similar bandying of topics between Sophokles and Perikles, for the benefit of literary cognoscenti, see V. Ehrenberg, *Sophocles and Pericles* (Oxford 1954), pp. 22–50.

8. However, *paidosporein* (literally, 'sow children') sometimes means simply 'have sex', 'ejaculate semen' (Pl.*Lg*.841d, cf. E.*Ph*.338); see Dover 1978, p. 163, n. 15.

9. Plato states his position on the wider question of equality between the sexes, 'There is, then, no pursuit in civic administration which belongs to woman qua woman, or to man qua man; but natural abilities are distributed alike in both sexes, and both women and men share in all pursuits by natural ability, though in all the woman is the weaker of the two' (*R*.455d). The statement has a sting in the tail; for a logical resolution of Plato's position, see Calvert 1975.

10. The dependence of the household, as well as the state, on the physical strength and potency of the adult male for its protection and survival—there being no professional police force—is possibly the reason for the presence at each front door of a statue of the god Hermes, represented with erect phallus—a warning symbol of a strong male presence within.

11. Breach of distinction in voice is always significant, implying that the woman is the dominant partner (E.*Med*.606, Antiph.46); some may see this as 'sexism' in language.

BIBLIOGRAPHY

M. B. Arthur, 'Early Greece: the Origins of the Western Attitude toward Women', *Arethusa* 6 (1973), 7–58

B. Calvert, 'Plato and the Equality of Women', *Phoenix* 29 (1975), 231–43

A. Cameron and A. Kuhrt (eds), *Images of Women in Antiquity* (London 1983)

P. Cartledge, 'Spartan Wives: Liberation or Licence', *Classical Quarterly* 31 (1981), 84–105

A.-H. Chroust, *Aristotle* (London 1973)

W. den Boer, 'Private Morality in Greece and Rome' *Mnemosyne* (1979)

E. M. Craik, *The Dorian Aegean* (London 1980)

G. E. M. de Ste Croix, 'Some Observations on Property Rights of Athenian Women', *Classical Review* 20 (1970), 272–8

G. Devereux, *Dreams in Greek Tragedy* (Oxford 1976)

J. Donaldson, *Woman; her Position and Influence in Ancient Greece and Rome, and among the early Christians* (London 1907)

K. J. Dover, 'Classical Greek Attitudes to Sexual Behaviour', *Arethusa* 6 (1973), 59–73

— *Greek Popular Morality in the Time of Plato and Aristotle* (Oxford 1974)

— *Greek Homosexuality* (London 1978)

V. Ehrenberg, *The People of Aristophanes* (2nd edn, Oxford 1951)

E. Fantham, 'Sex, Status and Survival in Hellenistic Athens: a Study of Women in New Comedy', *Phoenix* 29 (1975), 44–74

A. W. Gomme, 'The Position of Women in Athens in the fifth and fourth Centuries', *Classical Philology* 20 (1925), 1–25; repr. *Essays in Greek History and Literature*

J. P. Gould, 'Law, Custom and Myth: Aspects of the Social Position of Women in Classical Athens', *Journal of Hellenic Studies* 100 (1980), 38–59

A. R. W. Harrison, *The Law of Athens. The Family and Property* (Oxford 1968)

S. C. Humphreys, 'The Nothoi of Kynosarges', *Journal of Hellenic Studies* 94 (1974), 88–95

— *Anthropology and the Greeks* (London 1978)

J. E. Karnezis, *The Epikleros* (Athens 1972)

H. D. F. Kitto, *The Greeks* (Harmondsworth 1951)

W. K. Lacey, *The Family in Classical Greece* (London 1968)

— 'The Family of Euxitheus', *Classical Quarterly* 30 (1980), 57–61

R. Lattimore, 'Themes in Greek and Latin Epitaphs', *Illinois Studies in Language and Literature* 28 (1943)

R. J. Littman, 'Kinship in Athens', *Ancient Society* 10 (1979), 5–31

H. Lloyd-Jones, *Females of the Species* (London 1975)

G. Lowes Dickinson, *The Greek View of Life* (London 1896 and repr.)

H. McClees, *A Study of Women in Attic Inscriptions* (New York 1920)

D. M. MacDowell, *The Law in Classical Athens* (London 1978)

— 'Love versus the Law: an Essay on Menander's Aspis', *Greece and Rome* 29 (1982), 42–52

G. R. Morrow, *Plato's Cretan City* (Princeton 1960)

S. B. Pomeroy, 'Selected Bibliography on Women in Antiquity', *Arethusa* 6 (1973), 125–7

— 'Feminism in Book V of Plato's Republic', *Apeiron* 8 (1974), 32–5

— *Goddesses, Whores, Wives and Slaves* (New York 1975)

— 'Plato and the female Physician', *American Journal of Philology* 99 (1978), 496–500

D. M. Schaps, *Economic Rights of Women in Ancient Greece* (Edinburgh 1979)

C. Segal, 'The Menace of Dionysus: Sex Roles and Reversals in Euripides' Bacchae', *Arethusa* 11 (1978), 185–202

C. Seltman, *Women in Antiquity* (2nd edn, London 1957)

B. Simon, *Mind and Madness in Ancient Greece* (Ithaca and London 1978)

P. E. Slater, 'The Greek Family in History and Myth', *Arethusa* 7 (1974), 9–44

B. Snell, *Poetry and Society* (Bloomington Indiana 1961)

A. M. Snodgrass, 'An historical Homeric Society?' *Journal of Hellenic Studies* 94 (1974), 114–25

L. S. Sussman, 'Workers and Drones; Labor, Idleness and Gender Definition in Hesiod's Beehive', *Arethusa* 11 (1978), 27–41

W. E. Thompson, 'The Marriage of First Cousins in Athenian Society', *Phoenix* 21 (1967), 273–82

— 'Attic Kinship Terminology', *Journal of Hellenic Studies* 91 (1972), 110–13

P. Vellacott, *Ironic Drama. A Study of Euripides' Method and Meaning* (Cambridge 1975)

J.-P. Vernant, *Myth and Society in Ancient Greece* (London 1980, trans. of 1974 edn)

P. Walcot, 'Herodotus on Rape', *Arethusa* 11 (1978), 137–47

D. Wender, 'Plato: Misogynist, Paedophile, and Feminist', *Arethusa* 6 (1973), 75–90

R. F. Willetts, *The Law Code of Gortyn*, Kadmos supplement 1 (Berlin 1967)

— 'A Note on Plato *Lg.*773b', *Journal of Hellenic Studies* 92 (1972), 184–5

H. Wolff, 'Marriage Law and Family in Ancient Athens', *Traditio* 2 (1944), 43–95

III

Free or not so Free?
Wives and Daughters in the Late
Roman Republic

A. S. Gratwick

Department of Humanity, University of St. Andrews

I

Roman women, everyone knows, were formidable characters. They insisted on and enjoyed a greater degree of freedom than Greek women; and the law of marriage was unusually liberal. For while there was a form of marriage contracted *cum manu*, 'along with control', whereby the wife and her property belonged absolutely to the husband's family as has been normal in many other patriarchal societies before and since, there was another; in a marriage *sine manu*, 'without control', the wife was not regarded as a member of her husband's family at all but of her father's, and in certain circumstances and respects could take initiatives and act independently of her husband and his relatives. By the second century B.C. this 'free' form of marriage had risen rather rapidly in prominence so that it was now the norm, at any rate among the Roman aristocracy, and so it remained in the Imperial period. Roman women had a better deal from the law than in any patriarchal society before our own enlightened times. Marriage *sine manu* was a good thing.

Such is received opinion, and if one asks why this interesting and important change in *mores* happened, while the more judicious will hold their peace (so Crook 1967), two quite different though not incompatible suggestions are conventionally offered. According to Balsdon (1962) and numerous essays by students, Roman women were simply not prepared to put up with the kind of subjection to a husband that marriage *cum manu* entailed. The change was due to some kind of 'women's movement', though what arguments it advanced and how it exerted its power (what power?) are unrecorded. According to Schulz (1951) and a smaller number of student-essays (for too few students read Schulz) the change came at men's initiative. A small but highly influential group of the Roman nobility, headed by Scipio Aemilianus, had liberal and progressive ideas about the proper ordering of society and were in a position to put them into effect by precept and example. According to Schulz, their Roman *humanitas* included disapproval of the traditional subjection of the Roman wife in marriage *cum manu*, and it was Scipio and his enlightened friends who, as he puts it, 'thrust marriage *sine manu* into the foreground', whatever that exactly means, and persuaded Roman men in general that justice and fairness demanded that they should give their wives the greater degree of freedom which *sine manu* marriage is supposed to have afforded. This is represented as a decisive step forward in civilisation and ethics for which the Romans deserve our applause and gratitude, for a society's treatment of women is a touchstone of its civilisation, and, according to Schulz and his followers, there is here a specifically Roman advance from Greek attitudes to wives and women.

It is true that Roman women were in some ways less closely restricted to domestic activities than Greek. But one must be careful in assessing the 'freedom' of what Schulz and Balsdon call 'free Roman marriage' if one is not to be seriously misled by modern ideas of 'freedom', individual, female, and political. For they both discuss marriage *sine manu* without reference to the most remarkable and pervasive feature of Roman domestic life, the axiom of *patria potestas*, 'power in the father's line'; Roman *humanitas* never saw anything wrong with that. As for the explanations which they severally offer for the rise in importance of marriage *sine manu*, it will be seen that they are essentially moralistic and general in character, and there is in fact no corroborative external evidence whatever for either of them. If, however, we reject them as implausible or inadequately grounded, why was it that Roman men surrendered their traditional dominance over their wives in marriage *cum manu*, and allowed them the apparent independence of marriage *sine manu*? What was in it for them?

II

Our best starting point will not be the assumptions and values of the present, but the world of our great-great-grandfathers. In chapter 20 of *The Egoist*, George Meredith makes the Reverend Doctor Middleton muse uncomfortably about his daughter:

> . . . However much he liked her character, the dread of her sex and age was constantly present to warn him that he was not tied to perfect sanity while the damsel Clara remained unmarried. Her mother had been an amiable woman, of the poetical temperament nevertheless, too enthusiastic, imaginative, impulsive for the repose of a sober scholar; an admirable woman; still, as you see, a woman, a firework. The girl resembled her. Why should she wish to run away from Patterne Hall for a single hour? Simply because she was of the sex born mutable and explosive. A husband was her proper custodian, justly relieving a father. With demagogues abroad and daughters at home, philosophy is needed for us to keep erect. Let the girl be Cicero's Tullia: well, she dies! The choicest of them will furnish us examples of a strange perversity.

Meredith's irony is as always delightful and delicately tuned. The Victorian *paterfamilias* depicted here is learned, but 'no reader of persons':

he thinks in well-worn, comfortable stereotypes. The reader is expected to catch the allusion to a hackneyed Virgilian tag, and to observe how Dr. Middleton assumes that (of course) he embodies that perfect blend of the practical and theoretical life which (of course) Cicero had been; and he is also expected to know about Cicero's daughter Tullia. Such knowledge is hardly more widespread now than when Meredith wrote; but the external facts of Tullia's life are brief to relate, and will serve conveniently to focus our attention on the richest and most authentic evidence for the family life and relationships surviving from any time before the Renaissance, namely Cicero's letters.[1]

Tullia was born in 79/8 B.C. when her father was twenty-seven or -eight and her mother Terentia, a fairly recent bride, was about sixteen. In 67 B.C. the parents arranged the betrothal of the girl, now eleven or twelve, to a young nobleman C. Calpurnius Piso Frugi. The marriage took place in 63 B.C., the year of Cicero's consulship, when Tullia was fifteen or sixteen. This year was the high point of Cicero's career; a couple of years previously Terentia had borne a boy, their only son Marcus, and Cicero's fortunes seemed set fair. He himself was a provincial aristocrat, the 'new man' from Arpinum, but he had married into the Roman nobility, made an excellent match therein for his daughter, acquired a healthy male heir, and reached the second-highest office of the Republic, at what proved to be a crucial time. For it was in Cicero's consulship that Catiline and his well-born but impoverished associates attempted a *coup d'état*, and Cicero won great prestige for acting decisively (for once) in quelling the attempt and having Catiline put to death. In succeeding years, however, Cicero came under increasing criticism from his political enemies—his intrusion into the charmed circle of the Roman nobility was resented, and Catiline was not without surviving friends—for having put citizens to death without formal trial. It was later claimed that Terentia had persuaded Cicero to act against Catiline, and that she instigated his opposition to the populist aristocrat Clodius. However that may be (and some forceful women of Terentia's class and generation did influence high matters of politics) Clodius forced Cicero to go into exile in 57 B.C. His wife and family stayed in Italy, and suffered no small insecurity and anxiety. Tullia and her husband appealed on Cicero's behalf to the consul, who happened to be a kinsman of Piso's, but to no effect; and young Piso soon died.

When Cicero was eventually pardoned in 56 B.C., he was met at Brundisium by his daughter, now a childless widow of twenty-one or -two, but not (it was noted) by his wife Terentia—perhaps the first public sign of stress in the marriage. There was no question of Tullia's remaining single. Social convention expected, Cicero's career-interests urged, and parental duty demanded another match. Tullia was married to the rich and noble Furius Crassipes in 56 B.C.; unfortunately nothing is known of the manoeuvres (which will certainly have involved both parents and their friends) which led to this wedding, or of its course; for reasons unknown it had ended in divorce before 51 B.C., and there were still no children.

By 51 B.C., then, Tullia was a widow and a divorcee of twenty-seven or
-eight years of age; getting on, to be sure, but too young for the shelf, and
even if we set aside the matter of her personality and looks (for our only
witness on this is plainly biased) still able to make several important people
think twice and more about marrying her; for she would bring a substantial
dowry, a valuable connection with a senior politician and the undisputed
master of the law-courts, and credibility and credit at the money-lenders'
offices.

The evidence for the dealings which led to Tullia's third marriage
comes in deliberately guarded and fleeting allusions in Cicero's letters to
Pomponius Atticus, Caelius Rufus, and Appius Claudius written between
May 51 B.C. and December 50 B.C. when Cicero was the somewhat reluctant
governor of Cilicia in what is now the east of Turkey. The archive is too
bulky for quotation here, but is well worth close reading as the best
evidence we have for the realities of Roman domestic life, touching as it
does on the disharmony of the marriage of Pomponia (Atticus' sister) and
Quintus (Cicero's brother), and on Cicero's nascent suspicions of his wife's
honesty in money matters.

By way of illustration we quote only the first of the letters, written on
5 May when Cicero was *en route* from Rome to Brundisium to sail east.
His brother Quintus was to accompany him on his staff as an experienced
soldier and administrator, and both their sons, now in their early teens and
ripe to be about men's business, were to go with them. It went without
saying that the ladies (Terentia, Tullia, Pomponia) would stay at home.
Cicero had arranged what he hoped would be a good-humoured family
party; but in the event he had to report the following embarrassing incident
involving Pomponia to her brother Atticus at Rome:[2]

I come now to the short postscript in the margin advising me about Pomponia.
This is how things stand. As soon as I had got to the shire and my brother had met
me we had a serious conversation in which you were the main subject, from which
I steered to what you and I had been saying privately at Tusculum about her. I've
never seen anyone so reasonable, so conciliatory as Quintus was towards your
sister, so that even if there was some score left over on the reckoning, it didn't
show. So much for that day. Next morning we left the shire. The holiday[3]
required Quintus to stop off at Arcanum; I stayed at Aquinum, but we dined at
Arcanum—you know the farm I mean. When we had arrived, Quintus with
perfect affability said, 'Pomponia, you entertain the ladies, I'll drum up the
lads.' But Pomponia answered so that we could all hear, 'I am a guest here
myself.' I suppose this was prompted by the fact that Statius had gone on ahead
to oversee the dining-arrangements. 'There you are', said Quintus; 'That's what
I have to put up with every day.' What did all that amount to? A lot. She had
offended me too: her response and her expression were so pointlessly rude. I tried
to hide my annoyance. We all took our places except her; Quintus however had
some food sent to her from the table, which she refused. All in all, I thought no-
one could have been kinder than Quintus or more offensive than Pomponia—and
I pass over a good deal that at the time needled me more than Quintus. I then left

for Aquinum. Quintus stayed at Arcanum overnight and met me early next morning. He told me that Pomponia had refused to spend the night with him and that at the very moment of her leaving for Rome she had been exactly as I had seen her. So there you are: you can tell her from me that in my judgement her behaviour that day was quite brutish. I have told you all this, possibly in more detail than necessary, to show you that you too have your role as guidance-counsellor.

Mutual embarrassment is clear. The marriage between Quintus and Pomponia had been in the first place an expression of the *amicitia*, 'alliance' as much as 'friendship', of the Tullii Cicerones and the Pomponii Attici, an alliance which derived from the warm and personal friendship of the senior males, Marcus Cicero and Atticus: they were responsible. But the match had never been happy, and ended in divorce in 44 B.C. In modern times Pomponia has acquired a reputation for shrewishness,[4] but this may not be altogether fair. The marriage, probably instigated directly by Marcus and Atticus, only lasted as long as it did because of their determination as elder brothers to see it work out. Besides, Quintus had been home in Italy for only two of the last ten years, serving first as praetor in Asia and later on Caesar's staff in Gaul: he can have seen very little of his son while he was growing up, and Pomponia, who seems to have had Quintus junior, her only child, quite late, was already middle-aged. And here was her husband, proposing at his brother's instigation to spend another two or three years away, and, besides, to take her son with him. Her comment 'I am a guest here myself' had more point than Marcus Cicero cares to admit.[5] She would be on her own: unlike Terentia, who was several years younger than Pomponia, she had no daughter to keep her company. One can sympathise with her. On the other hand, it would be facile to blame the Cicero brothers for insensitivity. They were merely taking for granted that the *res publica*, *officium, gloria* and the boys' education came first; and one must remember that Marcus Cicero was himself most reluctant to undertake the appointment anyway.

Let us return to Tullia. Cicero had raised the delicate matter of her marriage with at least three friends before he left Rome—Sestius,[6] Caelius Rufus, and of course Atticus, who, however, was to be away in Greece at what turned out to be critical stages. Cicero still felt himself the 'new man' in the Roman nobility, though Terentia was herself well-connected in the right circles. Snobbery is relative. To confirm his own position and to satisfy Terentia's expectations he wanted a match with someone from the same aristocratic background as both Tullia's earlier husbands. Atticus, however, advised that he should go for a good solid man of affairs from the equestrian order, the next rank of Roman society. Some five maybe six people are alluded to as 'possibles' in the letters, and these are not necessarily all who came to somebody's mind.[7] In May 51 B.C. Cicero wrote to Atticus describing *A* as *faute de mieux*, *B* as probably unacceptable to the girl, and speculating that *C*, the son of the current consul Ser. Sulpicius

Rufus, might be tried with the discreet aid of Servilia (step-sister of Cato, mistress to Julius Caesar, mother of Brutus, and mother-in-law of Cassius).[8] We have here a rare glimpse of what must have been a major industry among Roman *matronae*—marriage-broking. Late in the year Atticus wrote encouragingly about *C*, and this seemed good to Cicero 'since Pontidia is being silly'. But soon something happened which made Atticus change his mind and write recommending Pontidia's candidate, who could be identical with *A* or someone else again *D*.[9] This Pontidia was from Arpinum, and her man was apparently from the equestrian order, Cicero's 'old gang' as Atticus approvingly puts it. But in spring 50 B.C. Cicero was directly approached by *E*, Ti. Claudius Nero, future grandfather as it turned out of the Emperor Tiberius. This young nobleman acted rightly in approaching the *paterfamilias* directly, but had not it seems done the wise thing and broach Terentia at Rome first. Cicero jumped at the chance, and wrote approving the suit to Terentia and Tullia at Rome. But letters took six or seven weeks to get from Cilicia to Rome,[10] and when the message arrived, Tullia was already married to *F*—P. Cornelius Dolabella (May–June 50 B.C.).

News of this only reached Cicero at the beginning of August 50 B.C. when he reached the port of Side, where a packet of mail was awaiting him; and it came as an unpleasant shock. He spent a couple of days at Side writing embarrassed letters to those concerned.[11]

Dolabella was not unknown to Cicero, who had twice defended him successfully in court on serious charges (their nature is unknown); according to Roman ideas, this should have put Dolabella under a lasting obligation to Cicero, and in the sequel Cicero deluded himself that he would be able to exploit this in Tullia's interest. Although the news of the marriage was a complete surprise, he certainly knew that Dolabella had expressed interest in Tullia already before he left Rome for Cilicia, and perhaps that Terentia favoured the suit. For Dolabella's name had evidently come up in a conversation which Cicero had had with his friend Caelius Rufus. This is the more remarkable, for, at the time, Dolabella was still married to a Fabia, a kinswoman of Terentia. Caelius alludes to this conversation in a letter written in February 50 B.C. and received by Cicero in April that year.[12] The news was that Dolabella had divorced Fabia; but, urged Caelius, it would be most imprudent to offer Dolabella any sign of encouragement—he was indiscreet anyway, and, more particularly, he had undertaken to prosecute Cicero's predecessor as governor of Cilicia, the aristocratic Appius Claudius Pulcher. It was politically important for Cicero not to offend this grandee in any way. Caelius' advice was to wait and see how Dolabella came off from this inconvenient sally. About the same time Cicero received at least one letter (now lost) from Appius himself complaining that there were rumours at Rome of a forthcoming engagement between Tullia and Dolabella. Cicero replied to this, or these, strongly repudiating the very idea of a match with Dolabella:[13] by now (April–May 50 B.C.) he had seen Ti. Claudius Nero and resolved to accept his offer. It is evident that Terentia had been giving encouraging signs to Dolabella from early in 50 B.C.; and though in his letter to Appius Claudius written at Side in early August[14] Cicero says that he had given Terentia his authority to act as circumstances required because of the difficulty of communication, there was room for suspicion on his part that she had in fact simply ignored his wishes.[15] He was now in a particularly embarrassing position with regard to Appius Claudius, and in this letter of explanation he could not evade the point that as head of the family he had the right to repudiate the connection with Dolabella whenever he chose.[16]Arrived back in Italy, and reunited with his family, Cicero's last word on the whole affair to Atticus was that maybe it would turn out for the best; Tullia seemed happy, and Dolabella's manners were charming; and anyway, all the suitors except the one Atticus had backed would have seen Cicero go bankrupt. This, though cynical and splenetic, is significant. For all their fine lineage, the candidates Cicero had considered were encumbered with debts, and were really after the use of Tullia's dowry and of Cicero's name to get credit at the bank.[17] In point of fact, that is exactly why Dolabella married her.

Though Terentia obviously liked Dolabella, Cicero's male friends all had misgivings about his character, politics, and finances. He is said to have been born in 69 B.C.,[18] but that is too late. In modern times there is a perhaps romantic tendency to put Dolabella down as a specially *young* rake when he married the twenty-eight year old Tullia. But it can scarcely be right that he was only nineteen. Cicero calls him *adulescens*, slightingly, in his first letter to Appius Claudius, but Latin usage, the context, and the ages of Claudius and Cicero allow us to infer only that Dolabella was less than forty years of age. Caelius refers to Dolabella's unspecified 'faults' as 'shaken off with the years' (*aetate iam decussa*), which should mean that he was clearly past the age when the callowness of youth might serve as an excuse for wild oats. A story retailed by Quintilian has Dolabella remark drily on his first wife Fabia's claim to be thirty years of age, 'Oh yes that must be right—I remember you telling me that, twenty years ago'.[19] The story is no doubt apocryphal, but the attribution to Dolabella was maladroit unless he was married to Fabia for quite a long time. Indeed, it is hard to see how Dolabella could have been the defendant in a serious case twice *and* have been married for some time if he was only nineteen in 50 B.C.; on the whole, it seems that Dolabella was a *boulevardier* at least as old as Tullia and probably in the mid-thirties when he married her.

When the Civil War broke out at the beginning of 49 B.C., Dolabella promptly sided with Caesar; so much for his sense of obligation to Cicero. Tullia, now thirty, was pregnant; a boy was born prematurely in May 49 B.C., but died. After much hesitation Cicero embarked for Epirus to join the supporters of Pompey, leaving Terentia and Tullia at Rome. Dolabella returned to Rome after the defeat at Pharsalus of Pompey in 48 B.C. He was heavily in debt, and reports from Atticus reaching Cicero now at

Brundisium told him that Tullia was ill and left in severe financial difficulties by her husband, who, for his part, was insisting on prompt payment by Cicero of her dowry-instalments; further, that the patrician Dolabella was taking steps to have himself adopted by a plebeian family, the Lentuli, in order to enable him to stand for the Tribunate of 47 B.C. with a programme of debt-cancellation as a main ticket: for patricians could not hold that office.

Tullia's predicament mortified Cicero. Besides, he was now seriously at odds with his brother, and both of them were on increasingly bad terms with their wives. Marcus had now convinced himself that Terentia had been cheating him over money. It was in these lugubrious circumstances that Tullia joined her father at Brundisium in June 47 B.C.; on her arrival, he wrote to Atticus that 'her courage, thoughtfulness, and affection . . . grieve me beyond measure when I consider the unhappy lot in which she is cast, not through any misconduct of hers, but by grave fault on my part'.[20]

Over the following weeks, he and Terentia contemplated declaring Tullia divorced (the *paterfamilias* of a wife married *sine manu* could do this whenever he pleased) but they hesitated, for the connection with Dolabella, a Caesarian, seemed the family's only security as supporters of the wrong side in the Civil War. In the event, Caesar welcomed Cicero as a friend (September 47 B.C.); Dolabella was sent to Africa in December, and was briefly reconciled with Tullia on his return (summer, 46 B.C.). But they had been divorced before Dolabella left again, this time for Spain, at the end of the year, and Cicero divorced Terentia about the same time. This meant that he had to repay her the substantial dowry which she had brought, while Dolabella owed him Tullia's,[21] who, to cap it all, was pregnant, but had no prospect of bringing the child up as her own, because there was no question under Roman law of custody being awarded to a divorced mother. The child would be a Lentulus, because of Dolabella's adoption into that family.

To put it no more strongly, Cicero must have been suffering severe emotional stress in the last months of 46 B.C., and marrying someone rich seemed the only solution to his own immediate financial problems. After all, many another had recently solved his problems that way at least *pro tem*. He raised the matter with Atticus, who, probably unenthusiastic about the whole idea, suggested two 'possibles' whom he perhaps knew Cicero would reject.[22] Then we suddenly find Cicero married to the sixteen-year-old heiress, Publilia. The match was certainly made without Atticus' approval, and attracted much adverse criticism at the time; and it was a fiasco. Cicero divorced her within a matter of weeks against her and her family's wishes,[23] shortly after Tullia had died in February 45 B.C. For meanwhile Tullia had borne Dolabella's child in Rome at the house of the Lentuli, who were virtual strangers, had contracted puerperal fever, and, having travelled to Tusculum, inconsiderately died in her father's presence. And so ends our gloss on Dr. Middleton's allusion.

III

Cicero's misery and remorse following the death of his daughter is apparent over the following months, during which scarcely a day goes by without an anguished letter addressed to Atticus, sometimes two.[24] It became an obsession of Cicero's that he should buy some land, preferably at Rome, on which to erect a shrine to Tullia's memory, and what he calls an ἐγγήραμα, a 'place to grow old in' for himself. His family life was over. As for the Publilii, Cicero will have simply severed his connection and surrendered all Publilia's money without any argument, for he had no claim at law to it[25] and the point of the divorce was to correct, publicly if ineptly and painfully, an irrational error.[26]

Reduced to a record card, Tullia's *curriculum vitae* would read:

Born, 79/8 B.C. (mother c.16, father c.28 years of age); betrothed age 11/12; married at 15/16; widowed at 21/22; remarried at 22/3; divorced at 25–8; remarried at 28/9; premature baby at 30/1; divorced while pregnant at 32/3 at the same time as her parents (now c.49 and 60 years of age); father remarried; baby born but did not survive; died of complications Feb. 45 B.C. before father's second divorce.

The general pattern of Tullia's life, though unusually tragic in the event, is unremarkable from the Roman point of view in its chronology, and not just for Tullia's class or time. Indeed Cicero's family as a whole—see the Family Tree, page 48—is fairly representative, at any rate for the nobility; this is the only class for which we have any detailed evidence about family-structures. It would be imprudent to generalise too freely. The aims, motives, calculations, moves, and considerations involved in match-making at different levels of society obviously differed. Cicero's family is very typical of the late Republican nobility in certain respects, e.g. low fertility, which, with the manifold public and private tragedies of the Civil War, eventually led to extinction, and a high rate of politically calculated marriage and divorce. In fact, five broken[27] out of six marriages in Cicero's immediate family is probably unusual even for the nobility. It does not follow that, for example, the solid peasantry will have behaved likewise; for them, children were a working asset and the aims of match-making were not the acquisition of instant political ends or cash, but of necessarily long-term securities in the form of neighbouring lands and their produce; though for them too the Civil War was a domestic as well as public disaster, as, for example, Virgil's first Eclogue makes movingly clear. Augustus later set himself the task of increasing the size of families and stabilising the life of hearth and home by well-known legislation which, however, had very little real effect.

No direct religious sanctions about the sanctity of marriage could be invoked, because there were none. Basic Roman assumptions about marriage were in many ways like Greek, as one might expect. To be sure, the various ceremonies of marriage were, as any other important step in life, marked by various more or less quaint rites and observances which attracted the curiosity and attention of Greeks because they differed from their own.[28] But this is unimportant. The institution itself was secular and non-sacramental. As far as the State was concerned the purpose of marriage was the production of citizens—future mothers, farmers, soldiers—and therefore it was only available to citizens. Laws of marriage and inheritance were formulated only to sort out who was who and who was to get what. Although there was a feeling that great honour was due to the wife who lived her life with one man only, who was obedient, fertile, a good mother and a practical housekeeper,[29] the rationale for this would be cast in terms of social utility, not religious or ethical terms. The gods might be said to be angry with Rome, but their anger was managerial annoyance at a decline in efficiency and productivity rather than at infringements of a decalogue or a code of conduct; after all, they had never issued such directives.

The families involved in arranging a particular match naturally hoped that it would prove to be a mutually advantageous alliance in this world, and the sooner the better; however, it was understood that if things went badly wrong it could be terminated without too much drama. As in Greece, the father or her family normally supplied the bride with a dowry; how much affirmed and perpetuated finely-graded class-distinctions. At Rome this was treated as the husband's property during a marriage, but except in the case of marriage *cum manu* it did not simply become his or his family's outright; there were complex rules by which it had to be wholly or partly restored if a divorce took place, and these depended partly on hard-headed stipulations made at the time of betrothal and partly on the circumstances of the divorce. By the late Republic a man who divorced his wife married *cum manu* without good reason would have to surrender not only his wife's dowry but all her property (Cic. *Top*.4.23). Thus dowry was an expression and sustainer of class-gradations, for a rich man would rarely marry a poor wife, while a rich father would have nothing to gain by supplying his daughter with a large dowry in marriage to a poor man; from the man's point of view it was an incentive to marry, and from the woman's it was an insurance against frivolous divorce by her husband.

In these matters Romans and Greeks made broadly similar assumptions. Further, it was widely held in both Greek and Roman society as a self-evident truth that most women were unreliable: they were emotional, irrational, and lacked the detachment of judgement and constancy of purpose which men claimed for themselves. *Varium ac semper mutabile femina*: the view of Dr. Middleton. They were unfitted by nature to participate in government not only physically but also intellectually and morally; and an elegantly circular argument to prove this was that, generally, they were uneducated in the law and rhetoric, and so could not participate directly in public affairs anyway. These now unpopular attitudes were not, as Schulz claims, an essentially un-Roman importation from Greece.[30] They were as deeply rooted in Roman Society as anywhere else, and are of course implicit in the national epic. Creusa, Dido, Juno, Allecto, Venus, the Harpies, Amata, and Lavinia are your typical females. There are good qualitities in some of them—housewifeliness, grace, tact, the ability to blush and not be heard; but the catalogue of the foibles and failings with which Nature has endowed most of them is a good deal longer. Some women paradoxically display *uirtus* 'manliness', but when they do, it is by suppression of their female nature (the Sibyl) or by tomboyish imitation of the lads (Camilla, Diana). And so it was with the exceptions in real life, as when Cornelia mother of the Gracchi used the tone and rhetoric of Cato the Elder in 'open letter' dissuading her last son Gaius from standing for the Tribunate,[31] or when a resolute Roman wife showed her hesitant husband how to die a Stoic suicide (*'Paete, non dolet'*).[32] But mostly women needed to be in the firm control of a man and follow his lead, as the vine needs the elm. It does not follow that women were despised: it is simply that the Romans had very tidy ideas about the proper *prouincia*, 'job, sphere of action', of men and women just as they did about the various gods and everything else. A wicked male conspiracy? If so, it was so subtly engineered that women, uneducated for the most part beyond the elementary stage, humbly accepted that men really did know best or more cunningly pretended to accept that they did, and behaved accordingly with sometimes disquietening subtlety and manipulative skill.

Romans, then, of both sexes just as Greeks took it as axiomatic that female citizens whose fathers or husbands were dead should have a *tutor*, 'guardian', at least to represent the woman at law. But there were important practical differences between the institution of 'guardianship' of women in Greek and Roman Society. An Athenian widow was expected to marry her husband's nearest available kinsman, and an heiress was regarded as the passive medium through which part of the clan's patrimony was passing: she had no initiative to dispose of it, and her guardian's authority over her was, in effect, the same as her father's. In Roman law it was quite possible that a woman might become *sui iuris*, 'of her own right', by a series of regrettable accidents, the nature of which will be examined in due course. A man *sui iuris* could acquire and dispose of property in his own name as he wished, make a will, and actively participate in the public religion and government. A woman *sui iuris* did not have the latter options, but she could take initiatives with her money and property. Unlike an Athenian guardian, the Roman tutor could not *tell* his ward to do anything, but he could stop her in certain cases, for his consent was necessary for important transactions involving what were technically known as *res mancipi*, land, slaves, and working animals, that is the 'invested capital' of an agricultural society. Primitively, when all Romans were peasant farmers, the guardian's duties will have included harbouring and protecting the woman, and safeguarding her patrimony in the interest of her heirs (probably himself or people close to him), and the guardian's veto on a woman's capacity to buy or sell *res mancipi* makes coherent sense in that context. However, it is rather silly in the setting of city-life, for there wealth might take many other forms, and the woman *sui iuris* never required the guardian's consent for dealings in *res nec mancipi,* which meant practically everything else. The obstructive powers of the guardian were eroded in various ways in the early Empire: a woman might apply for a substitute guardian, possibly a complete stranger, if her own were not immediately available, and a legal dodge was allowed by which a woman could have her *tutor* replaced permanently if the two were at loggerheads. Augustus exempted the *sui iuris* mother of three children from the necessity of having a *tutor* at all, the first breach in the principle that no woman should be without male authority. But he did not dream of exempting the mother of three children who was still under her husband's or father's *patria potestas* from that much more direct and active control. The aim of these and other adjustments of the law of tutelage was not to further a libertarian principle or to help the single businesswoman. It was specifically to limit the power of the *tutor* to interfere with a woman's ability to dispose as she wanted in her will; and to make life easier for guardians. For unlike the Athenian guardian, the Roman had legal responsibilities and moral duties without the power of enforcement, and the office was understandably unpopular. It may be asked why the institution did not simply disappear; the answer is that it could not, as long as women were excluded from the courts. One should not necessarily suppose that what the law allowed to those who knew how to exploit it was what actually happened in custom and practice. One of the problems of framing laws of 'women's guardianship' must have been that the kinds of relationship which had to be covered were extremely diverse, ranging from close blood-relationship (uncle–niece) through the accidental (teenage son of a deceased slave-owner—his father's freedwomen) to the artificial (complete stranger—rich heiress with good legal advisers). Only some women, the rich and well-advised, really stood to benefit substantially from being *sui iuris*: many women who happened to find themselves 'of their own right' in practice probably tended to treat their guardians' authority with the same deference as they had been trained to give to their *patresfamilias*. It was a matter of personalities and moral authority rather than of the law of statutes.

Some women, then, might become *sui iuris*; but this was a matter of pure accident over which the woman had no control (bar parricide). It might happen when she was young, old, or it might not happen at all; and it was only some of these who were *sui iuris* who had the means and the good advice to exploit a status for which their upbringing had ill prepared them. A citizeness could only be 'of her own right' if she was not in someone's *manus,* 'control'; and that could only happen if all the relevant males who might exercise that control were dead. There is nothing to suggest that the status was seen by women as intrinsically desirable or preferable to belonging to a family with a male head. This brings us to the two particulars wherein there is a radical difference between Greek and Roman Society— *patria potestas* 'power in the father's line' and marriage *sine manu* 'without control'.

The mere fact of marriage did not confer a patriarchal status on a Roman husband. A Roman family could only have one head, the *paterfamilias*, who was the senior direct ascendant in the male line. For males, the subordination did not end until the *paterfamilias* died, unless he had previously chosen to 'emancipate' them, e.g. by arranging their subjection to some other *paterfamilias* by sanctioning their adoption, or by cutting them off. There was no 'coming of age'. When the *paterfamilias* died, there were as many new *familiae* as there had been adult males immediately subject to him, 'adult' meaning 'past puberty'. My paternal grandfather has three sons. He dies: there are now three *patresfamilias* and *familiae*, even if both my uncles are bachelors. My father dies. My brother and I are now both *patresfamilias*, and there are four *familiae* in our corner of the clan of all those who share our patronymic (Tullius, Iulius, Publilius, etc.). The powers of the *paterfamilias* within the *familia* are very real; the law regards him as the absolute monarch of a tiny realm, and the regulations governing these tiny kingdoms are like international law written small. *Patresfamilias* are all expected to conform to certain rules of conduct, but their internal affairs are their own. Anything which I use—land, money, slaves—or which I produce—crops, earnings, children—are not mine but belong to my *paterfamilias*, and only become mine absolutely when I become *paterfamilias* myself by the combined decease of father, his father, his, and so back: meanwhile what I have is on sufferance. I cannot marry without his consent, and it would be difficult to avoid his explicit advice to marry X's daughter because of the pressures he could exert. It is he, not I or my wife, who decides whether on birth our children should be raised or got rid of. He can tell me to divorce my wife without having to justify his decision—though this would cost him money, because the dowry would have to be repaid. In scandals affecting the reputation of the family he is the ultimate authority recognised by the State, and he can sit with a family tribunal with the power of life and death over anyone in his *potestas*. It is essentially this 'freedom' of the *paterfamilias* that the Romans valued and meant by *libertas*, the right of the individual patriarch not to be interfered with in his domestic empire by other patriarchs, or by all of them collectively, i.e., the State. It is important to note that the descent of this *potestas* is restricted to the direct male line, that it is infinitely divisible, and that it cannot move 'sideways'. I cannot tell my younger brother what to do, I can only offer him suggestions. We are on a par as *patresfamilias* now that father and his ascendants are dead, and this is what Romans mean by equality before the law. Since men generally did not marry before their middle twenties, the breeding-cycle of males was roughly twenty-five to thirty years. Consequently, a young man could not normally expect to pass out of *patria potestas* before his middle years, if he lived that long, unless his grandfather and father should both die relatively young.

In Cicero's family, Cicero senior of Arpinum was still alive when Marcus and Quintus married, and he will have been formally involved in the betrothal-negotiations as head of the family. After their marriages, neither brother technically owned anything in his own right until their father's death, sometime in the sixties B.C., when they themselves were already in their forties. Of the three children they had between them, only Marcus junior ever became *sui iuris*, 'of his own right'; Quintus junior and Tullia remained *in patria potestate* all their lives, and this cannot have been unusual. A man's *patria potestas* naturally applied to his daughters as well as to his sons. It was not open to a girl to choose a single or a married life, for the relevant decisions were not hers but in theory the exclusive business of her *paterfamilias* and in practice of both her father and mother. Nor (see p. 47) did she automatically pass out of *patria potestas* by living to a certain age; it was, other things being equal, her natural condition for life. If the patriarch negotiated a betrothal *cum manu* the girl passed out of his family into the other patriarch's. She would cease to take part in her father's family-cult and would have no automatic right of inheritance in that family. Instead she became wholly a member of her husband's family, taking part in the cult of his ancestors and acquiring inheritance-rights on a par with her daughters if any. As the Roman lawyers paradoxically put it, she counted *filiae loco*, 'as one of her own daughters', for this purpose. If her husband was or became *paterfamilias*, she was called a *materfamilias*, a status which commanded deep respect; but technically she could own nothing, because she was *in manu*, and would continue so long as her husband lived; if he was not himself *paterfamilias* but subject to his own father's *manus*, she would continue in that condition until the old man died. On the other hand, if the woman became widow to the *paterfamilias* and her own father were still living, she would not be subject to his *potestas*; she and her children would be *sui iuris*. Thus the chances of a *materfamilias* becoming *sui iuris* were parallel to those of her sons, but due that much later in her life.

If on the other hand a woman's *paterfamilias* chose to have her married off *sine manu*, he kept control over her and she stayed in his family; she would not participate in the cults of her husband's family, she would acquire no rights of inheritance and her *paterfamilias* could tell her to divorce her husband at any time. But the children belonged wholly to the husband's family in this as in *cum manu* marriage and there could be no grounds in law for 'tug-of-love' disputes. Thus Tullia had no prospect of bringing up her child by Dolabella, even if they had survived. It might easily happen that the wife's *paterfamilias* would die during the marriage: in that case the wife would be *sui iuris*, perhaps even before her husband, and her affairs would be placed in the hands of a *tutor*—usually a representative of the wife's family, not the husband's, for one main point of *sine manu* marriage was to prevent the entangling of patrimonies. Terentia was *sui iuris* for all or most of her marriage to Cicero, but we do not know who was her *tutor*. It has been suggested that this is a symptom of the obsolescence of women's guardianship at Rome; for there is a good deal in Cicero's letters about her financial activities. But it is dangerous to generalise from the single case and with an argument from silence. For one thing, most of the transactions to which Cicero refers have to do with *res nec mancipi*, which would not involve the *tutor* anyway. For another, Terentia was a forceful personality and very rich by most people's standards; she may simply have dominated the man. Again, she had access, as most women did not, to the best legal advice and was in a position to exploit it to her advantage. What is clear is that she depended heavily on the skills and loyalty of a freedman Philotimus, whom Cicero could not abide, but over whom he had no authority. One would like to eavesdrop on Philotimus' conversations with Cicero's own right-hand-man Tiro. These relationships would have been materially different if Terentia had been married *cum manu*. All the progeny of his male line, including the daughters, would naturally be in the patriarch's *familia* and control; and so would his daughters, but not *their* children. For if he married off his daughters *cum manu*, that was the end of his formal authority over them: they would be in the *manus* of their new *patresfamilias*, who in turn would have the decision whether to marry these women's daughters *cum* or *sine manu*, and so on.

From the point of view of the *paterfamilias*, the main advantage of a marriage *cum manu* was that the daughter and her potential descent were off his hands: the patrimony would not have to be divided to take account of them. Good news for the girl's brothers: there would be more for them and their progeny. In a peasant society, and among the poor in a city, this must always have been an important consideration. On the other hand, there were very obvious advantages to a rich *paterfamilias* in arranging the marriages of his daughters *sine manu*. For if the patrimony was sufficiently substantial to stand sub-division, the patriarch might extend the realm of his political and social importance by determining whom his girls should marry, and being able to sever a connection of which he came to disapprove whenever he wanted. On his death the inheritance would be divided to the disadvantage of the male line(s), but that might be a secondary consideration, and these males would provide the *tutores* of the females anyway.

Current opinion has it that from the woman's point of view marriage *sine manu* was more desirable than marriage *cum manu* because thus she escaped subjection to her husband's authority. But this is hasty and superficial. Those who think so forget that she did not thereby escape the very real authority of her father; and in either case the prospects of a woman's becoming *sui iuris* depended entirely upon the number, health, and ages of the line of males in whose *manus* she happened to find herself. Sentiment and tradition accorded great respect to the *materfamilias uniuira*, the wife married *cum manu* to one man only; at the same time, society applauded the dutiful daughter who unquestioningly obeyed her parents. At least a wife married *cum manu* knew where she was supposed to stand: her loyalty must be to her husband's family; there was a clean break with her parents. But things were less clear for a wife married *sine manu*, and not just in such exceptional circumstances as those facing Tullia in 49 B.C., when her father and Dolabella were on opposite sides in the Civil War.

Her loyalty was divided: she was in many ways expected to behave like a *materfamilias* and be loyal to her husband through thick and thin, but at the same time there was no clear break with her father's family, of which she remained a full member, 'Daddy' might continue to dominate her not only psychologically but with the full backing of the law, while her husband's women kin would be wise to treat her with more reserve, as an 'outsider', than a *materfamilias* who would be wholly 'theirs'.

IV

We have considered a particular family and some general principles, and return to the questions posed at the beginning of this essay; how should we evaluate marriage *sine manu* as an institutional framework in comparison with others as Greek, or our own; and how do we explain its importance in Roman Society?

An objective answer to the first is really impossible, for any judgement we offer is based on the implicit assumptions and priorities of our time. In marriage certain things 'obviously' matter more than others; but the fact is that the relative priorities of these things is not at all obvious. We stand upon shifting ground. An answer to the second question, however, is perhaps possible, because it is a question of historical fact. Both points may be illustrated from Schulz's discussion of Roman marriage in *Classical Roman Law*, published in 1951.

According to him, 'The classical law of marriage is an imposing . . . achievement of the Roman legal genius. For the first time in the history of civilization, there appeared a purely humanistic law of marriage, viz. a law founded on a purely humanistic idea of marriage as being a free and freely dissoluble union of two equal partners for life . . . (it was) a creation of Roman *humanitas* and it is for this reason that it appeals to us as so amazingly modern . . .'. Against this he sets a representative nineteenth-century opinion, quoting the Dutch scholar Jhering who wrote in 1880: '. . . the traditional Roman matrimony in which the wife was *in manu-mariti* 'under the husband's control' grew out of fashion, and even where it continued to exist, *manus mariti* was dwindling to a mere fiction. Better natures, however, far from seeing progress in this evolution, rightly regard it as a sign of ever-spreading demoralization.'[33]

Meredith's Dr. Middleton would no doubt endorse Jhering's interpretation warmly, and it is not surprising that Jhering should express a typically 'Victorian' and patriarchal view. It is historically interesting that Schulz, writing in the immediate post-war years, should say that the general view among scholars was still that the rise in importance of marriage *sine manu* was a symptom and cause of moral degeneration. For only thirty years later received opinion is virtually the opposite; and here Schulz's interpretation was itself a symptom of changing attitudes. Contradicting Jhering and his ilk with no small passion, Schulz alleged that the 'free' form of marriage came to prominence through 'the strength of the Roman humanitarian movement' which had its origins in the small group associated with Scipio Aemilianus in the mid second century B.C., and adds that 'the law of marriage was indeed radically humanized in a surprisingly short time'.

This, and the view that the rise in importance of marriage *sine manu* was due to women's pressure (see p. 30), is implausible in itself and without any supporting evidence. Firstly, it is widely assumed and asserted, not only by Schulz and Balsdon, that we have to reckon with a relatively rapid rise in the frequency of marriages *sine manu*, and that this must have happened in the second century B.C., hardly earlier. But this goes well beyond what we really know. All that we can say is that when our evidence becomes reasonably abundant, that is in the first century B.C., marriage *sine manu* was already normal in the circles which it illuminates, that is the upper classes. It does not follow that the same pattern would be observed in other classes, or that the change in *mores* was either rapid or particularly recent. We do not have enough evidence about the betrothal-stipulations of marriages from an earlier period to assert that marriage *sine manu* was not already common in certain circles or circumstances long before the first century B.C. For, secondly, the legal mechanism by which *patresfamilias* of girls could stipulate a marriage *sine manu* goes back to the venerable XII Tables, and there was no legal reform of marriage-laws in the second century B.C. The humanitarian reformers envisaged by Schulz did nothing to change it, and, what is more to the point, they did not question or attempt to restrict the remarkable powers and authority of the Roman *paterfamilias*. Nevertheless, thirdly, Schulz claims that the allegedly rapid rise in the frequency of marriage *sine manu* was the fruit of a conscious policy of social reform in which legal minds played a leading role: they 'thrust it into the foreground'. This must mean by their own example, prestige, and pamphleteering; for which, however, there is not a scrap of evidence. Schulz wrote at a time when extravagant claims were still being made for the cultural and social importance of the so-called 'Scipionic circle', and he tends to envisage it as a kind of an elite and earnest movement like the Bloomsbury Group or the Cambridge Apostles of the 'thirties. But as Astin has emphasized,[34] the exclusiveness, cohesiveness, and self-consciousness of the 'Scipionic Circle' has been greatly exaggerated, and it is certainly wrong to attribute to its 'members' any comprehensive and radical plans of social reform. Scipio's own marriage was a miserable affair, scarcely an exemplary pattern of enlightened modern marriage.

The real reasons why marriage *sine manu* was frequent in the nobility is less edifying than Schulz suggests, and less 'relevant' than Balsdon would have it. A poor man with several daughters might well be inclined to make settlements for them *cum manu* because he would have to provide each of them with a dowry anyway and by stipulating for marriages *cum manu* his sons would benefit: his small patrimony would be divided among the boys, and the girls would inherit severally in the families into which they were given. Conversely in negotiating a settlement for a son, the poor man would have to consider carefully whether 'gaining a daughter' in a marriage-settlement *cum manu* was an advantage which outweighed the fact that she added to the number of persons among whom his estate would be divided, whether the dowry offered was large enough to offset this, and whether he would not be better off with a contract for the girl *sine manu*, perhaps with a smaller dowry; on the other hand this arrangement would give the girl's father rights of interference that might one day prove regrettable. . . . One can see that on both sides not only the size of the dowry but also the nature of the inheritance-rights and the definition of paternal *imperia* were involved in the calculations. The girl had to be in someone's *manus*; in whose was the subject of shrewd bargaining in which the girl's attitude and her potential happiness were only one consideration. The girl's father would be satisfied if he thought he had done the best he could both for the girl and for the family-interest; whether he had or not would of course remain to be seen.

The priorities of the rich and ambitious, on the other hand, might be very different. By the late Republic, they were less prolific breeders; they did not need large families, because they had plenty of slaves to do the work on their estates, and one way for a father to provide for the future prosperity of his heirs was not to raise too many of them. Besides, the marriage-market was a good deal wider for them than for the peasantry, whose choice was practically limited to their neighbours by the nature of their only substance, the local land. For the rich *paterfamilias* the division of his patrimony was a less urgently pressing consideration than for the peasant. Marriage-alliances were frequently the means of securing purely political advantages between families from widely separate parts of Italy. This is not to say that money did not matter. Far from it: the costs of what may politely be called election-expenses were very heavy, and a politically ambitious *pater-familias* might be more interested in acquiring for himself or his son the use of a substantial dowry and of the extended bank-credit which a respectable alliance would confer. However, since dowries had usually to be repaid in whole or part on the occasion of a divorce, the rich male divorcee would find that he could not afford *not* to be married, as a person today with a mortgage cannot afford to be without a job. The wealthy *paterfamilias* who had the disposal of his own or his sons' daughters had a good deal to gain by retaining control over his daughters in marriage—an *entrée* into the affairs of other families, with influence and power over the daughters, including the right to end the alliances at any time, if they became politically or otherwise inconvenient. The only thing which he would be giving away would be his daughters' children, if any, for these would be out of his control whatever form of marriage was arranged. Besides, in stipulating a marriage *sine manu*, the father of a daughter could argue (like a peasant) that since the girl would not become an heir in her suitor's family but in his own, a smaller dowry would be appropriate than if she were married *cum manu*: marriage *sine manu* was less immediately expensive for

CICERO'S FAMILY
(simplified)

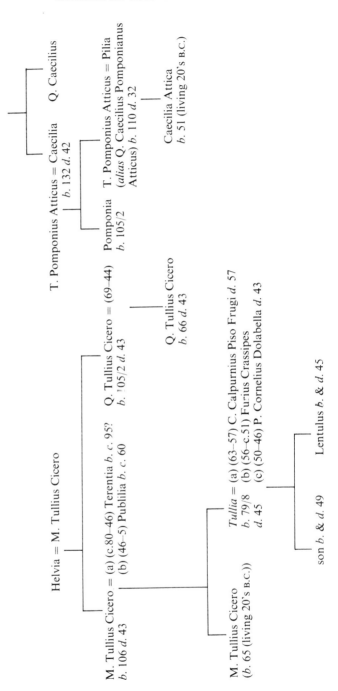

the girl's father than marriage *cum manu*, because a settlement for the latter would involve calculations of the potential burden the wife would represent as a co-heir in her new family. The noble suitor with a cash-flow problem would, naturally, prefer a settlement *cum manu* for this very reason, but it would be a foolish father who agreed lightly to this without careful probing. For it is evident that rich fathers of daughters of the right background could call the tune in the late Republic. Aristocratic suitors were likely to be encumbered by debts and, as pointed out above, were finding that marriage to *someone* was an economic necessity; and it may be suggested that there were not enough girls to go round, because of the general preference for male children. Whether there was such an imbalance of the sexes in the progeny of the aristocracy deserves investigation. However this may be, it is clear that marriage *sine manu* in aristocratic circles of the Republican period had nothing to do with some new conception of women's status, or with women's pressure. It was, in fact, an expression of the fundamental and lasting importance of *patria potestas* in Roman society. Schulz does wrong to underemphasise the reality of this power, and Balsdon worse when he describes marriage *sine manu* as 'a free form . . . in which the wife remained in the power of her father and after she was 25 years old only subject to a formal supervision by her guardian'.[35] That married women over twenty-five years of age should simply pass out of *patria potestas* would have been a revolutionary proposal to shock Roman fathers from Aeneas to Boethius, and amaze Tullia. But it never occurred to any Roman to make such a suggestion, let alone enact it.

NOTES

1. In chronological order: *ad Atticum* 5.1 (Shackleton Bailey [*SB*] no. 94), *Att.*5.4.1 (*SB* 97), 5.13.3 (*SB* 106), 5.14.3 (*SB* 107), 5.17.4 (*SB* 110), 5.21 (*SB* 114), 6.1.10 (*SB* 115), *ad familiares* 8.6.2 (*SB* 88), 3.10.5 (*SB* 73), *Att.*6.3.8 (*SB* 117), 6.4.2 (*SB* 118), *fam.*8.13.1 (*SB* 94), *Att.*6.7.1 (*SB* 120), 6.6.1 (*SB* 121), *fam.*3.12 (*SB* 75), 2.15 (*SB* 96), *Att.*7.3.12 (*SB* 126).
2. *Att.*5.1.3–4 (*SB* 94); the writer's translation.
3. The festival of the *Lares*, 1 May, requiring the master's presence.
4. So e.g. Balsdon (1963), p. 46.
5. Her word *hospita* covers more than 'guest': 'outsider', 'stranger' are also implicit.
6. *Att.*5.17.4 (*SB* 110). As Tribune he had promoted Cicero's return from exile in 57 B.C.
7. On what follows see J. H. Collins (1951/2), pp. 164–8, 186.
8. And a considerable power behind the scenes in Republican politics. See Balsdon (1962), p. 51 f.
9. Identified by Collins (1951/2) with *A*, Mr. 'Faute-de-mieux' of the previous May; but this is unfortunately not a context where Occam's razor is an appropriate instrument.
10. Cf. *Att.*5.19.1 (*SB* 112); Cicero reckons 46 days from Rome to the Taurus mountains (S.E. Turkey) a fast delivery, and a couple of months was usual (5.18 [*SB*] 111).

11. Appius Claudius, Caelius, Atticus; letters to the family were no doubt sent but do not survive.

12. *fam.*8.6.2 (*SB* 88).

13. *fam.*3.10.5 (*SB* 73).

14. *Att.*6.6.1 (*SB* 121).

15. Cicero wrote in June to tell Atticus among other things that he had written to Terentia about Tullia's *condicio* (here specifically meaning 'wedding settlement'), and immediately goes on to voice his first suspicions of his wife's honesty in a financial matter: *Att.*6.4.2–3 (*SB* 118).

16. *fam.*3.12 (*SB* 75); the whole letter merits careful reading: it must have been one of the most difficult Cicero ever had to write.

17. *Att.*7.3.12 (*SB* 126). 'You know whom we broached; except the one we made moves about through you, they would all be putting me in court; for no one would stand them any credit. But all this when I see you—it needs a good deal of discussion.'

18. Appian *B.C.*2.129.

19. Cic. *fam.*3.10.5 (*SB* 73), 8.6.2 (*SB* 88); Quint. *Inst.*6.3.73.

20. *Att.*11.25 (*SB* 231).

21. Tullia's various difficulties are frequently referred to in *Att.*11, *passim* (March 48 to August 47). There were problems in getting back her dowry instalments after her divorce (*Att.*12.8 [*SB* 245], *fam.*6.18.5 [*SB* 218], *Att.*16.3.5 [*SB* 413]; October 46, January 45, July 44). Bad feeling between Cicero and Terentia is said by Plutarch to have gone as far back as to Cicero's exile when Terentia conspicuously failed to meet Cicero at Brundisium along with Tullia (Plut. *Cic.*41.5), but the first we hear in the letters is in 50 B.C. (*Att.*6.4 and 5 [*SB* 118 and 119]) when Cicero reveals his suspicions of her freedman Philotimus' dealings; these only hardened over several years (*Att.*11.24.3 [*SB* 234], August 47). He had disapproved of certain dispositions that Terentia proposed making in her will (*Att.*11.16 [*SB* 227] June 47), and after Tullia's death there was some unpleasantness over a new will Cicero had recently made in which Tullia's baby Lentulus was named and to which Publilius, probably brother to Cicero's second wife Publilia, was a witness; the inference drawn by Terentia seems to have been that the Publilii were beneficiaries (*Att.*12.18a [*SB* 256], March 45). Neither Dolabella's debt to Cicero and Terentia nor Cicero's debt to Terentia had yet been sorted out in July 44 (*Att.*16.3.5 [*SB* 413]) and the whole sordid business was weighing heavily on Cicero.

22. Pompey's daughter (Cicero refers to her as incredibly ugly) and Hirtius' sister; *Att.*12.11 [*SB* 249] of late November 46.

23. *Att.*12.32 (*SB* 271), 28 March 45.

24. The letters run from 7–30 March and 2–31 May 45. On Cicero's plans see D. R. Shackleton Bailey, *Cicero's Letters to Atticus* vol. 5 (Cambridge 1966) Appendix III, 'Tullia's Fane', pp. 404–13.

25. Cic. *Top.*4.23, Watson (1967), p. 76.

26. Publilia is mentioned only in *Att.*12.32 (*SB* 271), where Cicero says (28 March 45) that she and her mother had written proposing to come and talk things over. Cicero wanted to avoid any such encounter. Plutarch *Cic.*41.5 reports that Tiro had written that Cicero married the girl not, as Terentia claimed, because of her looks, but to solve his money problems—mainly that is the problems of Tullia's and Terentia's dowries. 'For the girl was very rich and Cicero being left as an heir was guarding her property in trust. But owing many tens of thousands he was persuaded by his friends and οἰκεῖοι to marry the girl in spite of his age and pay off the creditors using her resources.' These friends do not seem to have included Atticus; the οἰκεῖοι

would appear to be the same as the *domestici* who witnessed Cicero's will (see note 21), and should mean in particular Tiro himself. Cassius Dio makes both the discrepancy in ages and the financial motive into slurs used by Antony (46.18.3, cf. Cic. *Phil*.5.19), and Quintilian *Inst*.6.3.75 tells the coarse joke that on being criticised on his wedding day for marrying a *virgo* at his age Cicero replied, 'That's no problem, she'll be a *mulier* tomorrow.' It is interesting that Tiro evidently thought marrying for money in this way less reprehensible than marrying at sixty for sex.

27. Both Cicero's, his brother's and two of Tullia's three. See the Family Tree, p. 48.

28. See Balsdon (1962) for an excellent account of what actually happened at a betrothal and wedding.

29. See Williams (1958).

30. Schulz (1952), pp. 180–4.

31. The authenticity of this letter has been much disputed, but the discussions impugning it are more interesting as a record of male assumptions and attitudes to women than they are productive of sound arguments. There is in fact no good reason to doubt its authenticity; and the document is a good deal more important than has been realised, for the point has not been made that if genuine it is the earliest extant prose by a woman in any language; if it is not genuine, it is at least a near-contemporary forgery in the authentic language and style of the period. As such, it would still be highly significant as evidence that the public *thought* it possible and plausible that Cornelia should have written thus. Cicero himself knew a collection of her letters, and had no doubts as to their authenticity (*Brut*.211). For a translation and brief commentary see Gratwick (1982), p. 146 f.

32. Pliny, *Ep*.8.23, cf. Tac. *Agr*.2.1.

33. Schulz (1957), pp. 103 f., 142.

34. Astin (1967), pp. 295–306 and *passim*; cf. Gratwick (1982), p. 123.

35. Balsdon (1962), p. 45.

BIBLIOGRAPHY

Works cited by author's name and date only

A. E. Astin, *Scipio Aemilianus* (Oxford 1967)

J. P. V. D. Balsdon, *Roman Women* (London 1962); cf. the reviews by F. Norwood, *Classical Philology* 59 (1964), 52–4, Lily R. Taylor, *Gnomon* 35 (1963), 840–1, T. Cadoux, *Journal of Roman Studies* 53 (1963), 207, W. K. Lacey, *Classical Review* n.s. 14 (1964), 87–9

J. A. Crook, *Law and Life of Rome* (London 1967); cf. S. I. Oost, *Classical Philology* 64 (1969), 200–1; A. R. Birley, *History Today* 17 (1967), 864–5; A. N. Sherwin-White, *Journal of Roman Studies* 59 (1969), 281–2

J. H. Collins, 'Tullia's Engagement and Marriage to Dolabella', *Classical Journal* 47 (1951/2), 164–8, 186

A. S. Gratwick, in *Cambridge History of Classical Literature*, ed. E. J. Kenney and W. V. Clausen, vol. ii (Cambridge 1982)

S. Riccobono and others, *Fontes iuris Romani anteiustiniani*, 3 vols. (Florence 1940–3)

F. Schulz, *Classical Roman Law* (Oxford 1951)

A. Watson, *The Law of Persons in the Later Roman Republic* (Oxford 1967)

G. W. Williams, 'Some Aspects of Roman Marriage Ceremonies and Ideals',
Journal of Roman Studies 48 (1958), 16–29

Cicero's Letters

D. R. Shackleton Bailey, *Cicero's Letters to Atticus* (6 vols., Cambridge, 1965–8;
text, translation, notes) and Cicero *Epistulae ad familiares* (2 vols., Cambridge
1977; text and notes only) is the most modern text; his excellent translation of
both the letters *ad Atticum* and *ad familiares* with very brief notes is published
by Penguin (2 vols., Harmondsworth 1978) as *Cicero's Letters to Atticus* and
Cicero's Letters to his Friends. These supersede the Loeb editions of the letters
ad Atticum (E. O. Winstedt, 3 vols., London and Cambridge, Mass. 1912–18)
and *ad familiares* (W. Glynn Williams, 3 vols., 1927–9), the only other
comprehensive edition with an English translation. Both Shackleton Bailey
and the Loeb editors retain the traditional arrangement of the letters by
addressee; the French Budé edition, with text and parallel French translation
(Paris, 1935 *et seqq.*; begun by L.-A. Constans and continued by J. Bayet and
J. Beaujeu) has the advantage of integrating the two collections and arranging
the letters as far as possible in chronological order; with tome 7 (Paris 1980),
the Budé edition has reached February 45 B.C. and covers nearly all the letters
referred to in this paper.

We refer in this essay to Cicero's letters in the traditional numeration with a
bracketed cross-reference to the numbers of Shackleton Bailey's translation
thus: *Att.*5.4.1 (*SB* 97), *fam.*8.13.1 (*SB* 94).

On Tullia, see W. Drumann, P. Groebe, *Geschichte Roms* (3te Auflage:
Leipzig 1929, repr. Hildesheim 1964), Bd. 6, pp. 614–27, and Collins (1951/2).

For detailed reference to primary sources concerning other members of
Cicero's family and his acquaintances the reader is referred to the appropriate
articles in Pauly-Wissowa's *Realencyclopädie* and in Drumann and Groebe.

Sources of Law

The single most important is Justinian's *Digest*, published in A.D. 533; on its
character and for editions, see the *Oxford Classical Dictionary* s.v. *Digest* and
Crook (1967), pp. 13–15. Gaius' *Institutes* as well as documentary evidence of
all kinds is put together in Riccobono's *Fontes* (1940–3). This is now seriously
out of date, as much new material has been discovered in the last forty years.
The best introduction to the material in general is Crook (1967) together with
the articles in A. Berger's *Encyclopedic Dictionary of Roman Law* (*Trans. of the
American Philosophical Society*, n.s. 43 part 2, Philadelphia 1953).

Historical and Sociological aspects of Roman Law

Again, Crook (1967) is the best introduction. Also: U. von Lübtow, *Das römische
Volk: sein Staat und sein Recht* (Frankfurt am Main 1955); W. W. Buckland's
Textbook of Roman Law from Augustus to Justinian (Oxford 1921; 3rd edition
revised by P. Stein, Oxford 1963, repr. with corrections 1974); H. F. Jolowicz,
Historical Introduction to the Study of Roman Law (Cambridge 1932, revised
1939), Schulz (1951). For the Republican Period, see apart from Watson
(1967), the same author's other books, *The Law of Property in the Later Roman
Republic* and *The Law of Succession in the Later Roman Republic* (both Oxford
1971), and *Roman Private Law around 200 B.C.* (Edinburgh 1971).

Women

Balsdon (1962); the only book on its subject, but not *the* book, which remains to be written. The second part is the better; see the reviews. Crook (1967), chapter four is important. An excellent introductory article is Gillian Clark's 'Roman Women' in *Greece and Rome* 28 (1981), 193–212; this covers a great deal of ground yet avoids superficiality. L. P. Wilkinson, 'Women's Liberation', in his *Classical Attitudes to Modern Issues* (London 1979), pp. 47–78 is less successful. Sarah B. Pomeroy offers a useful bibliographical survey of studies of Roman women in *Arethusa* 6 (1973), 144–52. Among articles which have appeared since then on particular aspects of the subject, see Barbara Rawson, 'Roman Concubinage and Other *de facto* Marriages', *Transactions of the American Philological Association* 104 (1974), 279–305, Susan Treggiari, 'Family Life among the Staff of the Volusii', *ibid.* 105 (1975), 393–401.

Patria potestas

See Crook (1967) *passim*, and his article 'Patria potestas', *Classical Quarterly* 17 (1967), 113–22.

IV

'Treasure in Heaven': Property and Inheritance Among Senators of Late Rome[1]

Jill Harries

Department of Ancient History, University of St. Andrews

I

In the late second century A.D. Lucilia Stratonice, a rich lady of Lyon, built on her estate and dedicated a shrine to house the body of her dead baby daughter.[2] The memorial expressed affection and loss in a manner which Cicero, who had done the same for his beloved Tullia over two hundred years earlier, would have understood. By the late fourth century A.D., when the Gallic Christian senator Paulinus of Nola laid his infant son to rest in a Spanish martyr-shrine under the patronage and protection of the 'very special dead',[3] times had changed. Paulinus was divided from Lucilia by the crisis which had caused the near break-up of the Roman Empire in the third century and, more important, by the transformation of upper-class attitudes initiated by the conversion of the emperor Constantine to Christianity in A.D. 312. From being the religion of a minority, with a strong social organisation in many cities after three centuries of growth but nonetheless liable to suspicion and sporadic persecution, Christianity had now become the 'official' religion, embraced and encouraged by influential patrons from the emperor downwards. All over the fourth-century Empire, new churches, martyr-shrines, baptisteries and, in time, monasteries testified to the pious enthusiasm of wealthy converts, who displayed their economic power and social prestige through ostentatious buildings, gifts and acts of public munificence, as they had always done, but in a Christian guise. The alteration in the religious landscape is exemplified by the building in the fifth century of the great church of St. Irenaeus of Lyon on the very site of Lucilia's memorial.

These developments did not in themselves pose any challenge to time-honoured practices and assumptions concerning marriage, property and inheritance. Although childlessness was no bar to the transmission of property as, under Roman law, property could be left by will to anyone, it was preferable that a marriage should produce male and female heirs in the direct line of descent, through whom both the line of the family and its landed wealth should be perpetuated. Under laws concerning intestate succession, which show how property was expected to pass in normal circumstances, the children had first claim, then those connected to the deceased by legitimate descent from a common ancestor through the male line (agnates), followed at some distance by the surviving spouse. This strict separation of the legal identities of husband and wife is rooted in Roman attitudes concerning the family in general, which gave chief importance to the blood tie and thus retained the links of the two partners of the marriage with the families into which they were born. However, as these principles applied only to intestacy, natural affection could easily supply a deficiency not catered for by legal provision. A widow could be left a portion of her husband's estate but the bulk of it, ideally, would pass to the children, thus continuing not only the wealth of the family but the status and opportunities for a distinguished career that went with it.

For many Christian senators there was no contradiction between piety and property or the conventional search for offices and honours; one very prominent Christian office-holder, Sextus Petronius Probus, who moved on from four praetorian prefectures to hold yet higher office in heaven (according to his epitaph), bequeathed both lands and distinction to his sons, who were consuls together in 395. Other senators, however, became increasingly troubled by what seemed to them to be a conflict between the unworldly demands of their form of ascetic Christianity and their retention of the lands, offices and honours essential to the conventional senatorial lifestyle. In the deserts of Egypt in the late third century, St. Antony and his followers had laid the foundations of the monastic movement which was, by the late fourth century, widespread; Antony's *Life* had been written and publicised in the West by Athanasius of Alexandria and it was known to Jerome, among others. In the 380s, Jerome himself was in Rome as the secretary to Pope Damasus and there gathered round himself a coterie consisting mainly of the female relations of senators, whose aspirations towards the renunciation of the world and the adoption of poverty and chastity he was to express and encourage. Other mentors of senators, such as Rufinus of Aquileia and Pelagius, were to follow him with similar doctrines which, if taken to their logical extreme, would have struck at the roots of marriage and inheritance among the greatest landowners of the Empire.

Eloquent and prolific, Jerome aimed through his writings to enhance by all possible means the glory and completeness of the sacrifices made by his eminent converts. As a literary source for the activities and attitudes of his lady patrons and friends, he is both informative and dangerous. Although ostensibly addressed to individuals, Jerome's letters were designed for a wider readership and exploited to the full accepted conventions of rhetoric and literary artifice. In flattering his ladies by, for example, translating their earthly 'nobility' into celestial terms ('noble in birth but nobler in sanctity' is almost formulaic in Jerome), he echoed an idea which permeates late Roman literature and art. Like all propagandists, he enhanced aspects of his saintly protegées most favourable to his message, while playing down or discarding facts which showed them to be more mindful of traditional obligations than he would care to admit. It is therefore the more significant that, behind the fervent affirmations of renunciation, we can still detect the tenacious presence of property and its transmission along conventional lines.

The letters and poems of Paulinus of Nola, who was related to Roman disciples of Jerome and Pelagius, show the process of ascetic conversion from within. Paulinus, governor of the fertile Italian province of Campania in 381, renounced his wealth and public career in the early 390s and caused a considerable stir in the Senate. His Aquitanian parentage, marriage with a Spanish wife and ownership of lands in Italy as well as Gaul and Spain serve as a timely reminder that, although Rome was the 'common fatherland' and many senators were based there with town houses, the lives of senators were also linked with their estates scattered through the provinces. The experience of Paulinus and others like him had a local provincial as well as a Roman dimension.

The most extreme rejection of conventional marriage and property-ownership was that of the last generation of ascetics to concern us, that of the younger Melania (as distinct from her grandmother of the same name) and her husband Pinianus. For them, we have the Latin and Greek *Lives* of Melania, based on her recollections as told to a monk, Gerontius, whom she met late in life in the Near East. The heavy emphasis on the need for heirs, the proper transmission of property and the question of its disposal, which is apparent in the early chapters, suggests that it was precisely this issue which sundered Melania and Pinianus from their peers and led them to leave Italy in, or soon after, 408, never to return. Unlike others (as we shall see), Melania and Pinianus took literally the oft-repeated advice of Christ to the rich young ruler, a cornerstone of Jerome's exhortations; 'If thou wilt be perfect, go and sell that thou hast, and give to the poor and thou shalt have treasure in heaven.'[4] In so doing, they ignored, or perhaps were not aware of, the ways in which their own relations' enthusiasm for the renunciation of worldly ties had been quietly modified by conventional expectations and practical realities.

II

The susceptibility of Jerome's ladies to ascetic influences was partly a result of the social and religious character of the age. As always in Roman history, women were officially debarred from an active political life, although women in the imperial family, wives, sisters and mothers of emperors, could wield enormous personal influence. Even the wives of imperial ministers, such as Serena, the wife of Stilicho under Honorius and friend to the younger Melania, were a force to be reckoned with. Their control over their own property seems in practice to have been con-siderable, with the result that women could engage in independent acts of patronage and endowment. But for most senatorial women, whose status derived from that of their fathers and husbands, the conventional outlets for their energies lay in their families, in the endless social round of the capital, which so wearied Jerome's friend Paula in the 380s, and in religious devotions and studies. Other diversions were less innocent. In the 370s, a number of senatorial women, as well as men, were implicated in charges of adultery, poisoning and magic and were executed, sometimes in horrifying ways. One Flaviana was stripped of all her clothes by the executioner before she was killed (although the offender was later himself burned alive for this). Another victim, Hesychia, while under house arrest smothered herself in her feather bed for fear of the tortures to come. A third, Anepsia, endured a long persecution from her accuser, in the course of which she surrendered to him all her wealth and much information implicating others in the hope of saving herself—to no avail. Rome became subject to a reign of terror in which even the innocent were not safe and 'the Eternal City mourned its dead' (Ammianus Marcellinus, *History* XXVIII.1.56).

Senatorial society was so far-flung that the ill-fortunes of one group needed to have had little effect on the tranquil existences of others. There is no known connection between the executions and, for example, the departure of the elder Melania from Rome for the East in 374. Yet the tragic events of the early 370s are symptomatic of the prevailing insecurity of the last centuries of the Western Empire. Renunciation of status, property or office-holding became easier and more desirable when those very things could be a source of risk. After a political and personal crisis, Paulinus of Nola sold up or surrendered his estates to reinvest the proceeds in splendid buildings for St. Felix of Nola, which he inhabited himself, secure in the belief that his patron saint would protect his own better than he, Paulinus, could do through his own unaided efforts. Past and rejected values were now, to Paulinus, no more than 'the empty image of an insubstantial shape' (*Poem* 21.497).

A sense of the transience of earthly things was not confined to the Christians of the Later Empire any more than was the belief that knowledge of a permanent truth conferred some form of special status. Various mystery cults and holy men had always found favour in aristocratic eyes, and initiates, male and female, recorded the fact on their tombstones, where were listed the things that had mattered (or were supposed to have mattered) most in their lives. One of the last of the Roman pagans was Fabia Aconia Paulina, wife of the celebrated pagan champion Vettius Agorius Praetextatus, most distinguished of senators, a special *bête noire* of Jerome's—and one of the few late Romans known to us with a sense of humour. Praetextatus' and Paulina's funerary inscription (*CIL* VI.1779) commemorated her as 'devoted to temples and a friend to the divine beings': she had experienced initiations in the cults of Iacchus, Ceres and Cora at Eleusis, of Liber, Ceres and Cora at Laerna, of the goddess at Aegina and of Isis the Egyptian goddess (also a favourite target of Christian polemic). Although any resemblance between Paulina and his Christian heroines would have been indignantly denied by Jerome, their religious attitudes were rooted in the same soil. No Christian could have found fault with Paulina's virtues as the ideal wife, 'modest, faithful, pure in mind and body, kind to all . . . , nurse of modesty, bond of chastity, pure love and heavenly faith . . . , gift of the gods who bind our marriage couch with friendly and modest ties . . . '. Like their Christian counterparts, Praetextatus and Paulina looked beyond earthly things:

> Why should I (Paulina) now speak of honours or of powers and joys sought by the prayers of men, which you, priest of the gods, valued only as small and transient things . . . ?

And, like the Christians too, Paulina anticipated for her husband a celestial palace (an idea highly offensive to Jerome), where she would be reunited with him.

Within their Christian context, Jerome's converts were part of a wider assertion of the values of celibacy and poverty which were endorsed by such mainstream Christian leaders as Ambrose of Milan, bishop of the imperial capital. On the issue of holy virginity, the Christian community had seized the initiative from the dying cult of the Vestal Virgins and polemicists delighted in contrasting the pure vocation of nuns with the sexual frustration allegedly suffered by the Vestals in their enforced confinement of thirty years; one Vestal, a certain Primigenia, was indeed convicted of taking a lover at this time (Symmachus, *Letters* IX.147 and 148). The issue, therefore, that divided the more extreme ascetics from moderate senatorial opinion was not the theoretical desirability of surrendering the world's goods and adopting a holy Christian life, but how that was best achieved in practice. Selling up and giving to the poor was out of the question for most senators and Jerome's use of the rich young ruler passage was explicitly criticised by Augustine in the early fifth century as taking no account of Christ's advice elsewhere to obey the commandments. By that time, however, Melania and Pinianus had already gone beyond the pale. Their isolation was no doubt partly the effect of Alaric's sack of Rome in 410, a symbolic catastrophe in which little actual damage was done, and the resultant new unity in the Roman senate, which could not be put at risk by irresponsible eccentrics. However, on a more mundane level the seeds of that isolation had already been sown by the cumulative effect of ascetic practices and teachings on three generations of senators, whose noble renunciations were emphasised by their propagandists at the expense of their unobtrusively exercised practical caution.

In the mid-fourth century, Melania the Elder was, like many daughters of senators, a teenage bride. At the age of twenty-two she lost her husband and two of her three sons. Only long after these tragedies could Jerome get away with his claim that she had promised her service to God the more readily because freed of the 'burden' of responsibility; 'how little she cared she proved in the case later of her only son, to whom she surrendered all she possessed and, with winter coming on, set sail for Jerusalem' (Jerome,

Letter 39.4). Even Jerome thus acknowledges that the son, Valerius Publicola's, rights as heir to the family estates were scrupulously observed, but Melania's duty to her son went beyond that. For twelve years after her husband's death she stayed in Rome to supervise his education under the auspices of the guardians to whom she had entrusted him 'that she might love her little son by neglecting him and keep him by sending him from her' (Paulinus of Nola, *Letter* 29.9). Only in 374, when her son was safely embarked on his career in his first office, as urban praetor,[5] did she leave Rome, first for Alexandria in Egypt, where she visited the monks of the desert, and thence to Palestine. Those twelve years from 362 to 374 may have been ones of inner turmoil and distress, but Melania was a consul's granddaughter and, as such, accepted that her son 'was to benefit from the wealth and honours of this world' (Paulinus, *ibid.*).

As heir, Publicola seems to have received most of Melania's property in 374, although she kept for herself money for her journeys and charities (supplemented later by contributions from her son) and still owned land in Sicily in 400. Whatever his early training, Publicola, as later events were to show, was as conscious as any senator of the need to transmit senatorial property intact through the generations and it seems from her actions that the elder Melania, in youth, thought the same.

Melania was to return to Italy at the age of sixty, confirmed in her vocation, hardened, perhaps embittered, a stark figure whose favoured mode of transport was a donkey. By then, the compromises of her youth were far behind her, and she was ready to criticise her son for not having followed her example, though others, like Paulinus,[6] were quick in his defence. Her spiritual journey cannot be traced in detail, but it could be that her hasty departure from Rome in 374 as the weather grew dangerous for sailing with the coming of autumn was the impulsive reaction of one who feared she had already delayed too long.

During the early 380s, a group of senatorial ladies headed by the *materfamilias*, Paula, was more directly under Jerome's influence. In many respects this was an exciting time. Famine and social upheaval threatened the city of Rome in 383, leading to an expulsion of outsiders (but the retention of a troupe of dancing-girls). In 384, the great pagan senator, Symmachus, exploited his office as Prefect of the City to further his petition for the restoration of the pagan Altar of Victory to the Senate-house, a request frustrated by the counter-arguments and influence of Ambrose. 384 was also the year that saw the young Augustine pass through Rome on his way to sit at the feet of Ambrose, and the historian from Antioch, Ammianus Marcellinus, perhaps[7] experience in person the frustrations of seeking senatorial patronage. But for Paula, her daughters and her associates, such as Jerome's childhood friend Pammachius or Pammachius' cousin Marcella, these interesting birds of passage might never have existed.

Paula's family claimed descent from the Scipiones and Gracchi, heroes of the Roman Republic, a line with origin distant enough to pass unquestioned. Paula and her husband, Iulius Toxotius, who seems to have been unexceptional by senatorial standards, had four daughters, Blesilla, Rufina, Paulina and Iulia Eustochia, and finally a son, another Toxotius. According to Jerome, Paula had performed her conjugal duties only in order to gratify her husband's wish for a male heir; whether she would have abstained from them thereafter is a moot point as she was widowed while her son was still a baby. 'So much did she weep for her husband,' Jerome recalled, 'that she all but died herself, and was thus converted to the service of God' (*Letter* 108.5).

Bereavement thus paved the way for renunciation of the past and a new life. Alone and tired by the unending social round of the capital, Paula found relief in the company of two visiting bishops, Paul of Antioch and Epiphanius of Salamis in Cyprus, in 384 and, under their escort she finally left for the East in the following spring. Her departure prompted emotional scenes at the harbour:

> The sails were set and the ship was being rowed out into the open sea. Little Toxotius was stretching out his hands on the shore. Rufina, of age to be a bride, in silent tears pleaded with her mother. Yet Paula turned her dry eyes towards heaven, overcoming her love of her children through her love of God (Jerome, *Letter* 108.6).

With Paula went her unmarried daughter, Iulia Eustochia, now vowed to perpetual virginity (her three sisters all married but died young and childless, the last Paulina, wife of Pammachius, in 396). Eustochia was still a very young girl when, under pressure from her mother and her admired mentor Jerome, she took her vows and disinherited herself so that 'far removed from her noble race, she left herself rich only in faith and grace' (Jerome, *Letter* 108.2). Eustochia's choice could be interpreted as a wish to avoid the possible traumas attendant on very early marriage or the dangers of childbirth—she was to survive the last of her sisters by over twenty years—but all the signs are that she was most strongly influenced by immediate emotion, as had been her mother and Melania, both of whom had experienced happy marriages and bitterly mourned their husbands' loss. For Eustochia, virginity was itself a marriage with Christ in the fullest sense—to be celebrated by Jerome in the words of the *Song of Songs*:

> trembling you will get up and say, 'I am wounded by love' (*Song*. V.8) and you will hear from him the reply, 'A garden shut up is my sister, my wife; a garden shut up, a fountain sealed' (*Song*. IV.12) (*Letter* 22.25).

And renunciation was to the greater glory not only of God, but of the convert:

> For truly what the Saviour promised to his servants and handmaidens is fulfilled in this. For she who despised the glory of one city is now famed in the opinion of the whole world; while she (Paula) lived at Rome, no-one outside Rome knew her

name but now, in obscurity in Bethlehem, barbarian and Roman lands alike wonder at her (*Letter* 108.3).

The motivation of the search for alternative status was thus openly acknowledged alongside others. Nor did it apply only to women with their limited opportunities for self-assertion. Paula's son-in-law, Pammachius, was a descendant of the noble Furii and of consuls, yet he never rose to be more than a minor provincial official. In the competitive world of the Senate, where so much depended on the holding of high office, Pammachius was far from conspicuous—before his conversion in 396:

> Before he served Christ with his whole mind, he had been prominent in the Senate, but many others too had proconsular insignia. The whole world is full of honours like this. He was indeed first, but only among others who were first. He preceded some in dignity but followed others (Jerome, *Letter* 66.7).

In matters of property, Paula had more regard for convention than even sympathetic (but biassed) observers would allow. Although she is supposed to have dispersed her wealth for charity before her departure (Jerome, *Letter* 108.5), Jerome also admits that she 'distributed her wealth' to her surviving children (excluding Eustochia) 'disinheriting herself that she might achieve her inheritance in heaven' (*ibid.* 6). As the claim of the children had, under the law of intestacy, priority over that of the wife, the younger Toxotius and his sisters may already have been in possession of much of their father's estate. It may also be assumed that the shares of Blesilla and Rufina, who both died in the mid-380s, would have passed on their deaths to Toxotius and Paulina, the wife of Pammachius, who was to leave her own property to her husband when she died in 396. As far as can be known, then, the line of succession of property in the family of Paula was not substantially affected by individual conversions in the family but, due to the high mortality rate, became concentrated in the hands of Pammachius, who had no close kin after 386, and, ultimately, of yet another Paula, Toxotius' daughter, who was the last of the line.

A different approach to the question of the disposal and inheritance of property was adopted by Pammachius' cousin, Marcella, and her mother Albina. Marcella, the first among Roman senatorial women to adopt the ascetic life in Rome, was descended from a family of praetorian prefects and consuls and, in the conventional way, married young, only to find herself a widow after seven months. Her mother, also widowed, tried to arrange a second marriage with a prominent senator, Neratius Cerealis, who could offer a connection with the imperial house itself; his sister was the mother of Gallus Caesar, cousin of Constantius II and half-brother of Julian the Apostate. He was advanced in years and very rich, and could be counted on to leave Marcella well provided for. But Marcella refused; 'If I wished to marry, and did not desire to devote myself to perpetual chastity, I would want a husband—not an inheritance.'

Apart from Marcella, Albina had no certain descendants (despite Jerome's witness to the contrary) and Marcella's refusal to remarry ensured that the line would end with her. Albina therefore took steps to guarantee the transmission of the property to heirs along conventional lines:

> So obedient to her mother was she (Marcella) that she acted against her own personal wishes. For Albina for some time made ready to neglect her own offspring and desired to alienate all her property from her own children and grandchildren to confer it on her brother's children (Jerome, *Letter* 127.4).

In fact Albina (as Jerome should have known) was following the principles of intestate succession by which the agnates, in this case her brother's children, would be the next heirs, in default of heirs by direct descent. Marcella's consent was rather beside the point, in that Albina was entitled to make a will which would preserve the family property within the family. Nor was Albina's own saintliness in doubt; she surrendered her wealth to adopt a religious life, thus carrying out both her vocation and her material responsibilities towards her family and its property.

Melania, Paula and Marcella were women without men and religion was one of their few acceptable outlets. For men, less subject to restrictions, the ascetic vocation might be expected to have had fewer attractions. Yet the 390s saw two spectacular conversions, those of Pammachius and Paulinus of Nola. Both men could have been strongly influenced by their pious womenfolk (Paulinus' wife was compared by a friend with the ferocious Tanaquil, wife of Tarquin the Elder), but their experiences reflect wider issues. Moreover, they signal a new development; in the course of liquidising their assets in order to dispose of the money in charitable or pious works, they may have sold their property outside the family.

As the husband of Paulina, Pammachius more than most would have been subject to pressures from a pious mother-in-law, wife and frail and fanatical sisters-in-law. Paulina's death in 396 left him 'heir both to her vocation and her property'. Conjugal affection thus counteracted the legal principle that the property of husband and wife were separate entities. Had Paulina made her brother Toxotius her heir, she would have, like Albina, observed the principle that a wife's property remained part of the holding of her original family. Pammachius himself was under no obligation to leave anything to his late wife's family, nor is he known to have had brothers or sisters who, or whose children, would be next in line under intestate succession. This lack of heirs is not emphasised in the sources, but it was probably the crucial factor in his decision to sell much of his lands and dispose of the proceeds in opulent works of charity. However, the fact that he remained a 'monk among senators' suggests that his sacrifice stopped short of reducing his holdings to below the senatorial census. And the splendour and ceremony of his feeding of the poor in St. Peter's, described in Paulinus of Nola, *Letter* 13, demonstrate that Pammachius had forfeited none of his senatorial habits of mind.

With Paulinus of Nola, we move outside the confined world of the 'Romans of Rome'. After his governorship of Campania in 381, he returned to his estates in Aquitaine to pursue the life of culture and leisure appropriate to an educated aristocrat. Then, in 389, soon after the fall of the Gallic usurper Magnus Maximus, disaster struck. His brother died violently and Paulinus, filled with self-reproach, removed with his wife to their estates in Spain. There his son was born, to die when barely a week old. Gradually after this Paulinus moved closer to the adoption of a religious vocation, his estates were put up for sale and, at Christmas 394, he was ordained a priest at Barcelona. But his heart was with his patron saint, Felix of Nola, and in 395 he made his last long journey to Campania to find rest 'in safe harbour' at the feet of his saint, whose praises he was to hymn in annual poems, the *Natalicia*.

Like so many other conversions to asceticism, that of Paulinus resulted from personal tragedy. His case is the more significant because it is bound up not just with the hazards of mortality but with the political vicissitudes of a dangerous age, in which both usurpation and religious heresy could prove fatal to those on the losing side. Paulinus' reaction against all his past life and interests, including the whole of classical culture, was intense and for a while he had little time for those like his kindly old teacher, Ausonius, who did not share his views. But there was also in his conversion an emotional element which Jerome had recognised in Paula, a profound weariness of the world:

> ... But advancing age and a character loaded with honours from its early years brought deeper seriousness in maturity, and besides the weakening of my body and the drying up of my flesh wore away my eagerness for pleasures. Moreover, my mortal life itself often exercised in trials and difficulties created in me a hatred of disturbance and increased my cultivation of religion in my need for hope and fear of uncertainty. And so, undistracted by public affairs and far removed from the clatter of the forum, I celebrate rural leisure and the Church in the pleasant and peaceful seclusion of my home . . . (Paulinus, *Letter* 5.4).

It is not clear how Paulinus went about disposing of his estates during this period of retirement. Paulinus' old tutor, Ausonius, complained that Paulinus' 'kingdom' was subdivided into a hundred lots, indicating that there were many different purchasers, and that Paulinus therefore allowed much of his land to pass outside his family. On the other hand, fifth-century Aquitaine was still populated by prosperous Pontii,[8] who could have been related, albeit perhaps distantly, to Paulinus, and who may have had first option when the lands were put up for sale. Certainly, Ambrose appears to contradict this hypothesis when he hailed Paulinus' sale as a lesson to his unworthy fellow-senators who would bemoan 'the interrrupted line of succession of a noble family', but this was to ignore the fact that the succession had been interrupted anyway and that the deaths of Paulinus' brother and son (and probable vows of religious continence on the part of Paulinus' wife) had left him without immediate heirs. Selling up to

collateral branches of the family, if that was the expedient adopted, would
have freed the convert of responsibility for his lands, kept them within the
gens (the rights of which may have been recognised by convention although
no longer in law), and of course provided the convert with funds for church
building and other charities. As Paulinus elsewhere seems to have accepted
obligations towards heirs, as in the case of Aper, whose wife took over the
management of their villa on behalf of their children who would inherit
(Paulinus, *Letter* 44), he is likely to have followed the same principle in his
own case. If so, his respect for family claims would have paralleled that of
the ascetic Hilary, later bishop of Arles, who settled his inheritance on his
brother (*Life of Hilary* 6) before becoming a monk on the island monastery
of Lérins, sometime in the early 420s. It would also be in accordance with
the practice followed towards property and heirs by the other Roman
ascetics already discussed.

As the fourth century drew to a close, the divisions between ascetics and
their opponents widened. Already in the 380s, concern had been shown at
the excesses in Paula's family. Eustochia's aunt, Praetextata, tried in vain to
counteract Jerome's influence, tempting the little girl (a notably unkempt
object at this time) with pretty clothes and a new hairstyle. More serious
was the reaction of the Roman populace in general to the early death of
Blesilla, whose materialist life was transformed by a brief marriage,
widowhood and a dangerous illness from which she recovered to adopt an
ascetic life, only to die after four months. The mob at the funeral had no
doubt where the blame lay:

> 'Isn't that just what we always said? How long before they expel that hateful crew
> of monks from the city? Or stone them? Or throw them in the river?' (Jerome,
> *Letter* 38.5).

By late 384, Jerome's doctrines had isolated him from the majority opinion
in the Senate and from the Roman clergy. His way of life was investigated
by the new Pope, Siricius, and he was virtually driven from Rome in August
385.

Meanwhile, in Gaul and Spain, asceticism had become tainted with
heresy and the capital crime of magic. In 386 the charismatic heresi-
arch, Priscillian, along with two noblewomen among his following, were
executed by the usurper Maximus at Trier. Two years earlier, another
probable Priscillianist, Urbica, had been lynched at Bordeaux, and at one
point the witch-hunt for heretics threatened to take the form of a general
persecution of ascetics, who were to be detected by their pallor and poor
attire. From Rome, Pope Siricius continued the offensive, castigating
monks in Spain (a hotbed of Priscillianist sentiment) for using their
monasteries as covers for sexual immorality, and forbidding the ordination
of 'vagrant monks'. When Paulinus passed through Rome in 395 on his
way to Nola, Siricius refused to see him, a 'haughty discretion' which
grated on Paulinus' sensitive feelings. Whatever Siricius' reasons, his

attitude hardly boded well for ascetics, whether inside or outside the Senate. For the senatorial ascetics themselves, their avoidance of social contacts with the uncommitted, the uncompromising teachings of the new instructor of senators, Pelagius, and the cumulative effect of years of ascetic doctrines and practices, all contributed to a more rigid approach. Paulinus and Pammachius had turned their backs on the senatorial rat-race for offices: the next generation were to reject the conventions on property.

When the Elder Melania returned to Italy in 400, she was met by a glittering welcoming party of relations, which perhaps included her son, Valerius Publicola, and her granddaughter, the younger Melania. During his mother's absence, Publicola had added to his offices with a governorship of Campania, where an inscription (*CIL* IX.1591) commemorates him as an hereditary patron of Beneventum. His correspondence on religious questions with Augustine establishes his credentials as a good (if not especially literate) senatorial Christian, but his piety stopped short of renunciation of senatorial property, office or lifestyle. His daughter, Melania, however, took after her grandmother. While the Elder Melania lamented on Publicola's death that he had been cut off before he had abandoned his worldly ambitions, the younger Melania's views on her father are filtered through her devout biographer, the eastern monk Gerontius, who recorded her recollections in her old age and represents Publicola as one of the many stumbling-blocks placed in the way of Melania's vocation—although he did repent on his death-bed. Gerontius' early chapters on the opposition encountered by Melania and her husband make it clear that it was the issue of property above all others which sundered them from their peers.

First for the younger Melania came the unwelcome necessity of marriage, into which she was forced by her parents:

> Her parents, being distinguished leading members of the Roman Senate and in the hope that their line of succession might be continued through her, exerted great pressure to force her into marriage with her blessed husband, Pinianus (*Life of Melania* 1).

Once married, she tried to persuade Pinianus not to sleep with her,[9] even offering to surrender all her wealth to him if he would 'curb the ardour of his youth'. Pinianus, although sympathetic, was also mindful of his family duties:

> 'As soon as, by the will of God, we have two children to inherit our possessions, then together we will both renounce the world' (*ibid.*).

The first child of Melania and Pinianus was a girl, who was dedicated to virginity in infancy; unlike Eustochia, she was allowed no choice in the matter. Pinianus, being 'still distracted by a desire for worldly reputation', insisted on his second child. Melania considered leaving him and her property altogether to take up a religious life but was dissuaded by her religious advisers, who held out the hope that she might redeem him as well as herself. While pregnant with her second child, Melania participated in all-night vigil in the chapel of St. Laurence and soon after suffered a serious miscarriage. As a result, her life was despaired of, and Pinianus was compelled to promise continence in future if his wife was to recover. Soon after, the daughter also died and the couple were left without direct heirs. Dangerous illness, loss of children and the (perhaps misleading) example of their elders all contributed to the resolution of the young couple to give up one of the largest family fortunes of the Empire.

At this point, the parents of both intervened. Gerontius ascribes their opposition to fear of 'the reproaches of men' (*ibid.* 6), but concern over the transmission of property among senators went far deeper than simple regard for popular opinion: their way of life and the standing of their families depended on it. Even a hunger strike by the young would-be saints failed to break Publicola's resolve:

> For the devil had pushed her father, man of great virtue though he was, so far that he was ready to commit a great sin on the pretext of its being good. For he had it in mind to take their possessions and hand them over to his other children (*ibid.* 12).

Although Gerontius' wording is imprecise—Publicola had power only over Melania and had no other children—the intention to disinherit is clear enough:

The intention, however, was never carried out. The *Life* ascribes this to a last-minute change of heart, but there may also have been practical difficulties. Melania was, by law, Publicola's *suus heres* (an 'heir' (*heres*) being more the equivalent of a modern executor of a will) and she would have had to have been excluded from her inheritance by name, which would have been scandalous. Moreover, an *heres* had come to be entitled, as a rule, to a quarter of the estate, or that part of the estate for which he was responsible as executor, and Melania could probably have challenged the will, had this quarter not been left to her (although by Justinian's time in the sixth century, this provision could be circumvented). As his father's only surviving son, Publicola could not turn to brothers or their children for agnate succession, and of course his wife's family had no claim on his property, even though Publicola did have a distinguished brother-in-law. At the last, these considerations may have weighed as much with Publicola as religious scruples.

On Publicola's death in about 407, Melania was at last freed from paternal restraint, but the troubles of the couple were by no means over. As they pressed on, they found themselves faced with a revolt of slaves on Pinianus' suburban properties:

> While they were making these plans, the devil, the enemy of truth, confronted them with a great test. Grudging the young people such burning ardour towards

God, he prompted Severus, brother of the blessed Pinianus, and he persuaded
their slaves to say, 'No, we will not be sold; but if we are forced to the point when
we are sold, your brother Severus is our master and he himself shall buy us'
(*ibid.* 10).

Melania and Pinianus, however, responded by appealing to Serena, the
wife of the chief minister Stilicho, and her intervention not only nullified
the challenge of Severus but also led to the speeding-up of the sale of the
estates in the provinces, which were extensive and for which the provincial
magistrates were made personally responsible.

Unsuccessful though it was, Severus' challenge has important implications. By exploiting the fears of the slaves on the estates (which turned
out to be groundless, as Pinianus freed many of them), Severus was exerting
pressure on Pinianus to dispose of the lands to the man who was now, since
Pinianus was childless, his next of kin, the man with the best claim in the
event of intestate succession. By the purchase, Severus would have been
able to unite and preserve the property which he and Pinianus had jointly
inherited from their parents. Far from being 'prompted by the devil',
Severus was acting, if in a somewhat unorthodox way, in accordance with
traditional senatorial values. His claims for consideration would have been
the stronger if, as suggested above, previous sellers like Paulinus had, out of
courtesy, offered the first option to their next of kin, as Hilary of Arles was
to do. In the man's world of the Roman senate, Pinianus' ignoring of his
obligations was the more serious and his breach of protocol would have
been more glaring than that of Melania. The setting aside of Severus'
claims, although not a violation of law, was a breach of conventional family
solidarity unlikely to appeal to moderate Christians in the Senate.

Therefore, when a further crisis came, they found little support:

And when they were leaving Rome, the Prefect of the City, a man of strong pagan
convictions, resolved in concert with the whole Senate that their goods should be
vindicated to the public treasury. He was pressing on with putting this plan early
into effect when, by the Providence of God, the people rose against him because
of a bread shortage; and thus he was maltreated and lynched in the heart of the
city and all the rest were terrified into holding their peace (*ibid.* 19).

As usual, Gerontius' version of events needs qualification. The Prefect of
the City of Rome, Gabinius Barbarus Pompeianus, was indeed a prominent pagan, among whose acts was an attempt to restore public subsidies
for the celebration of pagan cults when the city was menaced by the Goths.
However, his paganism had little to do with his measure on the property of
Melania and Pinianus. As Gerontius admits, Pompeianus had the support
of the whole Senate; there was a financial crisis because of the need to find
money to buy off the Gothic invaders of Italy who blockaded Rome itself in
the winter of 408–9; and Melania's patroness Serena had been suspected of
treason and executed by order of the Senate. To some extent, then, Melania
and Pinianus were victims of circumstances outside their control, but they

were also vulnerable at a time of political and military uncertainty because their behaviour had alienated them in the eyes of an increasingly defensive Senate. So far from being a spiteful pagan offensive against Christians, Pompeianus' measure would have had support among moderate Christians in the Senate, as Publicola had been, who combined Christian belief with a tenacious adherence to the rights of property.

Yet Melania and Pinianus should not be seen purely as starry-eyed fanatics, isolated from society by idealism, quarrels with their family and the special conditions of the early fifth century. Pinianus had begun by trying to reconcile ascetic vocation with family responsibility and his attempt only ceased when both his prospective heirs were lost. Like other senators, he took pride in his family and ancestry; Paulinus of Nola in 407 praised him as a 'young pine tree', boasting descent from one of the first consuls of Republican Rome. In the disposal of his property too there was a practical consideration. The policy of Stilicho, to compromise with barbarian invaders by buying them off, ended with his fall and execution in 408. To all but a few, Alaric's invasion of Italy late in the year was predictable, and Melania and Pinianus had the satisfaction of having liquidated their Italian assets before he arrived. The exception was Pinianus' Roman mansion on the Caelian Hill. This he could not sell but 'after the passage of the barbarians (in 410), it was a burnt-out shell, which they gave away for less than nothing' (*Life of Melania* 14).

From a long-term standpoint, an unsympathetic observer could dismiss the senatorial challengers to accepted views of marriage, property and inheritance as an isolated group of neurotics or unfortunates whose senses of bereavement or failure were channeled in the direction of renunciation by skilled and fanatical teachers. But both in their reaction against conventional priorities and in their unobtrusive observance (as a rule) of practical considerations, their response has wider social implications. Traditional values were not rejected so much as transformed. The 'nobility of sanctity' no longer looked to honours, wealth or the dangerous friendship of princes, but they had not thereby renounced claims to special status in their new vocation. With the money realised from the disposal of their assets, a process that could take years, senatorial 'saints' endowed churches, hospices and monasteries—and expected their due reward hereafter. Paulinus of Nola, for example, built a hospice and churches at Fundi as well as St. Felix's splendid complex of churches at Nola; Pammachius added to his feeding of the poor in St. Peter's the building of a hospice at Portus Romae; Melania and Pinianus fed the poor, ransomed prisoners, enriched local African churches, especially at Thagaste (the see of their and Augustine's friend, Alypius), with lavish presents, and endowed monasteries in Africa for eighty men and one hundred and thirty women from the number of their own freed slaves. Acts of Christian patronage on this scale, while a continuation of senatorial munificence under the Empire, were also an extension of the Church's benefactions to its flock in the cities on every social level.

In broader terms, although ascetic converts were a minority in the Senate, their rejection of the world was part of a wider response to the competitive, hazardous and brutal character of the age. Behind the comfortable senatorial façade of polite correspondence, elegant presents and holidays in such fashionable watering-places as Baiae, or hopeful predictions of the dawning of the 'Christian Age', lurked a belief in the imminence of the Apocalypse, a fear that sooner or later the 'old age of the world' (*senectus mundi*) must end in death. The unpredictability of imperial politics had affected Paulinus and perhaps destroyed his brother; unscrupulous officials had exploited the suspicions of emperors to bring even the innocent to torture and the scaffold, as the executions of the 370s had once again demonstrated; even Melania's own patroness, Serena, had succumbed in 408 to political intrigue. At her interview with Serena, Melania had been made to sit in her rags on a golden throne, from which she had drawn the moral, from St. Peter (I Peter 1.24), that 'all the glory of men is as the flower of grass . . .': even then, Melania must also have seen that her own choice of life would ensure, if not sanctity, survival.

NOTES

1. I would like to thank Elizabeth Craik, Wolfgang Liebeschuetz, John Matthews and Susan Treggiari for reading and commenting on earlier versions of this paper. The generosity of the British Academy enabled me to profit from a stay at the Foundation Hardt pour l'Étude de l'Antiquité Classique, where much of this chapter was written.
2. Lucilia's dedication offers cult *to* as well as *for* her baby daughter. The shrine was later linked with the burial place of two Christian martyrs, Epipodius and Alexander, between whom was then interred Bishop Irenaeus of Lyon. See W. Seston and Ch. Perrat, 'Une basilique funéraire paienne à Lyon', *REA* XLIX (1947), 139–59.
3. See Brown, *Cult of the Saints*, ch. 4. The transformation of the role of the dead in the eyes of the living is a central theme of Brown's book, as is the 'special relationship' which men like Paulinus claimed and felt with their saintly protectors.
4. Matt. 19.21; Luke 18.22. Compare the exhortations of the equally austere but more practical Bishop Caesarius of Arles (early sixth century), *Sermon* XXIII on *caritas*, 'A man is not told, "Fast beyond your ability, keep watch beyond your strength"; it is not laid on him to abstain from wine or meat if he is too frail in body. And if he cannot achieve perfection, he is not compelled to sell all he has and give to the poor.'
5. Jerome, Chronicle, *anno* 374, where the manuscripts read 'unico tunc praetore urbano filio derelicto', having left her only son *as* urban praetor. Some editors have wanted a dative, *praetori* for *praetore*, suggesting that Melania left her son under the guardianship of the urban praetor, in accordance with Paulinus, *Letter* 29.9, stating that he was left under the guardianship of his powerful relations.
6. Paulinus, at Augustine, *Letter* 94, recalls Publicola as a 'true imitator of Christ'.
7. Ammianus, *History* XIV.6.12–24 contains a diatribe against the unreliable and discourteous treatment meted out to an 'honourable stranger' by senators. The

passage, which also refers to the expulsion of strangers from Rome, could well be autobiographical.

8. One Pontius Leontius owned a fortified villa, described by Sidonius Apollinaris, Poem XXII, at Bourg-sur-Gironde in the fifth century. Various other Paulini were active in the area in the fifth and sixth centuries.

9. The 'virgin bride' was also something of a literary motif (compare Jerome on Paula, above). A more successful attempt at continence was recalled in the provincial church of Clermont in central France in the sixth century (Gregory of Tours, *History of the Franks* I.47). Two scions of the local nobility are united by their parents in the hope of heirs. On the wedding night, the bride confesses her longing for perpetual virginity, her bemused young husband makes a few faltering protests about their families' wish for heirs to inherit their property but is finally overruled. The bride promises him a share in her eternal reward and they go to sleep hand in hand.

BIBLIOGRAPHY

P. Brown, *Religion and Society in the Age of St. Augustine* (London 1972) collects important articles on this theme first published elsewhere

— *The Cult of the Saints* (Chicago and London 1981) is a wide-ranging and challenging survey of changes in late Roman ideas and society

W. W. Buckland, *A Text-Book of Roman Law from Augustus to Justinian*[3] (Cambridge 1963) covers the legal background

J. N. D. Kelly, *Jerome* (London 1975), for a balanced and readable account of Jerome's life and thought

J. Matthews, *Western Aristocracies and Imperial Court* (Oxford 1975), on the Christianisation of the Roman aristocracy and the changing role of the Senate in its wider context

The *Theodosian Code, Constitutiones Sirmondianae* and *Novellae* of Valentinian III, text edited by Mommsen and Meyer (1905), contains texts applicable to the fourth and fifth centuries. See also translation of these by C. Pharr, *The Theodosian Code* (Princeton N.J. 1952, repr. N.Y. 1969). These are to be supplemented by earlier and later laws preserved in the compilations of the emperor Justinian (*Code* and *Digest*) put together in the first part of the sixth century.

V

Marriage and the Status of Women in Norse Society

Barbara E. Crawford

Department of Mediaeval History
University of St. Andrews

There has been a somewhat romantic view of the pagan past among Scandinavian historians, regarding the pre-Christian Viking period as their Golden Age. The high status of women in Norway and the Viking settlements established in the Atlantic area has been mentioned as a feature of this Golden Age (Du Chaillu 1889, pt. II, p. 1). A slightly antagonistic attitude towards Christianity has also attributed an evident decline in women's status to the introduction and spread of the new religion in the eleventh and twelfth centuries. The actual situation may not have been so simple as this interpretation would imply, and although the change of religion probably did affect the position of women—but whether for better or worse is a matter of debate—an equally important factor lay in the social and economic circumstances of the different societies in the Norse world. Where economic decline can be perceived with some degree of certainty, as in Iceland, it also seems to have had a constricting effect on women's position.

'In the two superior social classes, women enjoyed high esteem and full freedom, as Norse literature abundantly testifies' (Brøndsted 1960, p. 242). This introduces straight away the problem of the evidence, for most statements about women's position are based on Icelandic Saga material, which, it is now fully recognised, cannot be relied on to give us accurate evidence about the position of women in the Viking Age, and which also has to be treated with caution when one is discussing social 'mores' at the time when the sagas were written (Jochens 1980, p. 378). In the absence of documentary evidence (which is sparse from the North throughout the Middle Ages, and non-existent prior to the twelfth century), past historians have used the corpus of Icelandic Saga evidence uncritically. This certainly gives more information about the role of women in society and more detailed comment on the institution of marriage than any other body of mediaeval documentary material. But apart from the problem of dating the attitudes portrayed or the information about women's situation there is the problem of knowing whether the women described can be regarded as in any way typical of the Norse 'housewife' of the ninth century. It would seem far more likely that the characters portrayed were remembered for their exceptional qualities or their unusual position—which made them such suitable subjects for the saga teller's art and for the entertainment of the audience. Apart from the literary material the historian is almost entirely restricted to legal clauses in the early Norwegian law-codes for reliable information when making an assessment of the position of women in pre-Christian society in the North. There is also the archaeological material such as graves which can provide most impressive evidence for the status of certain women, and the remarkable number of rune-stones commemorating women has recently been commented on (Roesdahl 1982, p. 27). These demonstrate that women might be highly respected, although such memorials to women are not of course restricted to the Norse pagan period. The law-codes help to inform us about the legal position of women in general. Being a twelfth-century amalgam of customary practices they are hardly a reliable basis for concluding about a situation two or three centuries earlier. Nonetheless, the details regarding marriage arrangements are one part of the law-codes which may be accepted as representing pre-Christian custom about this important personal matter in a woman's life.

Marriage was a very important part of tribal custom, and in looking at pre-Christian Norse society we are dealing with a tribal society, in which the power of the kindred was the motive force. Marriage alliance with another kindred was an important way of boosting the power and influence of the family, for it established peace and friendship with the obligation to support one another's feuds. The marriage pact was treated as a legal contract between two groups of kindred. Obviously therefore the question of marriage partner could not be left entirely to the woman's own choice, and there is no doubt that the leaders of the kindred had full power to decide whom she would marry. This is not to say that a woman had no power and significance in such a society. Indeed, it is possibly true to say that a woman's role in a tribal society was likely to be more politically significant than her position in a later mediaeval society where the growth of State and Church structures allowed little room for female participation. But at the same time any significance that she may have had in a tribal society certainly would not have given her any control over her own marriage.

Marriage arrangements as we read about them in the law-codes were evidently laid down by ancient custom. The most important feature of the marriage contract was the bride-price paid by the bridegroom for the bride before the marriage. It was called the *mundr* and was stipulated by law, as none of the other payments was. One of the law-codes gives the fixed sum of twelve ounces of silver (this equalled $1\frac{1}{2}$ marks or one *baugr*—a monetary element which appears in the oldest fine lists; this is thought to indicate its antiquity). The marriage was not legal until this sum had been paid, originally to the bride's guardian, but under the influence of Christianity it went to the bride, and was turned into a gift rather than a payment signifying purchase. There was, however, no attempt by the Church to abolish this *mundr* immediately after conversion; when trying to eradicate polygamy the Church laid down that a man's only legal wife was the first one for whom he had paid the *mundr*. All consequent bride purchases were illegal—but not apparently the bride price itself. However, the word is avoided in nearly all the later law texts (KLNM, *sub mundr*).

None of the other monetary transactions was laid down by law in quite the same way, but they were open to negotiation between the two families. The woman brought a dowry (*heimanfylgja*) with her from her family, and the groom had to match this with an additional gift (*tilgjǫf* or *þridjungsauki*) which in the western parts of Norway may have had to be as large as the dowry if the woman was a virgin, or half its size if she were a widow. Later in the Middle Ages these gifts were made in the form of landed possessions, not money. They were the woman's personal possession, although administered by her husband, who, however, had no legal right to inherit them, for they passed to the children of the marriage if there were any; if not, the dowry went back to the woman's family.

These arrangements were made in the presence of witnesses and when completed the betrothal ceremony took place, finishing with the betrothal ale-feast. The woman's *giftingsmann* or male relative responsible for her marriage repeated some verbal formula and joined the couple's hands together with his own on top, while all those witnesses present did likewise. This was called the *handarband* ceremony and was similar to procedure after any business transaction. In the later Christian laws the groom had to pledge himself to his bride without the mediation of the *giftingsmann*. The betrothal was considered binding and could not be broken by either party without payment of some penalty. The marriage itself had to take place within the year unless the groom was away abroad, and if he was away longer than three years then the bride could be married to another (KLNM, *sub Festermal*).

There is no doubt at all that in pre-Christian times a man could ally himself with more than one kindred by marrying more than one woman. The attempt to eradicate this is clear from the Christian laws, and it was one of the first breaches made against pagan custom. Adam of Bremen, writing *c*.1070, says unequivocally about the Swedes that 'a man according to his means has two or three wives at one time; rich men and princes an unlimited number' (Tschan 1959, p. 203). It is an open question whether this debased a woman's status; that all wives were considered equal seems clear from the right to inheritance of all sons of all wives. All wives had a special legal status which made them quite different from the *frillur* or concubines also maintained by the powerful and wealthy: these presumably were not protected by any legal contract, and their children—although freeborn—came long after legitimate children (and *their* offspring) in the line of inheritance (KLNM, *sub Slegfred*). But there appears to have been little idea of shame attached to the status of concubine, and such women could be well-born. Even in thirteenth-century Iceland there was no stigma from extra-marital relations and women who had been involved in such unions went on to marry other men (Jochens 1980, p. 384) while the children of these unions were often highly regarded and could be brought into the family if the father so decided, then do well in the inheritance stakes. A recent study of the saga evidence for illicit unions in thirteenth-century Iceland concludes that they were of 'extraordinary frequency' (Jochens 1980, p. 383), and although the evidence suggests that women may not have had quite the sexual and marital freedom of men nonetheless there was 'an astonishing degree of sexual permissiveness among both sexes' (*ibid.* p. 385). The author thinks it highly likely that this was a continuation of ancient custom even though the Family Sagas do not themselves portray much extra-marital sexual activity relating to an earlier age.

The twelfth-century Norwegian law-codes have clauses relating to concubines suggesting that this social custom from pagan times continued well into the Christian period.

> If a man keeps a bondwoman as a concubine and keeps her by his own fireplace, or whatever kind of woman he keeps in addition to his wife, and if he is accused and convicted of this, he shall pay a fine of twelve ounces (of silver) to the bishop and he shall go to confession and do penance; and he shall forsake the woman (Larson 1935, p. 55).

From the small fine imposed it appears that the practice was not only common but, further, still had no social stigma attached to it. Indeed a clause allows for the recognition of the legality of a relationship with a concubine that had continued for twenty years, and for the ability of the children of such a union to inherit legally. This sounds like the Church attempting to tidy up what was evidently still a very loose attitude to marriage. Presumably the extra-marital relationship was determined entirely by personal and sexual needs and circumstances, not circumscribed by the needs of the kindred or by any other external requirements such as the need for the two partners to be socially compatible or *jafnrædi* as the term was in the Icelandic law-codes, an apparently important aspect of the betrothal arrangements for formal marriage (KLNM, *sub Festarmal: Island*).

The question of divorce in the pagan period is complex because there is probably a gap between legal clauses and actual social practice. Most commentators stress the belief that divorce was easy and simple to go through with, and quote the Law-codes to the effect that only a statement before witnesses by either husband or wife was required for the dissolution of a marriage (Jochens 1980, pp. 378, 380). It seems unlikely that such a step would be lightly undertaken by either party however considering the economic implications and the enmity which would be earned from the partner's kindred. There are, of course, known examples of divorce by husband or wife in the corpus of saga evidence, but these examples may not be representative of the norm, or indeed representative at all. They may well have been remembered and retold because they were unusual and memorable events, as well as being the culmination of some domestic strife, a favourite theme of the sage-teller.

All the indications are that the effects of conversion and Christian teaching were felt but slowly; and that particularly in Iceland it took a long time before social conventions regarding marriage were widely changed. Nonetheless, it might be expected that the adoption of a male-orientated, monotheistic religion, having a male priesthood and preaching the desirability of the chaste life would mean the devaluing of the role of women in society. Frey and Freyja, god and goddess of fertility and crops, were potent members of the Norse pagan pantheon, and there is some evidence to suggest that women were particularly associated with the cult of these gods in Iceland (Guthmundsson 1967, pp. 88–90). Women apparently held divination ceremonies and were the practitioners of witchcraft, certainly functions which the Christian church frowned upon. The heathen cult in the north seems to have been kept alive mainly by social feasting, on which occasions the tribal, family bonds would have been strengthened, and the suggestion that the women's role on these occasions was a very important one is surely right (Steffensson 1967–8, p. 182). The tribal leader was also probably the religious leader, offering up sacrifices for the health of the kindred. In a tribal society fertility cults are always central to religious belief because of the necessity of continuing procreation and the strength and health of the kin. In all these aspects of pagan religion the female sex obviously played a very important part.

By contrast the Christian religion entirely transcended the tribal nexus, its priesthood was meant to be a caste apart and women played no part in the service or ritual. The Church had to maintain a constant struggle to break the control of the local kindred group over church and priest. That priests should be celibate was recommended from the mid-eleventh century, but the Church found it very difficult to put this into effect, particularly in Scandinavia. Most parish priests probably married until the late thirteenth century and even after that the practice of keeping mistresses seems to have been maintained, assuring the priests' comfort and meeting domestic needs. Jochens has not been able to find a single example of a celibate priest in the literary or historical evidence from mediaeval Iceland (Jochens 1980, p. 383), although church leaders constantly showed their disapproval, and fines were demanded in payment for each child born (Johanesson 1974, p. 218). Such an attitude of disapproval may well have reflected disadvantageously on the role and function of women in general and spread beyond the rank of priests' mistresses.

From the very beginning of Christian conversion in the north there was an evident concern with marriage and the many regulations concerning it in the law-codes suggest that there was some reduction of the kindred's total control over this important matter of tribal life. The new Christian morality also interfered in the most intimate relationships of husband and wife, for which there is plenty of evidence from the many legal regulations of the Christian church (Payer 1980, pp. 353–76). But as there is a total lack of any corresponding evidence of moral codes or sexual taboos from the pagan period, it is very difficult to know how this changed sexual practices and the relationship of husband and wife. The Church was particularly concerned to forbid marriage within the kindred, and a regulation about this was one of the provisions of the very earliest ecclesiastical lawcode which St. Olaf and Bishop Grimkell introduced in their arrangements for the establishment of Christian worship in Norway c.1024 (Larson 1935, p. 245), while the twelfth-century provincial law-codes all include strong prohibitions about marrying within the seventh degree of blood kinship. The concept of incest does not seem to have been frowned on in the pagan period, when marriage within the kindred may well have been encouraged. Christian restrictions extended also to relations by marriage—forbidding those related within the fourth degree from marrying; and to spiritual affinities, that is, god-parents and god-children. These restrictions must have complicated the choice of partners for the young generation, and although there were probably few problems connected with recognition of one's sixth cousin in a society which treasured its genealogies, there must have been many problems in finding people to whom one was not related in a sparsely populated country. That such problems were insurmountable can be seen from a papal dispensation for either Greenland or Iceland which allowed marriage within the fifth degree in 1160, and which was extended generally by the Church in 1215. But the penalties for incest were high, and they were exacted (Hovdhaugen 1976, p. 22).

The Church strove hard in the eleventh and twelfth centuries to instil the idea of monogamy and to restrict the customs of concubinage. But the evidence shows that it took a long time for the idea to become accepted. References in England in the eleventh century to the custom of marrying 'after the Danish fashion' suggest that there was a well-known distinction between the Scandinavian custom and the regular version in the more Christianised parts of Europe. It certainly points to a traditional union in which the church had not been involved, and may also imply more than one wife. Virtually every Norwegian king during the eleventh, twelfth and thirteenth centuries had extra-marital relationships and illegitimate children (Hovdhaugen 1976, pp. 32–3). It must have been almost impossible for the Church to impose its ideas of moral conduct when the highest social levels constantly offended against them. The Norwegian archbishops fought tirelessly to inculcate the new teaching and several letters from Archbishop Eystein to chieftains in Iceland have survived in which they are individually castigated for their moral behaviour, being told that in their private lives they were 'no better than the beasts of the barnyard' (Johannesson 1974, p. 187). This was followed up by letters from Pope Innocent III (Jochens 1980, p. 386).

The English archbishops concerned themselves similarly with the morals of the petty kings of Ireland, where easy divorce and marriage within the kindred were also customary (Sellar 1978–80, pp. 470–1). Norse and Irish attitudes to these matters seem remarkably similar and in the kingdom of the Isles the two strands blended, as can be seen from the regulation of the marriage of the king of Man in 1176 by a legate of the apostolic see, Vivian Tomasini, Cardinal priest of St. Stephen's, Monte Coelio. He was sent to the island of Man 'and in the discharge of his office caused Godred IV, king of Man, to be united in lawful marriage with his 'wife', the daughter of MacLoughlin, son of Murrough, king of Ireland, with the abbot of Rievaulx conducting the marriage ceremony (Goss 1874, p. 77). The two had been living together for some while for there was a son and King Godred had to pay compensation for this irregularity, granting land, on the day of his marriage, for the founding of a monastery in the island. Godred's father, Olaf, is said by the same monastic chronicler to have been a devout king, 'zealous in promoting the divine service and acceptable to God and man, except in as much as he indulged too much in the domestic vice of kings' (Goss 1874, p. 63). At least the Church was able to pressurise Olaf's son into undergoing a Christian marriage ceremony.[1]

Gradually the Church's teaching that marriage was a God-instituted sacrament, which created an unbreakable bond and placed a sanctity on the union of the sexes made its impact throughout Scandinavia. Although the teaching about the seven sacraments does not appear to have been very important before the late twelfth century in the Christian Church generally, there are definite indications in the early Norwegian laws (c.1150) that a priest ought to be associated in the marriage ceremonies. Eventually it became customary for the couple to be blessed at the church door and a bridal mass to be held in the church afterwards. During the service, a 'pell' or cloth supported on four poles was sometimes held over the bridal pair (Hovdhaugen 1976, p. 16). Thirteenth-century church laws say that banns must be read out on the three preceding Sundays so that any impediments to the marriage could be brought forward—a procedure particularly necessary when the forbidden relationships were so wide-reaching. But the church blessing was not absolutely necessary and many marriages took place without it. The betrothal established the marriage and not until late in the sixteenth century is there any mention that the church blessing was the only legal form of marriage (Hovdhaugen 1976, p. 17).

The church taught that the sacrament of marriage was an agreement between two individuals and this is an attitude entirely at variance with the tribal contract of pagan custom. Did this allow a woman any more freedom of choice than she had exercised under the older kindred system? There is evidence that a marriage was considered lawful by the Church only if the agreement of both partners had been secured. It is clear from two of the Norwegian provincial law-codes that a marriage was considered to be unlawful by the Church if a woman's opposition to it was made in the presence of witnesses; although the absence of these particular clauses from the other two law-codes suggests that there were diverging views in different parts of Norway on this matter c.1200.[2]

There are five famous marriages in saga literature which took place against the stated will of the girl concerned. All five were unmitigated disasters, ending with the death, maiming or divorce of the husband. From this evidence the conclusion has been drawn that 'while a woman's consent did not count for much, it was unwise to marry her off against her wishes' (Frank 1973, p. 477). Doubts have already been expressed about taking such literary examples as typical of the situation of Icelandic women in general. One is given the distinct impression of some very powerful and exceptional women, who dominated the society in which they lived as well as the menfolk about them: and that is probably exactly why they figure in the sagas. They have been interpreted as representing an older social type than the period of saga-writing in the thirteenth and fourteenth centuries and as also representing an older moral force in Icelandic society, remaining loyal to pre-Christian ideals in which revenge figured prominently. But it is not wise to treat them as typical of women in Norse society as a whole or to draw any generalised conclusions from them about the impact of Christianity on marriage in this society.

The Church in general is thought to have exercised a loosening process on the tribal society of pre-Christian Scandinavia (Johnsen 1948, p. 100), weakening the family bonds and perhaps reducing the power of the kindred in many social and political matters. As regards the question of marriage, however, it is quite clear from the sources that a woman's *giftingsmann* retained the power and right to choose her marriage partner, which was still a very important matter for the family as a whole. There may have been some support from the Church for a woman who did not want to be forced into an unwelcome marriage. But a young girl would have to be particularly strong-willed to refuse an arranged marriage and her freedom to make a choice of partner was still exceedingly circumscribed, unless she was an heiress over the age of fifteen in Norway (twenty in Iceland). Widows were also economically independent, and, as in other parts of Europe, had much greater freedom in the matter of their re-marriage. This situation was probably experienced by many women eventually for the early age of first marriage for a girl meant that the likelihood of her having more than one husband was high, if she survived the rigours of childbirth.

As regards the question of divorce it would appear that this escape route from an unhappy marriage was denied to both men and women in the Christian period, for according to the Church's teaching, a marriage which had been contracted before God could not be dissolved. There were occasional grounds for separation, but neither party could marry another (Hovdhaugen 1976, p. 18). As always, the rich and powerful might get away with it: King Sigurd the Crusader managed to get a divorce from his wife in the early twelfth century on payment of a fine to the Church. It seems unlikely that this was a viable path to freedom for a woman, even though Icelandic evidence suggests that the pagan tradition of easy divorce may have survived there longer (Jochens 1980, p. 380).

In one respect the Christian church did offer women an alternative to marriage, in the possibility of devoting their lives to God and entering a convent. For the exceptionally gifted it may have offered some opportunity to develop their talents in a direction other than the home and children, and we have the well-known example of Ingunn, who taught Latin to the scholars in the Cathedral school at Holar and corrected their exercises while doing her needlework (Foote and Wilson 1970, p. 109). But the family had to be well-off to endow a daughter sufficiently well for her to enter a convent, and as far as Iceland is concerned, the evidence does not suggest that it was a much sought-after alternative. There were two Benedictine nunneries in Iceland, but the number of women in them seems to have been very small and to have included many previously married who had entered the convent in their widowhood. Virginity was not prized in Iceland; the term for an unmarried woman means 'unlucky' and the word for a bachelor also 'vagabond' or 'wretch' (Frank 1973, p. 482).

As suggested, the Icelandic evidence seems to tell us about the 'exceptional' rather than the 'normal'. It is very difficult indeed to acquire evidence of the 'normal' marriage and a woman's freedom of choice in the matter because there is always little reason to record the normal. However, a rune stick found comparatively recently under the floor of the mediaeval church of Lom in Gudbrandsdal does give us some positive indication of a more normal situation—so ordinary that we know absolutely nothing about the individuals involved in this personal matter as they are totally unrecorded in any other historical source. Carved on the rune stick is a message: in fact, a proposal of marriage: 'Havard sends Gudny God's greeting and his own friendship. And now it is my full intention to ask for your hand, if you do not want to be with Kolbein. Consider your marriage and let me know your will' (Liestol 1977, p. 37). It dates from the late thirteenth or early fourteenth century and is therefore evidence of the attitudes of provincial Norway at a time when Christian principles were fully in force. It is a most useful addition to the dry information of the legal codes which tell us so little of the practicalities of the process of choosing a partner in this society. Its formality would not be inappropriate to the eighteenth or nineteenth centuries, but it certainly gives us the impression that a woman has full freedom of choice between two suitors. Perhaps Kolbein has already asked for her hand and Gudny is hesitating—a situation known to Havard. He, at any rate, wants to know her feelings before he embarks on the process of entering into negotiations with her parents or guardian, and this is exactly what the Eidsivating Law-code says the man must do who is wishing to marry a woman. We know nothing of Gudny's situation, whether she is unmarried or a widow. The impression given is that she was of an age to know her own mind, and if she had already come into an inheritance then she would be very likely to have more than one suitor, and would have had some freedom of choice in the matter. She was of the richer section of the farming community for the stick was found near the choir where the top people sat (and incidentally on the north side, which was the women's side). But whether this message was sent to her during the church service or whether she had received it before and taken it to church with her we have no way of knowing. Had Havard had no opportunity to ask Gudny in person if she would encourage his suit or not? It may be that we have the eternal triangle situation and Havard is trying to force Gudny to make up her mind one way or the other. Whatever else we make of this piece of social history, it suggests that the situation as regards marriage conventions in fourteenth century Lom was little different from that in the nineteenth century. What we are still not able to say with any degree of certainty is whether it was much different from that in the tenth, although the open nature of the above enquiry does imply that the personal wishes of the woman counted for more than they might have done in a pre-Christian age.

We cannot assume that the situation in Norway, the home country, was the same as in Iceland or the other colonies. It is probably true to say that women in colonial societies anywhere tend to enjoy a higher degree of freedom than in the 'more settled, proprietorial and feudal way of life' (Allen 1960, p. 49). The Viking Age throughout Scandinavia was a period of upheaval and opportunity, when women must have been left in charge of the family and the farm during their husbands' absences on sea-faring voyages (Foote and Wilson 1970, p. 111). This situation would have given them the opportunity to use their own resources of organisation and judgement which they did not exercise to the same extent when occupying a subordinate position, and particularly so, since the farms of Scandinavia were isolated settlements without the security and reciprocal assistance available in village communities. Indeed, a certain class of farm-names thought to date from this period in Norway have a woman's personal name as the specific first element, which seems to indicate that she was the legal owner if not the founder of that farm (Hovdhaugen 1976, p. 12). But a more significant fact is the startling difference between the percentage of such names in Norway and in Iceland, providing unequivocal evidence for the standing of women in Iceland in the Settlement period.[3] The difference in the figures was originally accounted for by the difference in natural conditions of the farming terrain, Olsen suggesting that the pastoral conditions in Iceland allowed a woman to farm the land on her own, whereas the arable agriculture of Norway demanded more co-operative effort and the organisation of a patriarchal family group (Olsen 1928, p. 116). However, the evidence would seem to invite conclusions of a more radical kind about the nature of a woman's position in Icelandic society, although it is doubtful whether one can accept all of Guthmundsson's theories about these farms and their female holders being closely associated with religious centres where the cult of Frey and Freya was practised by priestesses who officiated at the religious ceremonies and lived in the *Stadir* farms round about (Guthmundsson 1967, pp. 148, 155).

Certainly Norse women were involved in the settlement of Iceland and the other colonies from the very beginning, for the numbers of pagan female graves are roughly equal to men's throughout the Norse world (except in the Isle of Man). In fact literary evidence gives us many examples of women themselves being settlers in Iceland, and taking land on their own account, substantiated to some extent by the Book of Settlements, the original version of which was written down in the twelfth century recording what was then traditionally remembered of the land-taking process several centuries earlier. It details the procedure to be followed for the hallowing of a land-claim by both men and women, the *Hauksbok* version saying that no woman could take more land than she could walk around between dawn and sunset on a spring day, leading a two-year-old well-fed heifer. This was different from (and perhaps more restrictive than) the procedure to be followed by a man, who had to mark off his boundaries by signal fires, taking only as much as he could encompass by kindling fires and keeping them burning between sunrise and sunset (Johannesson 1974, pp. 30–1). It is thought probable that these arrangements date from a period when the original land-takers or their descendants were having to divide up some of their huge estates among other settlers; otherwise the territory held, for instance, by one of the early settlers Aud the Deep-Minded in the Daleslands could not possibly have been walked around by her in one day leading a heifer. Nonetheless, the principle was laid down that a woman was legally able to do this herself, either for the original land-taking or for a later division when she was perhaps heiress to a large estate.

Aud is the most famous of all the Norse women of the Icelandic settlement period, because of the remarkable evidence for her independent status, her wealth and presumably her wisdom, implied in her nickname 'djupuðga'. Her father, Ketill Flatneb, was one of the famous early Vikings of the mid ninth century who took most of the Hebrides under his control, and she was married to Olaf the White, probably identical with the king of Dublin, who ruled the Norse communities in Ireland from 853–71 (Smyth 1977, p. 119). By birth and marriage therefore she was a part of the most powerful layer of Norse society in the west, and it was the mobile and exceedingly unstable political situation in that area which gave her the opportunity to live thereafter the life of an independent matriarch. As a widow, she accompanied her son Thorsteinn to Caithness which was an area of Norse expansion in the late ninth century. When he died she moved on via Orkney and Faeroe to Iceland which was then the uninhabited land which the Vikings were taking for settlement when they had exhausted most of the opportunities around the British Isles. Due to her family situation and wealth she was able to marry off grand-daughters in both Caithness and Faeroe, founding in the latter the wealthiest and noblest family of the islands. Arriving in Iceland with twenty freemen on board her ship as well as a good number of slaves she founded one of the most important dynasties in Iceland, along with other members of Ketill Flatneb's family. It is pertinent that it was in Iceland that she was able to take land where—unlike all the other areas of Norse settlement in the west except Faeroe—it did not have to be won from an indigenous population: this possibly allowed a woman more opportunity to become a land-taker herself. Aud is by no means an isolated example of a female settler in the Icelandic colony. There are so many other cases in Saga literature that one must assume that these accounts are based on some residual memory of the female founders of certain families—in which the custom of naming children after their mother seems to have been prevalent (Guthmundsson 1967, pp. 32–5). The place-name evidence already discussed would support this.

But the circumstances were exceptional, and they did not last. Iceland was traditionally believed to have been fully settled in sixty years, and although this can hardly mean that everywhere was fully cultivated in that time, it suggests that by the mid tenth century there was no room for pioneering activities on a large scale. At the same time the opportunities for raiding and acquiring surplus wealth throughout Europe were much reduced, quite apart from the fact that it was exceedingly difficult to replace the original ships with ocean-going craft in a country which lacked the necessary timber. These two factors changed the earlier situation of mobility which seems to have been favourable to the colonial Norse woman's evident independent status. An additional point is that when the male members of the household were away less often—and eventually not away at all—this cut down on the opportunity for the women to prove themselves capable of running the farm in the absence of the men, perhaps representing the family's interests at the public courts, and in the process earning for themselves the laudatory nicknames which seem to have been a feature of the pre-Christian period. Research suggests that this tradition was not maintained. Nicknames decline in number in the Christian period, and they also acquire an overtone of opprobrium, such as 'mare of the court-yard'. The declining number has been interpreted as 'evidence for the declining influence of women in Christian society'. Only eleven nicknames are known from the Christian period and the change in type of nickname is thought to indicate a 'complete change in the situation of women in society' (Steffensson 1967–8, p. 182) occasioned directly by the change of religion. Guthmundsson's theories suggest that some women may have had a very important role in pagan worship in certain parts of Iceland (1967, pp. 72, 119, 155), and certainly, as mentioned earlier, their involvement in preparing the food for the central ceremonies of the pagan cult must have closely associated them in the spiritual life of the tribe. The most immediate change of religious practice on acceptance of Christianity was the ending of sacrifices and of the eating of horseflesh, even although Iceland was exceptional in apparently being allowed to continue sacrifices in private for a while (Johannesson 1974, p. 139). The continuity of the traditional pattern of life and the failure of Christianity to impose certain ideas regarding monogamy and the celibacy of the priesthood have been discussed already, but the impact of the new religion in the area of ancestor worship and sacrifices was more immediate and eventually total. The suggestion that this may well have curtailed an important area of feminine activity cannot be refuted.

In one other respect the conversion to Christianity may have affected the social order and thereby helped to reduce the status of women; in its effects on the system of slavery. All Scandinavian societies were based on slavery and one of the main objects of the Viking raids was to enslave people from the countries raided and transport them back to Scandinavia or sell them to Muslim countries in Southern Europe. The settlers of Iceland brought large numbers of slaves with them, the majority captured in the British Isles; these would have worked on the original large estates thus giving the Norse women freedom from the daily chores of life. Conversion to Christianity helped to change this, not simply because it became incumbent on the Christian to free his slaves, but more probably because the forbidding of exposure of children rendered the perpetuation of slavery impossible (Johannesson 1974, pp. 353–4). The ensuing growth of the servile population to an intolerable level could then only be checked by liberation and the grant of a piece of land on which the freed slave could settle with his family and not burden his former owner with their maintenance. This resulted in the division of the original large estates among freeholders and the development of medium-sized farms which were all worked by the labour of the individual farmer and his family. This must have led to Icelandic women having to bear more of the burden of family and farming life on fewer resources and the ensuing decline of their former independent status. So it seems likely that conversion and economic change worked together to turn them into more subordinate and less highly-valued individuals in the community, a process glimpsed in the change of nicknames applied to them.

This development was from a situation of exceptional freedom for women to one which was certainly closer to that in the rest of Christian Europe. This is hardly surprising. Firstly, there is no similar population movement in early mediaeval Europe providing women with such opportunities to be powerful and independent. Secondly, the spread of the Christian religion was a pervasive force for standardisation of morals and establishment of cultural unity. Most commentators on women's position in mediaeval Norway or Iceland conclude that 'in a formal, legal sense women do not seem to have counted for much in what was essentially a man's world' (Foote and Wilson 1970, p. 110), although it seems this could be said of many other periods in history, including our own. A woman's legal rights may appear extremely limited (Frank 1973, p. 483), but this is no cause for surprise, particularly when, as in mediaeval Iceland, the implementation of a judicial decree depended on an individual's political influence and possibly in many cases the outcome of a duel (Johannesson 1974, p. 70). It is on the other hand surely significant that the Icelandic law-code specifically allowed women to transact business at the *thing* (the legal assembly) and negotiate with merchants on their husbands' behalf (Du Chaillu 1889, pt. ii, p. 29; Foote and Wilson 1970, p. 110), and although limitations on the value of goods which she could buy and sell on her own account were stipulated, this was presumably a safeguard for the redress of reckless spending of her husband's income rather than a fixed minimum amount beyond which no wife dared go. In Denmark, which was in fact more influenced by feudal ideas than the rest of Scandinavia, there are nonetheless records of women being involved in trading and dealing, not only in land, but even holding partnerships, in vessels and cargoes (Jexlev 1978, p. 35). Moreover, the custom of including daughters in the division of family lands seems to have spread from Denmark, where it may have been established some centuries earlier, to the rest of the Scandinavian world in the thirteenth century (KLNM, *sub Odalrett*). Women throughout Europe usually had their share of the family lands in the form of a dowry, but nonetheless it became the custom in the Norse world that daughters inherited lands to the value of half of their brothers' inheritance. This is a very definite legal advantage over women in the rest of Europe and must have contributed significantly to the Norse woman's independence, enhancing her position in society. She had, for instance, to be party to the many legal transactions which took place on the division of the family estates.

This sort of evidence suggests that a woman's legal position in the late Norse world may still have been significantly different from that which pertained in the rest of Christian Europe. Two documented cases from Shetland, a group of islands lying between Scotland and Iceland, show two women in the late thirteenth and early fourteenth centuries acting on their own account in lawcourts in a manner which suggests that they had an independent status and a legal standing contrasting markedly with what is known about other mediaeval societies. Shetland is a part of the Norse world not very often cited as having any particular interest for the social historian, because of the absence of documentary evidence in comparison with the Orkney Islands to the south and Iceland to the north. Shetland rarely figures in any saga material, and these documents are the first still extant to have been drawn up in the islands. They concern the period when Shetland was ruled directly by the Norwegian crown and not by the earls of Orkney, and particularly when it was under the control of a powerful individual, Thorvald Thoresson—a royal official who was probably also a native Shetlander—from the 1290s to c.1330 (Crawford, in press). There is some evidence to suggest that this man was a harsh and over-bearing official, who may also have been guilty of depriving his royal Norwegian overlord of some of his rents and dues. Certainly the first document records an occasion in the year 1299 when Thorvald was accused of not returning the rightful amount of royal rents from the island of Papa Stour to Duke Hakon of Norway (the brother of the king, who at that time held Shetland as a ducal fief). The document is drawn up by the Shetland Lawthing (the main legal assembly) recording the accusation which had been made about this by a woman on the island, Ragnhild Simunsdatter, and was evidently being forwarded to Duke Hakon with Thorvald's refutation of the accusation (Clouston 1914, pp. 67–8). She had accused him twice, and both occasions are carefully recorded. The first time was on the Monday in

Passion week when several individuals from the west side of Shetland along with Thorvald were gathered in the living-room of the duke's house on the island and Ragnhild complained that—in some way which is not fully comprehensible now—one of the farms on the island, Brekasetter, had not been properly accounted for in the duke's rental. Thorvald said that many others apart from himself had dealt with this matter of rent from Papa Stour, to which Ragnhild replied that it made no difference, they had all deceived the duke. The second occasion was a few days later outside the duke's house when Ragnhild, in what must have been a dramatic encounter, said to Thorvald, 'Thou shalt not be my Judas though you are the duke's'. Thorvald then made a deposition about the rental situation in the island, and, obviously concerned to clear his name, got the lawthing-men of Shetland to draw up an account for forwarding to the duke.

That is all that is recorded about that particular situation, although as Thorvald continued to act as royal official in the islands we must presume that he managed to clear his name sufficiently to retain his commission. Several factors about the incident are quite obscure, particularly who Ragnhild was, or why she was defending the Norwegian duke's interest so vigorously; although it has been suggested that she may have been the ducal 'housekeeper' on the royal farm (Munch 1859, p. 657). But whoever she was, she was appearing at some hearing or official meeting on the island and taking a very independent line of action, without any husband or male relative acting for her. For our present purposes it is enough that we have contemporary documentary evidence of a woman acting thus against a very powerful royal official and that he took her accusation extremely seriously.

The second case is rather less dramatic, but once more shows 'Herra' (Lord) Thorvald coming up against a woman who is not afraid to make a complaint about him and act on her own behalf at the main Lawthing assembly in Shetland. This time it was over a fine which the woman, Bjorg, *husfreya* (Mistress) of Cullievoe in Yell, had incurred against the crown. Once more it is a complicated story and involves Thorvald making private agreements with her for the payment of the fine—including the mortgaging of land to him in part-payment (which one suspects may have been a way of acquiring land for his own benefit). Eventually, and after she had attempted to redeem part of the land with a type of coin which the royal official would not accept, she appeared in the Church at Tingwall where the legal assembly was being held and lodged a complaint against him saying that she wished to rescind all the agreements that had been made for the payment of the fine (Clouston 1914, pp. 69–70). A compromise was worked out by the Lawman, but what happened thereafter is unrecorded. We have in this recorded case therefore evidence of a woman being considered herself responsible for a fine to the Crown, negotiating with the royal official over its payment and finally appealing to the public court—and appearing in the public court—for redress against what she thought was his evident harsh treatment of her in this matter. There is no way of knowing whether she was widowed or not; the title *husfreya* is customary for married women of a certain status. But there is no indication that the situation was considered to be in any way unusual. Indeed, the very fact that the two earliest (and only) legal records of the functioning of the legal system in Shetland before the islands passed to Scotland in 1469 *both* show women acting on their own behalf strongly suggests that it was not unusual. They date from a time when Norse law and custom were still fully operational in Shetland, and before the economic and political problems of the later fourteenth century produced significant changes in society.

These two case histories should serve to balance the view that women's legal rights were very limited in mediaeval Norse society. But can they be taken as evidence of a general situation throughout the Norse world? In an area so geographically extensive, it can hardly be expected that social and economic conditions or women's position would be exactly the same in every part. Five centuries after the Viking expansion and settlement of the islands in the Atlantic was long enough for very different social conditions to develop in the colonies from those of the home countries. The evidence examined above does suggest that a woman's position in Iceland was originally significantly different from that in Norway. There were, however, powerful factors working for uniformity, notably the Christian religion (as already mentioned), and the role of Norse law. If there was one common factor which gave these diverse communities any unifying stamp it was the importance of their laws and legal assemblies; these played a very important role in the social cohesion of communities geographically separate and with very different political structures. The island colonies all followed some variant of the Norwegian Law-codes from the beginning of the colonisation process, and as the kings of Norway increased their political control over them in the mediaeval period, so the local versions of the laws were tied in with the Norwegian codes and new amendments imposed. These two forces of mediaeval society—Church and Law—created comparable political and social frameworks within which women's status was defined. It is thus suggested that Ragnhild and Bjorg may be regarded as not totally exceptional in the Norse world, and certainly not as isolated examples of a peculiarly female-dominated Shetland society. Our sources of evidence about them are documentary survivals concerned with recording situations for a legal judgement, and not therefore subject to any personal interpretation or dictates of literary convention. Brief though the information is about the two women it is contemporary and factual, and thus of a very different order from the literary evidence of the Icelandic saga material. The problems of using the latter type of evidence to delineate an accurate picture of the status of Icelandic women in the pagan or Christian period have already been discussed. The impossibility of knowing whether the characters portrayed are typical or exceptional will remain. There is no doubting that many of these saga women are exceptional by any standards of judgement. But there is some supporting evidence for the exceptional nature of the opportunities that existed for women of wealth and standing in a colonial situation, and for the status of Icelandic women in the Settlement period. Although Ragnhild and Bjorg lived in different times from Aud the Deep-Minded, and their lives were certainly less rich in opportunity and more circumscribed by conventions of mediaeval church and society, nonetheless it may be suggested that they can be seen manifesting the same spirit of independence within the restriction of a legal context and a legal document. But the poverty of our sources prevents us from being able to draw any closer comparison between them and their ninth-century forebears in the Norse world.

NOTES

1. At a similar date pressure was brought to bear on the Norse earl of Orkney over the irregularity of his marital affairs. Earl Harald Maddadsson had taken as his second wife—while his first was still alive—the daughter of the earl of Ross and became involved in rebellious activities in Moray, perhaps as a result of prosecuting his wife's family's interests (Duncan 1975, p. 193). Both the Church and the king of Scots combined together to force this powerful northern magnate to submit to feudal and ecclesiastical authority and in 1196 he submitted to King William at Perth. One of the terms of his submission and conditions on which he was restored was that he put away his second wife and take back his first (which he refused to do according to one chronicler).
2. The best known example which proves that a woman did indeed have some freedom in this matter if she was powerful enough, is that of the sister of King Sverre, Cecilia. She was married to a Swedish nobleman by her brother's political opponents but when her brother got hold of the throne she returned to Norway and declared her intention of marrying a Norwegian *lendirmann* (noble). At first the archbishop set himself against this marriage, but Cecilia brought witnesses to prove that the earlier marriage had taken place against her will, and as a result it was declared illegal (Johnsen 1948, pp. 111–12). However, she managed to do this only once the political situation was such that she had powerful supporters and one is left wondering if this theoretical freedom meant very much in practice for the rest of the female population.
3. Out of 2500 *stadir* names of farms in Norway, perhaps 30 (or less) contain female names. In Iceland there are 1100 *stadir* names and more than 110 of these contain female names 'a percentage at least ten times as high as in Norway' (Olsen 1928, p. 115).

BIBLIOGRAPHY

W. E. D. Allen, 'The Poet and the Spae-Wife' *Saga-Book of the Viking Society*, xv (1960)
J. Brøndsted, *The Vikings* (1960)
J. S. Clouston, *Records of the Earldom of Orkney*, Scottish Historical Society (1914), 2nd series, 7
B. E. Crawford, 'Papa Stour: Survival, Continuity and Change in one Shetland Island' in *Northern and Western Isles in the Viking World: Survival, Continuity*

and Change, Publication of Bicentenary Conference of the National Museum of Antiquities, Scotland (ed. A. Fenton) (in press)

P. Du Chaillu, *The Viking Age* (1889)

A. A. M. Duncan, *Scotland: The Making of a Kingdom* (1975)

P. Foote and D. M. Wilson, *The Viking Achievement* (1970)

R. Frank, 'Marriage in 12th and 13th century Iceland', *Viator* (1973), 4

Rev. Goss (trans.), *The Chronicle of Man and the Sudreys* (Manx Society (1874), xxii)

B. Guthmundsson, *The Origin of the Icelanders* (1967)

E. Hovdhaugen, *Ekteskap og Kjønnsmoral i Norsk Historie* (Oslo 1976)

T. Jexlev, 'Wills, Deeds and Charters as Sources for the History of Mediaeval Women' in *Aspects of Female Existence* (Proceedings from the St. Gertrud Symposium, 'Women in the Middle Ages', ed. B. Carlé (Copenhagen 1978)

J. M. Jochens, 'The Church and Sexuality in Mediaeval Iceland', *Journal of Mediaeval History* (1980), 6

J. Johannesson, *A History of the Old Icelandic Commonwealth* (1974)

A. O. Johnsen, *Fra Aettesamfunn til Statssamfunn* (Oslo 1948)

Kultur Historisk Leksicon for Nordisk Middelalder (KLNM) (Copenhagen 1956–78)

L. M. Larson, *The Earliest Norwegian Laws* (1935)

A. Liestol, '"Will you Marry Me?"; Under a Church Floor', *Mediaeval Scandinavia* (1977), 10

P. A. Munch, *Det Norske Folks Historie*, i–v (1852–63)

M. Olsen, *Farms and Fanes of Ancient Norway* (1928)

P. Payer, 'Early Mediaeval Regulations concerning marital sexual relations', *Journal of Mediaeval History* (1980), 6

E. Roesdahl, *Viking Age Denmark* (London 1982)

W. D. H. Sellar, 'Marriage, Divorce and Concubinage in Gaelic Scotland', *Trans. of the Gaelic Society of Inverness* (1978–80), LI

A. P. Smyth, *Scandinavian Kings in the British Isles* (1977)

J. Steffensson, 'Aspects of Life in Iceland in the Heathen Period', *Saga-Book of the Viking Society* (1967–8), xvii, 2–3

F. T. Tschan (trans.), *History of the Archbishops of Hamburg-Bremen* by Adam of Bremen (New York 1959)

VI

'My Wife Shall Have It': Marriage and Property in the Wills and Testaments of Later Mediaeval England

Ann J. Kettle

Department of Mediaeval History, University of St. Andrews

The historian of English law, Sir William Holdsworth, wrote that:

> No legal system which deals merely with human rules of conduct desires to pry too closely into the relationship of husband and wife. Dealings between husband and wife are for the most part privileged. But some rules it must have to regulate the proprietary relationships of the parties when they both own property, and to regulate the fate of such property when the marriage terminates.

The wills and testaments of later mediaeval England provide an insight (seldom provided by other kinds of surviving documentary evidence) into contemporary attitudes to marriage and property. Wills reveal the ways in which property owners, anticipating the termination of marriage by death, attempted to provide for the surviving spouse within the restraints imposed by law and custom. Occasionally they reveal also individual attitudes to the marriage bond and attempts to exert control over behaviour from beyond the grave by exercising the sanction provided by the ownership of property. The extent to which testators relied on their spouses to carry out the provisions of their wills is another area of investigation, together with the question of variations in practices and attitudes between town and countryside. The material for this study comes from several thousand wills and testaments printed in a series of collections which vary greatly in the quality and accuracy of transcription and edition. The wills range in date from the second half of the thirteenth century to the end of the fifteenth century, with a geographical spread from Somerset to Northumberland. They contain, in the main, the last wishes and bequests of substantial property owners from the ranks of the nobility, gentry and merchants of later mediaeval England.[1]

Before considering the terms of the wills themselves it is necessary to examine briefly and in a much simplified way proprietary relationships during and after marriage and the law governing those relationships. Marriage was often the point of endowment of both men and women and thus the point of establishment of a conjugal estate. By the early fourteenth century the *maritagium*, land settled on the bride by her family, had largely gone out of use and, as K. B. McFarlane wrote, 'Daughters, unless they were heiresses, were not, in the later middle ages, an occasion for the dispersal of land' (McFarlane, p. 64). The *maritagium* was replaced by the marriage portion, the upper class version of the dowry. The marriage portion was a money payment which usually went to the father of the groom and was less a portion for the bride and more a payment for a son-in-law. The wills of members of the nobility and gentry often contained bequests of money for the marriage portions of daughters for whom no suitable marriage had yet been arranged; a fashionable charitable bequest was the provision of dowries for girls, often the servants of the testators, whose families could not purchase husbands for them. Although brides other than heiresses no longer brought land to a marriage the groom was expected to make provision in the form of land for the support of his wife in the event of his death. Dower, which had its origins in a voluntary gift of part of the husband's property at the time of marriage, developed in the later middle ages into an estate in land for the widow protected by the common law. The widow was entitled for life to one third of the lands held solely by her husband during the marriage. To secure an heiress as a bride it was often necessary, however, for the groom and his family to offer more than the prospect of dower rights enforceable by law. In most surviving marriage contracts the wife was given a jointure in part of her husband's lands; by this arrangement she was entitled, if she survived her husband, to hold for the rest of her life those lands which had been put in joint tenancy, in addition to her dower lands.

The property arrangements made at the time of marriage were thus designed to secure a suitable partner and to provide some security for the bride in the event of her widowhood. They were not designed to secure the economic independence of the bride during the marriage as English law allowed few property rights to the married woman. In contrast to most continental systems of law English common law rejected the idea of a community of goods between husband and wife. The wife could inherit or acquire lands during marriage but the husband controlled those lands while the marriage lasted and, if a child was born of the marriage, 'if a cry was heard within four walls', the husband who survived his wife was entitled to a life estate in her lands 'by the curtesy of England'. The widower's right of curtesy, which Frederick Maitland called 'a large, a liberal right' (Pollock and Maitland, p. 416), was thus more generous than the widow's right to one third of her husband's lands. During the marriage the wife had no power to grant away her own lands without her husband's agreement but her husband could alienate her lands without her consent, although the alienation could be revoked after his death by the widow or her heirs. The development of the law relating to dower gave the married woman some protection against the alienation by her husband of his lands during the marriage. The husband could not alienate lands to which his widow might have a dower claim without her agreement, signified by a final concord in which she renounced her title and claim to dower after a private examination before the royal justices. In towns, where borough custom often allowed widows a generous but not always clearly defined right to dower and where it was necessary for real property to be freely disposable, a married woman's acknowledgement of her renunciation of her rights could be recorded with less formality and expense by a deed registered in the borough court. Pressure by the common lawyers to standardise this procedure in the fourteenth century and prevent the registration of the deeds of married women in borough courts was resisted by the burgesses who preferred their customary procedures.

The married woman was allowed by law even fewer rights over movable property. Whatever goods the wife brought to the marriage and whatever goods she acquired after marriage became the property of her husband. English common law adopted, with all its implications, the rule that husband and wife could not own chattels in common. The wife could not even be said to own her paraphernalia, defined as the clothes on her back and the ornaments of her body, since her husband could sell or give these away during his lifetime. He could not, however, dispose of his wife's paraphernalia in his will, although some husbands did bequeath to their wives the only goods over which the latter might be said to have some tenuous right of ownership. In 1442 Edward Tyrell bequeathed to his wife 'all her own array that belongs to her body and all her attire without any diminution thereof' (*Chichele*, p. 634). The equivalent in the city of London of the common law paraphernalia was the 'widow's chamber', the name given to the bed-chamber, furniture and clothing which was set aside for the widow before the goods of those who died intestate were distributed.

The implications of the difference in the property rights of husband and wife can be seen most clearly in the arrangements made for the disposal of property when the marriage was brought to an end by death. Testators naturally wished to use their property, real or movable, land or chattels, to ensure the health of their souls and to fulfil certain social obligations, such as paying their debts and providing for members of their families and for other dependents. They had, however, only limited opportunity to use their property to exert influence after their deaths as law and custom imposed certain restraints on freedom of devise. Under common law land could not be bequeathed as 'God alone could make an heir' and the normal rules of inheritance could not be bypassed (Simpson, p. 59). In the later middle ages, however, landowners had increasing resort to a device which enabled them to evade this irksome prohibition on the devise of real property and to distribute their land as they pleased. The creation of a 'use' transferred the legal ownership of land to a group of feoffees while the enjoyment of the land remained with the former owner during his life; on his death the land was distributed by his feoffees according to his 'last will'. There was thus a technical distinction between the testament which bequeathed movable goods and chattels and the last will which contained instructions for the conveyance of land; as E. F. Jacob pointed out: 'The complete separation in

England between the law of inheritance to realty and the law of succession to personalty is implied in this distinction' (*Chichele*, p. xix). There is little evidence to support the idea that one of the purposes of the use was to deprive widows of their rightful dower. The common law courts would uphold the widow's absolute right to her third of the lands held solely by her husband during the marriage and to all of the land held by her and her husband in joint tenancy. In 1459 Sir Robert Hungerford asked his feoffees to dispose of his lands, 'always provided my wife have a sure estate in her jointure and dower according to the law of the land' (*Somerset Wills*, p. 192). According to J. M. W. Bean, the wife could be given by means of the use a life estate in her dead husband's lands greater than the dower to which she was entitled and surviving wills suggest that widows were in fact generously treated (Bean, p. 137). On the other hand, uses, which eroded the feudal concept of the heir and gave freedom of devise to property holders, became a matter of concern to those prospective fathers-in-law whose daughters could suffer if their husbands were prevented from inheriting according to the normal rule of primogeniture. After the mid-fifteenth century the fathers of heirs were frequently obliged to swear in marriage contracts that they would not alienate their lands or tenements and thus deprive their eldest sons and their wives.

In towns there was no prohibition on devise of lands and urban property could be freely bequeathed by testament. This freedom of devise was difficult to reconcile with the wife's claim to dower and in this matter, as in others, it has been pointed out that 'borough customs pursued an erratic and unsteady course' (Bateson, p. c). Initially in many boroughs it seems that the widow enjoyed her freebench, the right to continue to live in the house in which she and her husband lived at the time of his death Behind this right lay the idea of the continuation of the household in community. In many boroughs the right of freebench was lost if the widow remarried and by the fourteenth century most boroughs seem to have adopted the common law rule of the widow's quarantine, under which the widow could occupy the main house or chief messuage for 40 days after her husband's death, within which period her dower was assigned to her. In London at the end of the thirteenth century a widow could challenge the testament of her dead husband if he had deprived her of freebench by devising the capital messuage for sale; by the mid-fourteenth century she could protest in court only if no adequate provision had been made for her dower. Even though common law rules were adopted in theory, freedom of alienation and devise in boroughs made it difficult for widows to enforce a technical claim to dower. According to *Fleta*, a late thirteenth-century legal treatise: 'There would be found scarcely any citizens who would make great acquisitions in his lifetime if, after his death, he should be compelled against his will to leave his property to ignorant and dissolute children and to undeserving wives' (Richardson and Sayles, p. 193). This problem was probably met in practice by the husband making generous provision for his wife in his will. In 1384 a London mercer bequeathed his wife a life interest in his lands and tenements, £200 in cash, as well as her entire chamber, ornaments and personal clothing with the condition that if she would not accept the bequests 'in the name of dower' she was to have only what the law allowed her (*C.W.C.H.* ii.242). In London the husband could leave his wife a life interest only in his property but the number of cases in the late thirteenth and early fourteenth centuries in which widows had to renounce bequests in fee and accept only a life interest suggests that this was a custom of recent origin and another example of borough custom adopting common law rules. In London husband and wife could hold and acquire property jointly and widows frequently asserted their rights by challenging testaments in which their husbands had attempted to devise tenements which were held jointly. In one case a widow objected when she was left jointly-acquired property only for as long as she remained unmarried (*C.W.C.H.* i.264).

The position with regard to the bequest of goods and chattels was even less straightforward. Although the husband enjoyed outright ownership of goods and chattels during the marriage it seemed reasonable that he should be expected to make provision from those goods for his wife and children on his death. During the twelfth and thirteenth centuries a quota system was in operation by which the husband was expected to leave one third of his movable property to his wife, one third to be divided among his children, with the remaining third as 'the dead man's portion'; if there were no surviving children the widow was entitled to one half of her dead husband's goods. Although this scheme of partition was for a time accepted by the common law and was adopted by the church courts in cases of intestacy, it failed to become the general rule in the later middle ages and was established as a local custom only in the province of York, in Wales and in London. It failed to become a legally enforceable general rule because the logic of the common law doctrine of chattel ownership by husbands gave them freedom of alienation, a freedom which many extended in the fourteenth century to their testaments. As M. M. Sheehan points out, 'If they had outright ownership of all the movable property of the family, it seemed reasonable that they should be able to dispose of it all in their own way' (Sheehan, *Medieval Studies*, p. 123). Even though neither the common law courts nor the church courts, which were content to accept local custom in the matter, recognised the rule of *legatim* as generally enforceable, it still occurs frequently in wills in the later middle ages. Sometimes it took the form of the legal minimum for an unloved wife: in 1408 John Cable of Frome left his wife one third of all his movable goods 'in the name of her third of her pourparty' which she could claim by reason of his death (*Somerset Wills*, pp. 33–5) and in 1396 Sir Nicholas Dagworth left his wife a third part of his goods 'to be quiet' (*Test.Vet.* i.139). It must, however, have been a difficult rule to administer and even where testators stipulated a mechanical division of their goods to their executors, it is not clear that this was meant to be strictly enforced. In 1427 Thomas Earl of Salisbury directed that half of his goods were to go to his wife but the actual legacies amounted to much more than the specified portion (*Chichele*,

p. xxxvi). More often the threat of the legal minimum was used by husbands against wives who might be unwilling to accept a more generous provision or the conditions attached to such legacies. In 1408 a London mercer left to his wife 2000 marks, household utensils, plate and some land and tenements, 'by way of dower and her reasonable part . . . with which if she be not content she is to take nothing but what she can and ought to take according to common law and the custom of the city of London' (*C.W.C.H.* ii.398). How far the *legatim* rule was enforced or enforceable even in those areas where it remained the local custom until the late seventeenth or early eighteenth centuries is not known but it does appear to have been operated more as a sanction by husbands who, although often enjoying in theory free disposal of their goods, were prepared to accept the idea of a minimum level of provision for their widows, a minimum which was usually exceeded in practice, but which could be converted, if necessary, into a legal maximum in order to enforce acceptance of bequests with the conditions attached to them.

No such freedom of bequest of movable goods was allowed to married women and the very capacity of married women to make wills at all came into question in later mediaeval England as a further consequence of the refusal of the common law to admit community of goods within marriage. Legal opinion at the end of the twelfth century held that a wife could not, without her husband's permission, dispose of chattels which were her husband's even in her will but that it would be to the husband's credit if he allowed his wife to bequeath that third part of his chattels which would be hers if she survived him. Legal writers in the thirteenth century were of the same opinion but added that, for decency's sake, wives should also be allowed to bequeath their paraphernalia. The English bishops were opposed to this idea that the right to make a will was a privilege granted to wives by their husbands and continued to assert the canonical theory that married women had the same right as any other adult to make a gift of alms by testament for the sake of their souls. The re-iteration by thirteenth-century synods of the testamentary capacity of the married woman was easily countered by the common lawyers who could point out that since a married woman owned no chattels she could not make a testament disposing of property that she did not possess. In the course of a case heard in the court of Common Pleas in 1311 it was declared that 'no person can make a testament save he who can claim property in the chattels, but a wife cannot claim property and consequently cannot make a testament' (Turner, pp. 240–1). The church continued to uphold the rights of married women but a provincial statute on the subject in 1342 provoked a protest in parliament two years later to the effect that it was against reason that the bishops should sanction the making of wills by wives. The fifteenth-century canonist William Lyndwood was reduced to arguing that a wife should be able to bequeath at least her paraphernalia freely.

In spite of the logic of the common law position married women in later mediaeval England did make wills and they, and their husbands, evidently considered they had property which they could bequeath. The wills of married women, however, form a very small proportion of the surviving wills of the period and do not provide a clear picture of wives' attitude to the question of their testamentary capacity or supply much material for a view of marriage and property. The wills are brief and very much shorter than those of widows who had free disposal of their property; they are usually said to have been made with the licence of the husband and the husband is almost invariably named as executor or supervisor. The tone is generally submissive: in 1438 Lady Strange said that she made her will at the command of her husband (*Test.Vet.* i.235) and in 1459 Joan Twynyhoo stated that she had her husband's permission to will that he should find a chaplain to pray for her soul (*Somerset Wills*, p. 284). After provision had been made for the testator's soul, usually by the sale of her paraphernalia, the husband was nearly always the chief beneficiary, although Margaret Vaysy provided in 1391 also for masses for the soul of her first husband (*Early Lincoln Wills*, p. 83). Occasionally wives appear to take an independent attitude towards landed property at variance with the law: in 1414 Joan, widow of Lord Scales and wife of Sir Edmund Thorp, arranged for her debts and legacies to be paid out of the profits of a particular manor and instructed her feoffees to hold two manors for a year after her husband's death in order to pay his debts (*Test.Vet.* i.185); in 1460 Maud Conyers bequeathed the remainder of the manors she had received by inheritance and gift from her father (*Test.Vet.* i.298); in 1462 Joan Bruyn disposed of lands in Essex, Kent and London in her will (*Test.Vet.* i.298). In all these cases, however, the immediate beneficiary was the husband. There was a great variety of local custom concerning the wife's devise of urban property. It was decided in London in 1256 that married women could not devise tenements, even with the permission of their husbands, as alienations could only be made only by open surrender in court by wife and husband together. The wills of several London women were challenged on these grounds, including in 1386 that of Idonia Salesbury, who had made her will between marriages but who was married when she died (*C.W.C.H.* ii.274). The custom in other towns was more favourable to the married woman: in Bristol married women could and did include landed property in their wills with the permission of their husbands, while in other towns, such as Gloucester and Lincoln, the consent of the husband was not required.

The treatment of chattels in the surviving wills of married women is equally ambiguous. In one of the earliest surviving wills of a married woman, that of Agnes de Condet made before 1223, a distinction is made between the half of his movable goods granted to her by her husband and her own chattels (*omnium que mea sunt*) (C. W. Foster, pp. 293–5). In later wills this distinction is less clear, although the fact that many female testators left the residue of 'their goods' to their husbands indicates some current popular idea of chattel ownership by married women; only occasionally and then in the wills of women living in the province of York are the goods bequeathed said to be part of the wife's 'portion'. It is perhaps significant that when Thomas Earl of Warwick made his will in 1369, a month after his wife had made her own will, be ordered that her testament should be fully performed out of his goods (*Test.Vet.* i.79). It is important that, as Sheehan points out, 'although the common law of England steadfastly refused to enforce the will of the married woman, in fact she very often managed to distribute property at death' (Sheehan, *Medieval Studies*, p. 122); the available evidence, however, is too sparse to indicate whether there was a widely held view among married women about chattel ownership which was opposed to that of the common law and it seems that in general the testamentary capacity of the married woman was dependent on the permission and the co-operation of her husband.

It is from the wills and testament of the property-owning and property-controlling husbands of later mediaeval England that we can obtain some indication of contemporary attitudes to the marriage bond not revealed by other sources such as legal treatises and correspondence. In particular we can see the extent to which husbands made provision for their widows beyond what law and custom required of them and also how far they used their control of the family's property to attempt to influence the behaviour of their widows. Attitudes towards wives can be found in the nature and extent of bequests rather than in the language of the wills which seldom rises above the conventional 'loving wife'. Occasionally, however, strong feelings do surface: Richard Edy gave as his reason for making a new will in 1438, 'that Margaret, my wife, is nought loving to me, nor to none of my kin, God knoweth the truth' (H. Harrod, p. 331). On the other hand, Thomas Hampden, in his will made in 1482, praised his wife, 'whom of youth I have known well conscienced, and to me a true and loving wife' (*Test.Vet.* ii.387). Displays of affection were more often shown when reminding wives of their duties and promises: in 1396 Thomas Earl of Kent asked his wife to remember 'all of the love and trust that has been between us' when acting as his executor (*Test.Vet.* i.139) and in 1469 William Earl of Pembroke enjoined his wife to pray for him and 'take the said order [of widowhood] that you promised me as you had in my life, my heart and love' (*Test.Vet.* i.304). Affection could also be shown by the purchase of prayers for the souls of dead wives and for the 'good estate' of living wives and in the choice of burial place. In 1296 William Earl of Warwick asked that his heart should be buried wherever the countess, his 'dear consort', should decide to be interred (*Test.Vet.* i.52). The choice of burial place could present problems when a man had married more than once. Sir William Burton found a diplomatic solution in 1373: 'My will is that the bones of my dear wife Mabel (whom God pardon) be placed on the right of my body and on the left my dear wife Alianora, if she will consent to it' (*Early Lincoln Wills*, p. 37). Sir William Mamyon was less decisive: in his will made in 1390 he asked to be buried near the tomb of his second wife but in a codicil added two years later he changed his mind and decided to be buried next to his first wife (*Early Lincoln Wills*, p. 58).

Concern could be shown for a wife in arrangements for her maintenance immediately after the testator's death, before dower was assigned or the will executed. In 1459 Sir Robert Hungerford ordered that his wife and the rest of his household were to be maintained for six weeks after his death; at the end of this period he advised his wife to take comfortable lodgings and good advice (*Somerset Wills*, pp. 190–2). John Chelmyswyk, in his will made in 1418, provided for his wife to be supported for a year after his death, on condition that she kept herself 'sole without husband' during that period (*Early English Wills*, p. 34). Some husbands evidently doubted their wives' ability to look after themselves: in 1464 John Baker instructed his executors to place his widow in St. Bartholomew's hospital, Sandwich (*Test.Vet.* i.306) and in 1463 Walter Wyghthill left a bequest to a servant on condition that he remained with his widow 'until she is able to govern her own household' (*Early Lincoln Wills*, p. 193). Merchants seem to have shown more concern about the standard of living of their widows: the widow of John Browne of Bristol was to find for herself meat, drink and clothing during her life from her husband's estate (*Bristol Wills*, p. 148) and Nicholas Blakburn of York wanted his widow to have the livelihood of a gentlewoman while she lived, 'and a priest and a servant' (*Test.Ebor.* ii.20).

Widows could usually be sure of their dower and jointure which were protected by law and it has been seen how they were frequently provided even more generously with lands for life by means of the use. It was in the distribution of goods and chattels, and of urban property, that testators had more freedom of action; they had the opportunity here to act generously towards their wives and also to attempt to control their behaviour by imposing conditions on their bequests. The treatment of goods and chattels in testaments reveals the contradictions and ambiguities in the law concerning the ownership of goods within marriage. In 1345 Sir Richard de la Pole left all his and his wife's goods to pay his debts, except the ornaments of her head and body 'without a price put on them'; his wife was to have a third part of 'their' goods and his entire chamber, with the exception of his plate and weapons (*Test.Ebor.* i.7–8). In 1390 Robert Titlot bequeathed household utensils, animals, growing crops and a ship to his wife 'for her part of all our goods' (*Test.Ebor.* i.139). There seems to have been an accepted belief that a wife was entitled to the goods she had brought to the marriage, even if these had been enjoyed by her husband during the marriage and were his to bequeath. Sir John Neville's wife, by his will of 1449, was 'to have wholly all the livelihood that she is endowed in, even like as I have it' (*Test.Vet.* i.265). In 1483 Sir Richard Chokke bequeathed to his wife 'all the plate and goods he had with her' (*Somerset Wills*, p. 238) and in 1418 William Neel instructed his executors to deliver to his wife all her goods and chattels, just as on the day that he married her; if any were missing they were to be made up from his own goods provided she made no complaint and claimed no dower from his London property (*Chichele*, p. 151). Robert Didbrok of Bristol allowed his wife one third of his goods and the 200 marks which had been her dowry (*Bristol Wills*, p. 91). In 1339 a London woodmonger bequeathed his wife all the goods and chattels that had belonged to her before marriage (*C.W.C.H.* i.440) and in 1435 Richard Earl of Warwick left to his second wife all the silver, bedding and household stuff 'he had with her and whatever else she had acquired since their marriage' (*Test.Vet.* i.232). Richard Earl of Arundel's second wife was to keep, by his will of 1392, the headdresses which he had given her and she was also to be offered the presents which she had given him during the marriage (*Test.Vet.* i.131). On the other hand, Sir John Drayton in 1417 left to his wife goods which had been given to her by others (*Early Lincoln Wills*, p. 119). It was not uncommon for wives to be left household goods and, in towns, ships or merchandise, either for the rest of their lives or during good behaviour. It was also usual for wives to be allowed the whole or part of the residue which remained after the meeting of specific bequests. When Sir Giles Daubeny was asked on his deathbed in 1446 who was to have the residue which had not been mentioned in his testament, 'Forthwith, the said knight, without any tarrying said, "My wife shall have it"' (*Test.Ebor.* ii.114). The widow was frequently expected to support children from the residue or to use it for the good of her dead husband's soul; it also provided another sanction for her good behaviour after his death.

There were various ways by which a testator might hope to exercise some control from beyond the grave on the behaviour of his widow. A not uncommon threat was to reduce bequests to the legal minimum if the provision made for her in the will was not acceptable to the widow. This occurs most frequently in London wills: in 1345 a mercer gave his wife a choice between certain specified legacies 'and her share by way of dower according to the custom of London' (*C.W.C.H.* i.483) and in 1368 a pepperer left his wife £40, all the merchandise in his shop, their dwelling house and household goods, on condition that if she would not accept them as dower she was to forfeit them all and 'take only what the law allows' (*C.W.C.H.* ii.130). As dower rules in London were vague and claims to dower against executors could be inconvenient, such threats were probably intended to persuade widows to accept bequests which were not ungenerous. Similar threats occur in wills elsewhere, probably with the same intention of discouraging widows from making claims on executors: in 1431 Sir John Wodehouse asked his wife to accept some generous legacies 'so that neither for her dower nor for any other occasion shall she have any claim upon, nor impede the executors'; if she refused the legacies would be cancelled and she must 'stand to the common law' (*Chichele*, p. 444). In 1411 the wife and children of Sir William Langeford were told that if they were to insist on their reasonable part of his goods 'after course of law' they would be deprived of all their legacies (*Early English Wills*, p. 20).

Husbands were concerned not only to prevent their widows claiming more of their goods than they were prepared to allow them, they were frequently concerned also to persuade their wives to live 'sole, chaste and unmarried' after their deaths. Behind this concern was clearly the fear that the property of the testator or of the children of the marriage would be taken by the widow into a new marriage and would fall into the hands of the new husband. Bequests were frequently made to wives on condition they remained unmarried. In 1425 a London grocer left tenements to his wife for life, 'so long as she remain unmarried and well conducted and bring up his children becomingly' (*C.W.C.H.* ii.439); in 1398 the wife of John Muleward of Bristol was left half a bushel of flour a week 'so long as she shall live in pure widowhood' (*Bristol Wills*, p. 53); in 1490 Henry Burnell left items of plate to his wife with the conditions that if she remarried or lived 'unclean of her body against the laws of God' the plate was to go to their son (*Somerset Wills*, p. 293). Sometimes even more was expected of the widow: in 1424 Roger Flower instructed his feoffees to make his widow an estate for life in two of his manors on condition that she 'live sole without husband' but she had to make her intention clear by taking a vow of chastity and assuming the widow's ring and mantle (*Early English Wills*, p. 60). Widows were sometimes to be allowed to control the residue only if they remained unmarried and occasionally they were threatened with a monetary penalty if they remarried. In 1441, for example, William Brampton left his wife £500 if she lived sole after his death; if she remarried she was only to have £200 (*Chichele*, p. 606). Testators in the city of London could also threaten their wives with the loss of their right to live on in the main dwelling house if they remarried; sometimes they stipulated that their apprentices should remain with their widows only as long as they remained unmarried. In the middle years of the fourteenth century a series of wills of London tanners laid down that their widows could take over their tables 'in the house called Tanners' Seld' only if they remained unmarried or married another tanner.

The fact that provisions in wills imposing penalties for remarriage are not common suggests that such sanctions were difficult to enforce and there is no evidence that widows were discouraged from remarriage by such threats or that the penalties were actually imposed by executors. Most husbands probably took a realistic view of the possibility of their wives remarrying. At the end of the thirteenth century William Bukerell left his house in London to his wife whether or not she took another husband (*C.W.C.H.* i.36) and in 1439 Sir Ralph Rochefort provided his wife with 20 marks of rent a year in addition to her dower on condition that she kept herself 'in honest and worshipful governance' or was remarried 'to her worship and to her estate' by the advice of his executors (*Early English Wills*, p. 122). In 1400 a London bucklesmith asked his wife, with no threat of loss of legacy, to maintain a chantry for him for seven years after his death if she took another husband (*C.W.C.H.* ii.357). In London the interests of the children were more often protected by nominating a guardian other than the wife or by requiring, in the event of remarriage, the widow and her new husband to provide the executors or the city authorities with securities; thus in 1359 a chandler willed that his wife should have custody of his children and their goods as long as she remained a widow but if she married again she and her husband were to give security for restoring their property to the children on their coming of age or marriage and for their proper maintenance in the meantime (*C.W.C.H.* ii.13).

A man who made a will was naturally concerned that its provisions should be carried out and to ensure this it was necessary to choose conscientious and trustworthy executors. In view of the subordinate position of women at law it is remarkable how frequently husbands named their wives as executors. Between 1414 and 1443 Archbishop Henry Chichele or his officials proved 286 wills; 116 of these testators were married men with living wives and 90 of them (77.5 per cent) named their wives as executors. Of husbands with living wives whose wills are found in the Lincoln episcopal registers between 1280 and 1500 nearly 80 per cent chose their wives as executors and the proportion was even higher in Bristol: 82 per cent of husbands with living wives whose wills were entered in the Great Orphan Book between 1381 and 1500 named their wives as executors. It is sometimes possible to suggest reasons why wives were omitted from the list of executors. The allowance of only the legal minimum in goods and chattels to the wife or the provision of a guardian other than the wife for the children of the testator suggests a difficult relationship, while arrangements for the maintenance of the widow by the executors suggests incapacity. The fact that John Tostrong of Bristol left his wife half his goods but made another woman his executor and left her his lands in Ireland and the residue tells a different story (*Bristol Wills*, p. 45). In some cases it is clear that wives were not asked to be executors because they were expected to make difficulties about the performance of the will; for example, in 1415 Edward Cheyne instructed that his wife should lose any bequest made to her if she refused to hand over to his executors any of the goods which were described in his inventory and which were in her custody (*Chichele*, p. 47).

In only a small proportion of the wills was the wife named as the sole executor since most husbands were probably concerned that their widows should have help in carrying out their wishes. In 1449 William de la Pole, Duke of Norfolk, named his wife as his sole executor, 'beseeching her . . . to take the charge upon her for the weal of my soul, for above all the earth my singular trust is most in her, and I will for her ease, if she will and else not, that she may take unto her such a person as she like to name, to help her in execution thereof for her ease, to labour under her as she would command him' (*North Country Wills*, p. 51). There may also have been some concern that a widow acting alone might come under pressure from her family or friends. There was an attempt to operate such pressure when Thomas Betson, the business partner of Sir William Stonor, lay ill in 1479 and Stonor's friends tried to persuade him to change his will and make his wife, Stonor's step-daughter, his only executor (C. L. Kingsford, p. 88). Even where, however, a group of executors is named the wife is usually mentioned first or even named as the principal executor. It is clear that husbands usually expected their wives to take on the responsibility of helping to execute their wills and this is illustrated by the injunctions addressed to wives when they were nominated as executors or when they were given the residue to dispose of at their discretion. Some husbands took this opportunity to declare their trust and affection for their wives. Stephen Thomas, giving a codicil to his will in 1415 the form of a letter to his wife asked her, 'as my trust is wholly in you, over all other creatures, that this last will be fulfilled and all other that I ordained at home, for all the love that ever was between man and woman' (*Early English Wills*, p. 41). Others issued dire warnings about the consequences of ignoring their wishes: one husband in 1418 asked his wife to dispose of his residue as she thought best and as she would answer 'at the day of judgment' (*Early English Wills*, p. 29), while another, in 1447, warned his wife that she would be required to render account for her use of the residue 'on risk of her soul' (*Somerset Wills*, p. 160). More often testators seem to have had reciprocity in mind: in 1471 Richard Dekyn assigned his residue to his wife 'therewith to dispose for my soul in works of mercy and charity as she would I did for her in case like' (*Somerset Wills*, p. 222).

The duties which a widow was asked to undertake for her dead husband were often onerous. William Earl of Pembroke reminded his wife in 1469 of her promise to take the order of widowhood after his death, 'as you may be the better master of your own, to perform my will and to help my children' (*Test.Vet.* i.304). In 1412 Stephen Bettenham made his wife one of his executors and also stipulated that she was to act as supervisor until she died or remarried; in addition she was to use the residue for the good of his soul with the agreement of her co-executors (*Chichele*, p. 35). The distribution of the residue, particularly when it was to be used either for the benefit of the testator's soul or for the upbringing of his children, must have put widows in charge of a considerable part of family resources for long periods. The widow of Sir Thomas Arundel, by his will of 1485, was given authority to transfer his bones to the church of the Greyfriars in Dorchester and to erect a tomb there; she was also to collect all the debts due to her dead husband, to maintain his children until they were of age and then to marry them suitably. To accomplish these tasks she was made one of his executors and his feoffees were also ordered to make over his lands to her. He showed unusual trust in her as he allowed her discretion to alter his will as she thought best (*Somerset Wills*, pp. 256–7). Other husbands were not so happy to rely on the discretion of their widows and laid down their duties, especially charitable ones, in minute detail. The widow of Thomas Earl of Salisbury who died in 1428 was to hear three masses a day for the rest of her life and was also to feed three poor people a day on his behalf (*Test.Vet.* i.216). In 1348 a London goldsmith ordered his wife to distribute each month, from the time of his death for the rest of her life, 17 silver pennies among 13 poor men and one poor woman: one penny to each of 12 poor men, three pennies to the thirteenth poor man, who was to be more infirm than the others, and two pennies to the poor woman (*C.W.C.H.* i.519).

How far the duties which testators imposed on their widows were carried out is as difficult to determine from the surviving evidence in print as whether the sanctions imposed on widows who remarried were enforced. There are some indications in the records of the court of Husting of the city of London that all did not always go according to the wishes of the testators. Agnes Lucas explained in her will made in 1348 that she had retained certain tenements which her late husband had ordered to be sold for pious purposes but as she had spent a considerable sum of money on the welfare of his soul she wished the property to go to her daughter (*C.W.C.H.* i.517). In 1333 the son of William de Bosenham complained that his mother had delayed proving his father's testament for fifteen years and had thus deprived him of his inheritance; his mother, who had remarried, explained that her first husband had died so deeply in debt that she had been afraid to prove his testament and undertake the burden of its administration (*C.W.C.H.* i.387–8). The fulfilling of the last wishes of a husband could sometimes be a lengthy process: in 1436 Margaret Holyn made her will, with the permission of her husband, with the intention of carrying out the wishes of a previous husband who had made his will in 1421; her co-executors had died and she asked her own executors to carry out his wishes (*C.W.C.H.* ii.461, 501).

It has been said that wills, if read aright, provide us with some of 'the most important evidence of men as individuals' (McFarlane, p. xxxvii) and the wills and testaments of later mediaeval England provide material on attitudes to marriage and property which, although difficult to quantify, helps to modify the impression left by common law rules which were very unfavourable to married women. Although married women enjoyed few rights over property during marriage and were even prevented from making valid wills themselves unless they had the permission of their husbands, they were assured, if they were the survivor of the marriage, of an adequate provision by law and were usually even better provided for by the will or testament of their husbands. Although some husbands tried to discourage remarriage by threatening the withdrawal of legacies, even when not obliged by the law most husbands were prepared to arrange for the comfort and support of their widows. In return most of them expected their wives to undertake responsibility for carrying out their last wishes as executors of their testaments. In this way widows came to control some of the property of which ownership had been denied to them during marriage.

NOTE

1. References have been taken from the following collections of wills; quotations are given in translation or modernised spelling.

Bristol Wills   T. P. Wadley (ed.), *The Great Orphan Book and Book of Wills* (Bristol 1886)

C.W.C.H.	R. R. Sharpe (ed), *Calendar of Wills: Court of Husting, London*, 2 vols. (London 1889, 1890)
Chichele	E. F. Jacob (ed.), *The Register of Henry Chichele, Archbishop of Canterbury, 1414–1443*, ii (Oxford 1938)
Early English Wills	F. J. Furnivall (ed.), *Fifty Earliest English Wills* (Early English Text Society, original series, 78 (1882))
Early Lincoln Wills	A. Gibbons (ed.), *Early Lincoln Wills* (Lincoln 1888)
North Country Wills	J. W. Clay (ed.), *North Country Wills*, i (Surtees Society, 116 (1908))
Somerset Wills	F. W. Weaver (ed.), *Somerset Medieval Wills, 1383–1500* (Somerset Record Society, 16 (1901))
Test.Ebor.	J. Raine (ed.), *Testamenta Eboracensia*, i (Surtees Society, 4 (1836)); ii (Surtees Society, 30 (1855))
Test.Vet.	N. H. Nicolas (ed.), *Testamenta Vetusta*, 2 vols. (London 1826)

BIBLIOGRAPHY

For the common law of marriage and property

J. M. W. Bean, *The Decline of English Feudalism* (Manchester 1968)
W. S. Holdsworth, *A History of English Law*, iii (London 1909)
K. B. McFarlane, *The Nobility of Later Medieval England* (Oxford 1973)
F. Pollock and F. W. Maitland, *The History of English Law*, ii (reissue of 2nd edition, Cambridge 1968)
A. W. B. Simpson, *Introduction to the History of the Land Law* (Oxford 1961)

For borough custom

M. Bateson (ed.), *Borough Customs*, ii (Selden Society, 21 (1906))
G. H. Martin, 'The Registration of Deeds of Title in the Medieval Borough', in *The Study of Medieval Records: Essays in honour of Kathleen Major* (eds. D. A. Bullough and R. L. Storey (Oxford 1971))
E. W. W. Veale, *The Great Red Book of Bristol*, part i (Bristol Record Society, 2 (1931))

For the history of wills and testamentary procedure

C. W. Foster (ed.), *Registrum Antiquissimum*, i (Lincoln Record Society, xxvii (1931))
H. Harrod (ed.), 'Extracts from Early Wills in the Norwich Registries', *Norfolk Archaeology*, iv (1849)
E. F. Jacob (ed.), *The Register of Henry Chichele, Archbishop of Canterbury, 1414–1443*, ii (Oxford 1938)
C. L. Kingsford (ed.), *Stonor Letters and Papers*, ii (Camden Society, 3rd series, xxx)
H. G. Richardson and G. O. Sayles, *Fleta*, ii (Selden Society, 72 (1953))
M. M. Sheehan, *The Will in Medieval England* (Toronto 1963)
M. M. Sheehan, 'The Influence of Canon Law on the Property Rights of Married Women in England', *Medieval Studies*, 25 (1963)
G. J. Turner (ed.), *Year Books 5 Edward II, 1311* (Selden Society, 63 (1947))

VII

Some Aspects of the Law of Marriage in Scotland: 1500–1700[1]

A. D. M. Forte

Department of Private Law, University of Dundee

The present century has witnessed an almost continuous improvement in the legal condition of women in Scotland. The husband's right to administer his wife's heritable estate (*jus administrationis*) disappeared with the passing of the Married Women's Property (Scotland) Act 1920; then in 1981 the separate property rule, which permitted a husband to exclude his wife from the matrimonial home if he were the owner or tenant, was abolished by the Matrimonial Homes (Family Protection) (Scotland) Act 1981. Divorce has now retreated almost completely from adherence to the notion of matrimonial fault since the introduction of a single ground based on the irretrievable breakdown of marriage (Divorce (Scotland) Act 1976, s.1(1)). Add to this the abolition of irregular marriages *per verba de praesenti* and *per verba de futuro subsequente copula* (Marriage (Scotland) Act 1939, s.5) and some rationalisation with regard to the prohibition of marriage between persons related in a certain degree (Marriage (Scotland) Act 1977) and we have a law of marriage which is reasonably congruent with the needs of modern Scottish society.

The objects of these reforms have their roots, of course, in a much earlier period and developed in a different religious and economic climate. This essay will try to give some idea of the law of marriage in the sixteenth and seventeenth centuries. However, it is eclectic in its choice of topics and a comprehensive account of the law during this period still remains to be written. Moreover, one should enter the caveat that, on the whole, it confines itself rigidly to the law in the centuries under consideration and that in many of the areas of law discussed the picture does not become really clear until the eighteenth and nineteenth centuries. Nevertheless, our period is of great importance as the formative era of the Scots law of husband and wife.

It is proposed then to deal with the following topics, viz.: the pre-Reformation law, canon and secular; irregular marriages; matrimonial property; and divorce.

The Pre-Reformation Law of Marriage

Before the Reformation, the substantive law of marriage in Scotland was found partly in the canon law of the Catholic Church and partly in the writings and decisions of secular lawyers or in statutes. Both of these sources survived the Reformation and continued to exert some influence throughout the seventeenth century.

The central concerns of the canon law appear to have been betrothal, the constitution of marriage and impediments thereto. We are indeed fortunate to possess the *Lectures on Marriage* of William Hay (in Barry 1967), Principal of Aberdeen University from 1536–42 who, as Professor of Theology, lectured on the seven Sacraments of the Catholic Church including marriage. Hay's lectures reveal just how important in the Canon Law was the notion of consent:

> *Secundo requiritur quod sit mutuus consensus illarum personarum in datione corporum quia nec sponsalia sicut dictum est nec matrimonium possunt claudicare quia si deficit consensus alterius personae nec sunt sponsalia, sicut nec matrimonium*[2] (Hay's *Lectures on Marriage*, p. 16).

This stress on consent continues in Scots law to the present day and Stair, the father of modern Scots law, observes that:

> though the commixtion of bodies seem necessary for the constitution of affinity arising from marriage, yet the opinion of the canon law is true, *consensus non coitus, facit matrimonium* (*Inst.*I.4,6).

The canon law also laid the foundations of the irregular forms of marriage by declaration *de praesenti* and promise *subsequente copula* which were accepted by both Stair (*Inst.*I.4,6) and Erskine (*Inst.*I.6,5) as creating a valid marriage, albeit one irregular in form.

Divorce *a vinculo* was not recognised by the pre-Tridentine canon law and though the terminology used is at times confusing[3] the position can be stated with reasonable accuracy. Hay takes divorce to signify what Scots lawyers today would call separation *a mensa et thoro*; in other words the parties are relieved from their mutual duty of adherence. This was granted for adultery, cruelty and heresy but it did not dissolve the marriage and re-marriage was not permitted (Hay's *Lectures*, pp. 59–61). Thus in *Bayne* v. *Anderson* (1525) it is stated:

> *decernimus dictam Margaretam Andersoun a mensa et thoro mutua cohabitatione et servitute dicti Johannis Bayne sui sponsi separandum fore prout separamus*[4] (*Liber Officialis*, p. 32).

Decrees of nullity appear to be more common and a marriage could be declared null *ab initio* on a number of grounds: e.g., incapacity to give consent (*Leith* v. *Elphinstoun* (1523); impotency (*Myrtoune de Cambo* v.

Forsyth (1544); and, of course, a prior valid marriage (Hay's *Lectures*, pp. 91–103).

The Reformation, of course, effected changes and as time passed the influence of the canon law certainly waned. Nonetheless a fairly strong canonical sub-current continued to flow; and though stress has been laid on the development of native rules in the seventeenth century (Ireland 1958, Ch. VII) there is evidence which demonstrates the active application of the canon law in that century. The canon law as to the forbidden degrees of relationship as an impediment to marriage, for example, was notoriously complicated. Consanguinity and affinity prohibited and nullified marriage 'as far as the fourth degree inclusive' (Hay's *Lectures*, pp. 185–16) and relationship by affinity was not only created by licit intercourse with a marriage partner but could also be created by illicit coitus.[5]

Act 1567 *c*.14 (A.P.S. III, 25) purported to sweep away the canon law degrees as regards the 'abhominabill cryme of incest', relating the offence to the eighteenth chapter of Leviticus; and Act 1567, *c*.15 (A.P.S. III, 26) 'declairit . . . that secundis in degreis of consanguinitie and affinitie and all degreis outwith the samin . . . mycht and may lauchfullie marie at all tymes'. Despite the obvious intentions of the early reformers, we find that in 1628 a schoolmaster, George Sinclair, was 'dilaitit of contravening the actis of parliament maid aganis the committeris of incest and adulterie' and the law applied in his case was the canon law. Sinclair's offence was that first he had intercourse with one of his female pupils and then again with her sister, 'thairby committand notour and manifest incest'. The editor of the volume containing the report of this case (Gillon 1953) comments: 'The use of the word incest for seduction does not occur again.' With respect, this is truly a case of incest based on the canon law principle of affinity created by carnal copula. The eighteenth chapter of Leviticus, on the other hand, though the basis of the Scots law of incest in 1628, does not expressly prohibit George's conduct. In any event, the verdict was guilty and George Sinclair was sentenced to death by drowning.

In the area of matrimonial property, the secular, private law of Scotland held sway and, as with the canon law, it was able to exert some measures of influence over later developments. *Regiam Majestatem*, II.15 (in Cooper 1947), for example, deals with donations between husband and wife, and discussion of marriage contracts features prominently in the early legal literature (Balfour's *Practicks*, pp. 101–5 (in McNeil 1962); Craig, *Jus Feudale*, pp. 853–8 (in Clyde 1934)). A tocher, or dowry, consisting of money, goods or land was frequently given and was returnable should the wife die within a year and a day of the marriage (Balfour p. 99) or should there be a separation granted on the ground of the husband's adultery (*ibid.*). The Protocol Book of Master Gawane Ros, a notary in Ayr, which covers the period 1512–32 contains an example of an instrument (No. 353) embodying a marriage contract. The spouses were Gilbert Gibson and Margaret Tonok and the bride's parents promised to pay Gilbert, in name of tocher, the sum of twenty-two pounds. Gilbert's father promised him eight merks and to place him in a mailin (i.e. farm) as good as his own (Anderson and Grant 1908; *see also* Murray 1910).

In addition to the understandable concern of the early law with property in general and heritable property in particular, it was well-established by the beginning of the sixteenth century that the husband was clearly *dignior persona* and that his wife had no legal *persona*. Scanlan (1958, Ch. VI) has asserted that the Church proclaimed the equality of husband and wife. Perhaps it did, but the law of Scotland did not or, at least, did not put the notion into practice.

Irregular Marriages

The Reformation had only slight impact as regards the concept of marriage and the cardinal element of a valid marriage remained the parties' consent (Stair, I.4,6). The pre-Tridentine canon law, though it forbade clandestine marriages (Hay's *Lectures*, p. 31) because of the difficulty of proof and because, if subsequently invalidated, this could result in the children being regarded as illegitimate, nonetheless did not regard such marriages as null 'for it is not of the essence of marriage to contract it in the presence of the Church' (*ibid.*). The post-Tridentine Decree 'Tametsi' of 1563 declared null all future marriages not celebrated by an ordained priest but the Reformation had already taken place and it came too late to be applied to Scotland. Nevertheless, for the next three centuries, repeated efforts were made by both church and state to make marriage a public institution, requiring the publication of banns and celebration by ordained ministers of the established church. (*See*, generally, Ireland 1958, ch. VII, pp. 84–6.) By the sixteenth century, however, irregular marriages were recognised, though as we shall see, the matter was not without its difficulties. Irregular marriage took one of three forms during our period, viz. (a) declaration *de praesenti*; (b) promise *subsequente copula*; and (c) cohabitation with habit and repute.

(a) Declaration *de praesenti*

In 1564 Isobell Auldingstone applied to the Commissaries of Edinburgh, alleging that Robert MacWilliam had married her *per verba de praesenti* 'befoir famous witnesses and voluntarie obleist him yairto'. MacWilliam had intercourse with another woman and the Commissaries[6] ordered him 'to fulfil his faythfull promeis maid to hir, in manner above written and to solemnizat ye band of matrimoney in face of halie kirk' (*Auldingstone* v. *M'Williame* (1564)). Fraser (1846, p. 131) comments that although in his day this would constitute 'very matrimony' yet in 1564 it was merely a promise, a pre-contract, and the marriage was inchoate until solemnised *in facie ecclesiae*, though he adds that a subsequent marriage to another partner would be null. Another problem appears to have been whether a bare declaration *de praesenti* followed by subsequent *copula* would constitute a marriage (*M'Lauchlan* v. *Dobson* (1796)).[7] In *Murray* v. *Simpson* (1569) both parties 'be wordis of the present' declared their marriage and intercourse took place 'after the promeis foirsaid'. The pursuer concluded that the man should be compelled to solemnise the marriage.

Writing towards the end of our period Stair's view (*Inst.*I.4,6) appears to be fairly clear that consent *de praesenti* is enough.

> For clearing whereof consider, that it is not every consent to the married state that makes matrimony, but a consent *de praesenti*, and not a promise *de futuro matrimonio* . . . the matter itself consists not in the promise, but in the present consent, whereby they accept each other as husband and wife: whether that be by words expressly; or tacitly by marital cohabitation or acknowledgment; or by natural commixtion, where there hath been a promise or espousals preceding, for therein is presumed a conjugal consent *de praesenti*.

The consent had, of course, to be clear and unequivocal (*Macinnes* v. *More* (1781)).

Fraser (pp. 135 et seq.) doubted that Stair was correct in his view and cites Lord Elchies' report of *Forbes* v. *Countess of Strathmore* (1750) that 'though nothing could have the civil effect of marriage in Scotland but celebration *secundum legem loci*, yet consensus *et copula*, even in Scotland would make a good marriage'. Fraser took the view that consent *de praesenti* did not constitute a marriage until there was a formal religious celebration or at the very least where intercourse had followed.

The earlier decisions may well justify some doubt as to whether a declaration of marriage (not a promise to marry or a betrothal) actually constituted marriage but, on balance, one should still favour an interpretation which suggests that this was a marriage. Stair was certainly not ignorant of the canon law and nor were the Commissaries; and even though the canon law recognised a clandestine marriage *de praesenti* it urged, and in some instances entertained actions to compel the spouses to receive a blessing *in facie ecclesiae* (*Liber Officialis*, xvii). In other words, there were policy reasons for such an approach and there is no good reason why the mere fact of Reformation should have made it any less imperative in the minds of the judges to confer a greater decree of security, especially on the wife, by making the marriage public. Moreover, we have already noted the authorities' desire to make marriage a public institution and though the decree of the Council of Trent 'Tametsi' was not part of Scots law it would have been known to Scots lawyers and its message approved.

(b) Promise *subsequente copula*

A promise or engagement to marry (i.e. *sponsalia de futuro*; and see Decretals, Greg. IX, iv.I, *c*.30) followed by sexual intercourse on the faith of that promise was declared by Stair actually to constitute a marriage

(*Int*.I.4,6) probably on the basis of canon law support. Again the canon law might admit litigation to compel solemnisation *in facie ecclesiae* but there was no doubt that a marriage already existed (*Liber Officialis, passim*; and see Anton (1958). It is, then, not surprising to discover that the Commissary records witness many cases in which defenders were compelled 'to a public celebration' (*Dalrymple* v. *Dalrymple* (1811)).

In 1605, for example, Janet Waugh averred that Patrick Duncan had promised marriage, that she had accepted him and in consequence 'gaiff the use of hir body, and had carnall daill with him'. Janet asked the Commissaries that Patrick should 'accept the said complenar to his lawfull spousit wyfe and suld accomplishe the band of matrimonie with hir, in face of halie kirk, conforme to his said faithfull promeis, and carnall following yairupon'. Proof of the making of the promise was referred to the defender's oath and as he denied this the court had no alternative but to assoilzie (i.e. absolve) him (*Waugh* v. *Duncan*, 3 July 1605).

Controversy about the nature of promise *subsequente copula* really took hold in the eighteenth century and was not finally settled until the early years of the twentieth century. But for the same reasons as those given in support of regarding a declaration *de praesenti* as a marriage, there was nothing strange or inconsistent with the idea of an actual marriage, in the courts' ordering celebration. This, it is submitted, was also the view of the seventeenth-century lawyer, in the main.

(c) Marriage by cohabitation with habit and repute

Unlike both of the prior irregular forms, marriage by cohabitation with habit and repute is still permitted today. It may or may not enjoy a canonical provenance and in its earliest form fulfilled a purely evidentiary purpose (Act 1503, *c*.77: A.P.S. II, 252). The courts declined to treat the cohabitation and the repute as elements of the marriage and continued to emphasise that marriage was the product of consent. Many of the more interesting aspects of this form fall outwith our period and, therefore, discussion is precluded.

Matrimonial Property

During the period under consideration there is no doubt but that the position of married women was subordinate to that of their husbands with regard both to the acquisition and administration of property. In Hope's *Practicks* (in Clyde 1937) it is stated that '*vir est caput uxoris et censitur dominus omnium bonorum quae possidet uxor de jure nostro*, and therefoir may be denunced to the horn for her caus'.[8] Stair confers on the husband (*Inst*.I.4,9) power, not only over the wife's goods but also over her person, extending this to a right to 'recover her person from any, that would withdraw or whithhold her from him'. The husband was simply treated as *dignior persona*. Some idea of just how limited were a married woman's property rights can be gleaned by looking at the husband's *jus mariti* and *jus administrationis.*

Some seventeenth-century lawyers appear to accept, at least in principle, the idea of a community of property in marriage. Stair writes:

> there arises between them [i.e. the spouses] a communion of all moveables, except the habiliments and ornaments of the wife's body (*Inst.*I.4,17).

In *Cockburn* v. *Burn* (1679), 'Alexander Cockburn having pursued George Burn for exhibition of a bond granted by the Laird of Cockburn to umquile Christian Burn, while she was wife to the pursuer, and which she had assigned to George Burn her brother . . . the said Alexander craves the same to be delivered to him, and to be declairit his right, the sum being lent out by his wife, and which the law presumes to be his means. The defender alleged the foresaid presumption is taken off, wherever the wife has a separate estate *extra communionem bonorum.*'

It is highly probable that the notion of a *communio bonorum* was a foreign importation, brought back from France by Scottish students in the seventeenth century.[9] There is no reference to it in either Balfour or Craig; and Erskine (*Inst.*I.6,13) so qualified its scope by reference to the *just mariti* that, at best, its practical consequences can never have been very great. Indeed, Hope rejected the notion and one modern commentator has denied its existence in Scots law (Paton 1958).

After marriage the wife's moveable property, with certain exceptions, passed under the complete control of the husband (*Auchinleck* v. *Williamson* (1667)) and, according to Balfour (*Practicks*, p. 216) though 'ane woman that is fre, and not under subjectioun to ane husband, may mak ane testament of hir gudis and geir' a married woman could not make a will of her moveable property without her husband's consent 'because scho hirself, and all hir gudis, are at the dispositioun of hir husband'. This continued to be the case until the seventeenth century though, even as Balfour wrote, practice permitted her to make a will as to one-third or one-half of her goods depending on whether she had children or not, without the need for any formal consent by the husband (Ashley 1953).

It seems, however, that the operation of the *jus mariti* could be something of a two-edged sword for the husband, bringing not only benefits but also responsibilities and liabilities. On marriage he became liable for his wife's debts contracted before the banns were proclaimed, including her previous husband's funeral expenses and even the aliment of her illegitimate children. Moreover, there was no limit to this liability. Thus in *Gordon* v. *Davidson* (1708): 'The Lords thought Mr. Davidson's case very hard, to make him liable in the annual rents of the debts far exceeding the rents of his wife's lands; yet *ita lex scripta est*, the same was now turned into a fixed known custom and Law'. The husband's liability, however, only subsisted during the course of the marriage so that, broadly speaking, death or divorce ended it.

The *jus mariti* could, of course, be renounced either by an ante or a postnuptial contract[10] and, in any event, a transfer of property to the wife might expressly stipulate that it was to be free of the *jus mariti*. Stair had his doubts about the validity of renunciation and the seventeenth century cases do go either way (*see*, e.g., *Collington* v. *Collington* (1667)) but by the mid eighteenth century it was well-settled that renunciation was competent (*Walker* v. *Husband's Crs.* (1730); *Murray* v. *Dalrymple* (1745)).

The *jus mariti* did not extend to the whole of a wife's moveable estate. In 1582 the Mistress of Gray raised an action against the Master, her husband, to restore to her 'certain chains, rings of gold, and certain other things, whilk appertained to the ornament of her body *et quae fuerunt de mundo muliebri*'. The Master argued that chains and rings were not *de mundo muliebri* but the court treated them as the wife's paraphernalia and ordered their restoration (The *Mistress of Gray* v. *The Master* (1582)). Paraphernalia, however, did not only include a wife's clothing and personal jewellery which she brought with her to the marriage but also *ornamenta morganatica*, bridal gifts of clothing or jewellery, and gifts of a like nature given during the marriage by the husband (*Craig* v. *Monteith* (1684)). Ordinary domestic items gifted on marriage, perhaps by the bride's relatives, such as linen or furniture were not accounted paraphernalia; nor were jewels which were inherited as heirlooms. Thus in *Leven* v. *Montgomery* (1683), a jewel gifted to Alexander Lesley, first Earl of Leven and which descended, as an heirloom, to the Countess of Leven was held to be inalienable. The court found 'all the rest of the jewels *bona parapherna*'.[11]

The wife's paraphernalia, *stricto sensu*, her clothing and jewellery and the receptacles in which these were kept, could not be attached by the husband's creditors (Stair, *Inst.*I.4,17) but gifts of a paraphernal nature made before and during marriage were attachable for his debts (e.g. *Davidson* v. *Maccubin* (1610)). Moreover, though gifts made by the husband before marriage were irrevocable, he could still revoke paraphernal gifts made *stante matrimonio* (*Dicks* v. *Massie* (1695)). Finally, it may be observed that though excluded from the operation of her husband's *jus mariti* she did not enjoy complete power over them since by virtue of the *jus administrationis* she needed his consent to dispose of them.

Any moveable estate excluded from the *jus mariti* and the wife's paraphernalia and heritable estate, though her property, were subject to the husband's general power of administration as *caput et princeps familiae*. The *jus administrationis* did not, however, signify that women lacked capacity but rather that it was felt that the general character of the relationship created by marriage required that control of property should be in the hands of only one party (Balfour, *Practicks*, pp. 93 et seq.). The wife could not sue as regards her separate estate without his consent, nor could she be

persewit in judgment, in ony civil action or cause, except hir husband in likewayis be callit and persewit to fortifie, assist and authorise hir (Balfour,*Practicks*, p. 93).

As with the *jus mariti*, the *jus administrationis* could be renounced but this was not really regarded as competent until much later in the eighteenth century. In one case the fear was that the husband could 'unhusband himself, and renounce the privilege given him by the laws of both God and nature' (*Dickson* v. *Braidfoot* (1705)).

Dissolution by Divorce

The influence of the canon law persisted throughout the seventeenth century but in the area of divorce and remarriage the break with past tradition was total.[12] As we have seen the canon law had permitted separation *a mensa et thoro* on grounds of cruelty, heresy and adultery (Fraser, *op. cit.* and sources cited therein, p. 653) but it did not permit divorce *a vinculo matrimonii* (Hay's *Lectures on Marriage, passim*). This changed with the Reformation after which divorce was permitted on two grounds, namely, adultery and separation.

As regards adultery, divorce was permitted by the immediate post-Reformation common law for what are clearly doctrinal reasons. Thus Stair comments:

> All do agree, that adultery hath some effect upon marriage. The canon law doth not thereupon dissolve it . . . but only granteth separation. But our Savior's precept cleareth the contrary: who in relation to the custom that then was of divorce for light causes, resolves, that putting away was not lawful, except in the cases of adultery, and so in that case approves the divorce even as then used, Matt. 19 v. 9 (*Inst*.I.4,7).

At any rate, the early law of divorce for adultery was not created by statute but by the commissaries encouraged, no doubt, by the clergy.

Naturally adultery, *per se*, did not dissolve the marriage; rather it constituted a ground entitling the innocent party to seek a decree of divorce (Stair, *Inst*.I.4,7). Proof of adulterous conduct was needed though it could be inferred from the circumstances. In *Earl of Wigton* v. *Lady Margaret Lindsay* (1708) Lady Margaret's husband alleged adultery between her and Lord John Belhaven in that she had 'received John Lord Belhaven, naked or undressed, at unseasonable hours of the night or day, into her bed-chamber, where she was then lying in naked-bed, and that they there staid together alone, with close doors, untill the next morning'. The commissaries held these facts to be proved and sufficient to infer adultery. It is interesting to note the somewhat ingenuous argument put forward on Lady Margaret's behalf that 'the circumstances libelled are not sufficient in this cold country, to infer adultery'. This objection, understandably, failed.

The question of remarriage by a person divorced because of his or her adultery appears, during our period, to have been a vexed one. The Act 1600, *c.*20 (A.P.S. IV, 233) annulled marriages between adulterers and persons 'with quhome they are declarit, be sentence of the ordinar judge to

have committit, the said cryme and fact of adulterie'. The wording of the
statute appears clearly to be restrictive: it is only remarriage to a paramour
that is forbidden, and yet doubts persisted even to the extent of it being held
that the marriage of a widower, after his wife's death, to his paramour was
no true marriage (*Irvine* v. *Ker* (1695)). Stair, however, rejected the strict
approach and concluded that: 'With us marriage betwixt the two
committers of adultery is declared null. . . . But otherwise even the person
guilty may marry again' (*Inst*.I.4,7).

Unlike divorce for adultery, divorce for desertion was sanctioned by
statute (Act 1573, *c*.55, A.P.S. III, 81). The Act, however, states that since
the Reformation it had been the law to grant a divorce on this ground when
either husband or wife 'diverts from the other's company, without a
reasonable cause alleged or reduced before a judge, and remains in their
malicious obstinacy by the space of four years'.

Just why there should have occurred statutory intervention at so early a
stage in the case of desertion is unclear. Mackenzie (1686) thought that 'the
form of process here set down seems to be borrowed from the Saxon law'[13]
and there is a reference to a decretal of Pope Alexander III.[14]

Another, and perhaps more plausible theory, suggests that it may have
been passed to help the Earl of Argyle who was married to a bastard
daughter of James V and who, in 1571, had gone to the Commissary Court
seeking to divorce her on the ground of her desertion. Certainly the
procedure gone through by the Earl prior to raising the action for divorce is
consistent with that later prescribed by the Act (see below). The Court,
however, was confused. Contrary to the assertion made in the Act, that
divorce for desertion had been lawful since 1560, the Court did not know if
it had the power to grant decree.[15] Then, in April 1573, the Act was passed
and in June of that same year the Earl obtained decree in his favour.[16] The
retrospective effect of the Act, declaring that divorce on this ground was
granted 'in all times bypast' since the Reformation, was probably intended
to calm the Commissary Court's doubts and justify their granting a decree
to so powerful a member of the Reformation movement.

Yet a third theory, and one which might still be congruent with the
second, was that Act 1573, *c*.55 gave effect in Scotland, to Calvin's '*Projet
d'ordannance sur les mariages*' of 1545 adopted by the Genevan legislature
in 1561. Might not the occasion of the Earl's litigation have acted as a
necessary catalyst? (Baird Smith 1939).

The procedure for obtaining a divorce on this ground was extremely
cumbersome. First of all, the pursuer had to raise an action for adherence
and this was competent in the inferior commissary courts (Hume, *Lectures*
(in Paton 1939–58)). A decree to adhere might be granted after one year of
desertion. Erskine observes that:

Though the offending party must, by the words of this act, have deserted four
years before he can be cited in the preparatory process for adherence, the
commissaries *de praxi*, admit that action, and even pronounce sentence in it upon

one year's desertion; judging it to be a sufficient compliance with the injunction of the act if four years intervene between the first desertion and the decree of divorce (*Inst.*I.6,44).

Secondly, if the defender would not comply with the order to adhere, the pursuer could then apply to the Court of Session for letters of horning and the defender would then be denounced rebel for disobeying the order to adhere. Thirdly, if being put to the horn failed to bring the recalcitrant spouse to heel, the pursuer could apply to his or her local Presbytery to admonish the deserter, privately at first and, if this failed, to direct the minister of the parish in which the deserting spouse resided to publicly demand that he or she should adhere. If the offending spouse remained obdurate, sentence of excommunication could then be pronounced. Any deserter who resisted all of these measures to pressure him back into the marriage could, by any standards, be justly described as guilty of 'malicious and obstinat defectioun' and could be divorced in the Commissary Court of Edinburgh if the period of desertion had lasted for four years (*see*, e.g. *Wood* v. *Sinclair* (1756)).

The impact of divorce on property can be dealt with fairly briefly. Where the wife was the party in adultery she was treated as though she were dead. The tocher remained with the husband as did all her moveable estate and goods brought by her into the marriage and she forfeited her terce[17] (*Watson* v. *Gadderer*, Balfour, *Practicks*, p. 112). If the husband was an adulterer, then she could keep all goods gifted to her at and after the marriage and she enjoyed her terce and *jus relictae*[18] but she still lost her tocher (*Justice* v. *Murray* (1761)). Where the divorce was for desertion then by Act 1573 *c.*55 the party in desertion lost the tocher together with all *donationes propter nuptias*. Some doubt as to the return of the tocher existed in this case and the matter was probably not finally resolved until Stair's day.

One hesitates in a study as selective as this has been to draw any detailed conclusions but, perhaps, it has revealed two prominent features of the law in our period. The first point is that in the area of consistorial actions, e.g. declarator of marriage and divorce, the canon law continued to exert some considerable influence and the application of the law did not appear to discriminate against women. The second point is that the law of matrimonial property, during our period, operated in a way which did discriminate in favour of men and, moreover, was of an extremely complex nature.

NOTES

1. I am grateful to my colleague, Mr. James J. Robertson, for discussing with me some of the points raised in this essay. I accept full responsibility, however, for the views expressed.

2. 'Secondly it is necessary to have a mutual consent of these persons to the giving of their bodies for, as we have stated neither betrothal nor marriage should be one-sided because if either party withholds consent there can be neither a betrothal nor a marriage.'

3. Thus in *Regiam Majestatem* II. 16, 73 and 74, '*separata*' is used of divorce *a mensa et thoro*, '*ob aliquam sui criminis turpitudinem*' and of divorce *a vinculo*, '*propter parentelam*'.

4. 'We decern that the said Margaret Anderson should be separated *a mensa et thoro* from mutual cohabitation with and subjection to the said John Bayne, her spouse and to that extent let them be separated.'

5. This point was to arise in the case of Henry VIII, as Mary Boleyn had once been his mistress. This meant that Henry was related to Anne Boleyn, Mary's sister, in the same degree of affinity (i.e. the first degree) as he was related to Catherine of Aragon by virtue of her marriage to his brother (*see* Scarisbrick, *Henry VIII* (London 1976) ch. 7).

6. The Commissary Court of Edinburgh was created in 1563. There were four judges and they had general jurisdiction over the whole of Scotland in cases of marriage, divorce, legitimacy, etc. and also acted as a court of appeal from inferior commissary courts throughout Scotland. The Commissary Court of Edinburgh was abolished in 1836 though the inferior commissaries were not formally abolished until 1876 (Donaldson, 'The Church Courts', Stair Society, vol. 20, ch. 27).

7. Hereinafter cited thus: '*A. v. B.* (1781) M. 12681.'

8. Disobedience of the Court's order was treated as rebellion and the offender was publicly denounced as a rebel to the accompaniment of three blasts of the horn (*see* Maxwell, 'Diligence', Stair Society, vol. 20, ch. 28).

9. The suggestion is that the *coutumes* of Paris and Normandy may have had an influence on Scots Law (Paton, vol. 20, p. 100). It is possible that the former may have had, for its understanding of the principle of *communio bonorum* was as distorted as that of the Scottish jurists who advocated its existence (*Gordon v. Campbell* (1704) M. 5787, and see, generally, *Coutumiers de Normandie* (ed. Tardif), Soc. de L'hist. de Normandie (1881–1903), 2 vols., Rouen).

10. Such a renunciation was, however, treated as a gift and if made after the marriage it could, in the seventeenth century, be revoked by the husband. In this case, however, revocation was subject to the proviso that the wife had other resources to fall back on.

11. *Peculium* or Lady's Gown and 'pin-money' were also treated by some as paraphernal. For a fuller account of these *see* Paton, *loc. cit.* p. 103.

12. This does not, however, mean that the canon law did not still exert some influence. Thus the canon law defence of recrimination (Hay's *Lectures on Marriage*, p. 16), that the other spouse was also guilty of adultery, was admitted in some cases (see Balfour's *Practicks* at pp. 98–9). *Lenocinium*, or the active promotion of the other spouse's adultery, as a defence to a divorce action also has a canon law origin (Hay's *Lectures on Marriage*, p. 63).

13. The Confessio Saxonica of 1551 prepared by Melanchthon.

14. He, as Magister Rolandus, had taught canon law at Bologna.

15. The matter was apparently so difficult that Craig was specially consulted to discover what his opinion of the question was.

16. MSS Records, Com. Ct., 11 June, 22 June 1573, vol. VI. Fraser, *loc. cit.* p. 679 n.(i), observed that the records did not reveal one case of divorce for desertion prior to 1573 and, as far as I am aware, this is still so.

17. A liferent of one-third of the husband's heritable estate.
18. A right to one-third of the husband's moveable estate if there were children and to one-half if there were none.

BIBLIOGRAPHY

Scots law, unlike the Law of England, treats the writings of certain authors termed the 'institutional writers', as being a source of the law just as much as statute or case-law: 'When on any point of law I find Stair's opinion uncontradicted I look upon that opinion as ascertaining the Law of Scotland' (Drew v. Drew (1870) 9 Macp.163, per Lord Benholme at p. 167). In our period the institutional writers were Craig and Stair. Not everything written by an author who subsequently achieved institutional status can, however, be regarded as an institutional work. Thus, for example, though Erskine's *Institute* is a work of institutional character, his *Principles of the Law of Scotland* is not. The unique quality of these works justifies their separate treatment in this bibliography.

Case-law is also extremely important as a source of Scots law. During our period the only reports of cases were found in *Practicks*. 'Practick' means a decision or a precedent and, in the plural, signifies a collection of decisions. Some *Practicks*, however, including those of Balfour and Hope, were more than mere reports and contained additional material such as excerpts from statutes and other sources. Eventually the decision-Practicks were replaced by law reports and the digest-Practicks were eclipsed by the works of Craig and Stair. Many of the older cases are found in Morison's *Dictionary of Decisions* and I have preferred to cite this work throughout the essay.

The Acts of the Scottish Parliament prior to 1707 are taken from Murray of Glendook's *Laws and Acts of Parliament*, 1424–1681 and also from the Record edition of *The Acts of the Parliaments of Scotland*, 1124–1707. In the text I have given the Glendook citation first (e.g., Act 1573, c.55) and the Record citation second (e.g., A.P.S. III, 81). I have omitted any reference to the chapter numbers given in the Record edition since these do not correspond with the chapter references in Glendook.

Institutional Writers

Craig, *Jus Feudale* (1655) ed. and trans. Lord President Clyde, 2 vols. (1934) Edinburgh and London. This work was completed before 1603 but not published until 1655. Craig is the only Scottish institutional writer who acquired a reputation on the continent and an edition of the *Jus Feudale* appeared in Leipzig in 1716.

Stair, *The Institutions of the Law of Scotland* (1681, 1693, 1759, and 2 vols. 1826 and 1832; 1981). The 1681 and 1693 editions were under Stair's own hand. References to Stair in the text are taken from the 1981 edition by Professor David Walker and published by the University Presses of Edinburgh and Glasgow.

Erskine, *An Institute of the Law of Scotland*, 2 vols. (1773, 1785, 1793, 1805, 1812, 1824–28, 1838 and 1871). The references in the text are to the 1871 edition by Nicolson (2 vols.).

Case-law

Balfour's *Practicks* (1962, 1963) 2 vols. (ed. McNeill, Stair Society, Edinburgh). Balfour's *Practicks* cover the period 1469–1579. Balfour was, briefly, Lord President of the Court of Session in 1567–68. These *Practicks* were first published in 1754 and are highly regarded by lawyers.

Hope's *Major Practicks* (1937, 1938) 2 vols. (ed. Clyde, Stair Society, vols. 3 and 4, Edinburgh). These *Practicks* cover the period 1608–33.

Liber Officialis Sancti Andree (ed. Innes) (1845) Abbotsford Club, Edinburgh. This contains the reports and records of the Officials' Courts. This is a selection of the work of these Courts culled from several collections of reports and records.

Lord Hermand's *Consistorial Decisions*, 1684–1777, ed. Walton (1940) Stair Society, Edinburgh.

Morison's *Dictionary of Decisions* (1801–4). This covers the period 1540–1808 (though a few earlier cases are included). It is a compilation in 22 volumes of the decisions of the Court of Session. Brown's *Supplement* (1826) covers the period 1628–1794 and includes the cases omitted by Morison.

Other literature

An Introductory Survey of the Sources and Literature of Scots Law vol. 1. Stair Society (Edinburgh 1936)

An Introduction to Scottish Legal History vol. 20. Stair Society (Edinburgh 1958)

Anton, 'Handfasting in Scotland', *Scot. Hist. Rev.* (1958), p. 96

Ashley, 'Property in Relation to Marriage and the Family', *Juridical Review* 65 (1953), 37–69; 150–81; 262–93

Baird Smith, 'A Note on Divorce for Desertion', *Juridical Review* 51 (1939), 254–9

Fraser, *A Treatise on the Law of Scotland as applicable to the Personal and Domestic Relations* (Edinburgh 1846)

Gillon, *Selected Justiciary Cases*, 1624–1650, vol. 16. Stair Society (Edinburgh 1953)

Hay's *Lectures on Marriage* (ed. and trans. Barry), vol. 23. Stair Society (Edinburgh 1967)

Hume, *Lectures* (1786–1822) 6 vols. (ed. Paton), 1. 169. Stair Society (Edinburgh 1939–58)

Ireland, 'Husband and Wife', vol. 20, ch. VII Stair Society (Edinburgh 1958)

Mackenzie, *Observations on the Acts of Parliament* (Edinburgh 1686)

Murray, *Legal Practice in Ayr and the West of Scotland* (Glasgow 1910)

Paton, 'Husband and Wife: Property Rights and Relationships, vol. 20, ch. IX. Stair Society (Edinburgh 1958)

Protocol Book of Gavin Ros, N.P., 1512–1532 (eds. Anderson and Grant). Scottish Record Society (Edinburgh 1908)

Regiam Majestatem, II. 15 (ed. Cooper), vol. 11. Stair Society (Edinburgh 1947).

Scanlon, 'Pre-Reformation Canon Law of Marriage of the Officials' Courts', vol. 20, ch. VI, Stair Society (Edinburgh 1958)

TABLE OF CASES

Auchinleck *v.* Williamson (1667) M.6033

Auldingstone *v.* M'Williame, 24 January 1564, MSS Rec. Com. Ct., vol. I

Bayne *v.* Anderson (1525) *Liber Officialis*, Sancti Andree (Abbotsford Club, 1845), p. 32

Cockburn *v*. Burn (1679) M.5793
Collington *v*. Collington (1667) M.5828
Craig *v*. Monteith (1684) M.5819
Dalrymple *v*. Dalrymple (1811) 2 Haggard's Consistorial Reports, 54 per Lord
  Stowell at p. 82
Davidson *v*. Maccubin (1610) M.5802
Dicks *v*. Massie (1695) M.5821
Dickson *v*. Braidfoot (1705) M.10,396
Drew *v*. Drew (1870) 9 Macp. 163
Forbes *v*. Countess of Strathmore (1750) Elchies' *Decisions*, 27 February
Gordon *v*. Davidson (1708) M.5789
The Mistress of Gray *v*. The Master (1582) M.5802
Irvine *v*. Ker (1695) Hermand, 91
Justice *v*. Murray (1761) M.334
Leith *v*. Elphinstoun (1523) *Lib. Off.* p. 26
Leven *v*. Montgomery (1683) M.5803
Macinnes *v*. More (1781) M.12683
M'Lauchlin *v*. Dobson (1796) M.12693
Murray *v*. Dalrymple (1745) M.5842
Murray *v*. Simpson, 28 April 1569, MSS Rec. Com. Ct., vol. III
Myrtoune de Cambo *v*. Forsyth (1544), *Lib. Off.* p. 88
Walker *v*. Husband's Crs. (1730) M.5841
Watson *v*. Gadderer, Balfour *Practicks*, p. 112
Waugh *v*. Duncan, 3 July 1605, MSS Rec. Com. Ct., vol. XXXIV
Earl of Wigton *v*. Lady Margaret Lindsay (1708) Hermand, 45
Wood *v*. Sinclair (1756) Hermand, 71

VIII

'A Mere Matter of Business': Marriage, Divorce and the French Revolution[1]

Jennifer Birkett

Department of French, University of Dundee

In marriage there is more than the union of name and property. Ought the legislator to admit that these are the chief reasons of marriage, and not the outward personality, moral qualities and all those things which excite sentiment and animal affection? . . . You must not treat marriage as a mere matter of business. . . . After all, the dowry is only an accessory; the union of husband and wife is the essential point (Napoleon Bonaparte, cit. A. C. Thibaudeau, *Bonaparte and the Consulate*, pp. 181, 183).

By property, every man has something which is exclusively his, of which he is lord and master: his wife, his children, a piece of land, house, furnishings, money (Nicolas-Edmé Restif de la Bretonne, *Le Thesmographe*, p. 81).

The characters seem to have picked up the wrong scripts. Bonaparte, the hard-headed legislator, insists that marriage is chiefly a question of sentiment, while Restif, the new man of feeling and disciple of Rousseau (according to Grimm, the 'gutter version'—'Rousseau du ruisseau') unhesitatingly defines it as a sub-section of the wider and far more important problem of property. But there is no mistake; and when the two texts, and their respective authors, are brought together what they throw into relief is the main point of contention in late eighteenth-century marriage: how to reconcile relations of property and relationships between feeling individuals or, in other terms, the claims of the social order and the demands of individual desire. The purpose of the present essay is to juxtapose the work of the lawmakers and that of one of the objects of their legislation, in order to bring into focus some of the issues and controversies that lay behind the arid prescriptions of the *Civil Code* of 1804 and helped to generate the policy options that made the *Code* into a viable piece of social legislation. This account of the legal and political background to the *Code*'s provisions on marriage, from the *ancien régime* and throughout the upheavals of the Revolution, will be examined in the context of the work of Restif de la Bretonne (1734–1806), whose own experience of marriage and divorce provides much of the impetus of his novels and short stories. Such writings, being fiction, can in no way be said to 'illustrate', in the sense of directly reflecting, the day-to-day experience of marriage in his period. But what the sum of Restif's work does provide is an expression of attitudes— an ideology of marriage—which adds considerably to our understanding of the forms of sensibility with which the legislation engaged.

For the lawmakers and for Restif, the main issue is the relation of the individual to the family unit, which is seen as the microcosm of the relationship of individual to state. Individuals first understand themselves and their place in the wider social order as part of a family unit, so that a nascent state, intent on creating a new category of citizen-subjects, must begin its social engineering by securing appropriate patterns within that unit. There are two main objects to consider. The first is the rights of the individual, with his new demands for autonomy and personal happiness— and, indeed, *her* demands, for the question of women's rights became, for the first time, a focus of attention in the legislation of the Revolution. The second is property, and its ownership and transmission. For the private citizen, this is largely a question of getting and keeping a grip on the economic resources that secure day-to-day survival and personal freedom of action. For the state, the regulation of property has much further-reaching implications as a political instrument for confirming or re-distributing power. In every case, for Restif and for the Napoleonic State, as it expresses itself in the *Civil Code*, the way to achieve satisfactory social structures is to build on an assumption of the subordination of women. Within the family, both agree that this alone provides individual happiness (for both sexes) and maintains order and authority; and it is clear from the development of the laws regulating the division of family property that the broader interests of an increasingly conservative state required also that women be refused individual rights equal to those of men. The languages in which Restif and the revolutionary legislators formulated their versions of the question of marriage were very different, but they engaged on one substantial point: the nomination of a category which, by accepting the status of *object*, 'annexed to the male' (*Les Françaises*, below), allowed both men and the state to come into being as *subjects*, free and self-defining entities. The inequality Restif demanded in his personal relationships was also needed to establish the hierarchies which constituted the Napoleonic State.

The greater part of Restif de la Bretonne's wild and prolific oeuvre (novels, short stories, philosophical utopias), deals with property and power relations between men and women, expressed in the sexual act, the marriage contract, or both. Much of it claims to be based on first-hand observation and experience of contemporary life but compared, for example, with Louis-Sébastien Mercier's *Tableau de Paris* (1781–8) it is only relatively unmediated reportage. Whatever Restif writes on male and female relationships is coloured by his own and his daughter's unhappy marriages, and is conspicuously the product of a domineering personality and an unusually unrepressed libido. Its value, however, resides precisely in that personal dimension that might seem to reduce its documentary worth. Restif's texts must be recognised as a caricature, but a representative one, of a common male (and female) view of marriage at his period. In terms of political sensibility, he is fairly representative of the new middle ground in which the *Code* of 1804 was eventually to be established. As Le Roy Ladurie has pointed out, Restif was one of many young men of well-to-do and respected peasant family, come to Paris to seek their fortune, whose experiences at the bottom of the 'urban pyramid' stirred a revolutionary fervour that co-existed with a nostalgic longing for the security of the familiar hierarchy back home, and the firm hand of paternal authority (in *Histoire de la France rurale, t.II*, p. 477). Desirous of reforms, eager in his utopias to argue for more equality and a better organisation of property, he is nevertheless also aware of present advantages and the dangers of change, and terrified of the passions of the people—one of the solid majority without whose consent there is no revolutionary change, but who can also act as a brake on progress.[2] In a statement of 30 July 1789, as the King and the Third Estate jockeyed for position at the Estates General and the rioting intensified, he carefully hedged his bets:

> I am no supporter of slavery and despotism. I have proved myself a good patriot. But I love my king, and I am delighted to applaud the wise reforms instigated by the enlightened and vigilant members, friends of the public weal, who constitute the Estates General of this kingdom. I love order, peace and justice; I hate everything that might threaten these things, and I would sacrifice the last drop of my blood to maintain the laws (*Le Thesmographe*, p. 367).

As a 'good patriot', he regularly changed his position to match the changing leadership of the nation; but the bloodshed of the Revolution terrified him. When Bonaparte and the Directory came to power, he was pleased to disown the anarchies of the Jacobin Republic. Reforms, however desirable, were not worth the cost: '[Men] are better off staying as they are. People talk about Revolution. Sheer foolishness! All men will get from it is the suffering that always comes with change' (*Monsieur Nicolas*, vol. VI (1797), p. 97).

In every sense, Restif offers himself as the eighteenth century's man in the street, and especially the back streets of Paris, of which he became the haunter and historiographer. The terms in which he sets the marriage question might well be seen as the back streets of the law.

His attitudes, a mixture of the liberal, the humane and the authoritarian, mirror the contradictory politics of the period. Radical in his demands for male autonomy, and in the freedom and explicitness of his sexual fantasies, Restif is also wedded to order, rule and institution. He reconciles the two in a concept of the importance of the family unit and strict family hierarchy which differs very little from the more conservative versions of the *ancien régime.* His main concern is to deal with the challenge represented by woman. In his thinking, woman is essentially that which is defined and governed by man, endlessly observed, classified and categorised in the entire sequence of civil conditions—daughter, spinster, wife, mother. Her acquiescence in this subordination confirms his sense of selfhood. The process is the same as in Rousseau's *Contrat social,* where the state is formed through its definition of individuals as citizens, and through those individuals' 'free' renunciation of their private rights, including both personal property and individual autonomy. Totalitarianism pervades Restif's writing.

In his pornographic texts, women are clearly victims. Conquette, in the *Anti-Justine* (1798), undergoes a multiple subordination, not only prostituted by her husband, but the (acquiescent) object of incestuous approaches from her father. The prostitute holds the centre of his stage, the paid object most easily regulated, both in Restif's social studies (*Le Palais-Royal,* 1790) and in his utopian legislative designs. As early as 1769, *Le Pornographe,* a whole volume devoted to a project for state-run brothels, shows with startling clarity the link between sexual and social hierarchies. The state brothel would not only serve to check the spread of venereal disease and improve public morality, but act as a nursery ('une pépinière') to form new and useful citizens for the state.

A married woman has obviously far better social status than a prostitute, but in many respects her relationship with the male is not dissimilar. The observations and anecdotes of *Les Contemporaines* (1780–3) and *Les Françaises* (1786) give a detailed picture of Restif's views on marriage in the 1780s. Marriage implies primarily social responsibilities; it is the institution through which men and women must reinforce the existing order, by accepting their place in the established career and property structures. A mismatch may secure short-term personal happiness, but abdicating one's social position makes an ultimate tragedy inevitable. The hero of 'Le Nouveau Pygmalion' (*Les Contemporaines*) loves Lise, the servant he has trained into his own mould, but recognises that marrying her will mean rejection by society, his own family, and their future children. If he marries suitably, his future is assured:

> I shall be approved by everyone; I shall make my way; get advancement; supported by the family I ally myself to I can claim Court favour, serve the state, acquire a reputation. That's not all; one day my children will thank me for having given them origin in two equally famous sources (I, 48).

Lise, not surprisingly, approves his decision:

> You belong to a condition with certain laws and certain advantages. Either give up the second or conform to the first. That's what my heart tells me. You belong to a particular condition. You must fulfil all its duties. One of those duties is a suitable and fitting marriage. You must fulfil that (p. 51).

Man is the principal partner in marriage, and woman naturally subordinate. The heroine of 'L'Epouse aimant un autre' (*Les Françaises*) receives from her father the cautionary tale of a wife who is tempted, falls, repents bitterly and is nevertheless justifiably buried in a convent. In addition, her father invokes the views of the Chinese and the Turks:

> Women do not have the principle of life; it is annexed to the male and is his glorious prerogative. He is the one who gives it, to be developed in woman. I refer you to this physical truth, my child, so that you can found on it the respect you will have for your husband, so that your submission to him will be easy, voluntary and pleasant, and so you can think it reasonable and natural, and therefore necessary and indispensable (III,63–4).

Women must learn that their sole function is to please men. 'The first sex (mine) is made for work and business, to acquire experience and enlightenment. Pleasing is not its essence' (p. 69).

Even the most intelligent wives should not interfere with the business side of a marriage. 'L'Epouse-mère' (*Les Contemporaines*), a talented woman with an amiable incompetent of a husband, runs a harmonious, if impoverished, household, by acquiescing in all his most foolish enterprises. In her view, society would be destroyed if women started to seek responsibility in their own right:

> I think it's bad for a woman to have a rank or title that isn't held through a man, like those spinster Countesses in Germany. A woman should only have civil status through her union with a man. I strongly disapprove of the steps taken by a certain ex-Minister of Finance, who thought it his duty to set up professional guilds for women. I may be wrong, but I think that is one of the things that are basic to manners and morals, and are liable eventually to lead a nation into false and destructive principles. The end of all good legislation must surely be to make the two sexes dependent on one another, and especially to make the first sex the necessary support of the second. But if the door to titles and distinctions is opened to the second sex in the upper classes, and women in the common classes given the means of independent establishment and subsistence, female celibacy is bound to make destructive advances (VII,211–12).

A wife without a dowry is easier to control; with the support of a dowry, she will be impertinent and spendthrift. A poor woman can be moulded by her husband and his parents, and readily 'worship' him ('La Petite Amoureuse', *Les Contemporaines*, vol. I). Maximilienne, 'La Femme impérieuse' (*Les Françaises*), will not entertain the idea of a joint dowry:

> Father, I don't see it like you do. Buy the land yourself and give it me; let M d'Ange give his son something else. ... You must realise that nowadays marrying with separate property (*séparés de biens*) is important, and I would very much like to keep all my income in my own hands. Besides, I like the idea of saying 'my property', and I'd rather have nothing than be reduced to 'our property at ***' (II,11–12).

She also persuades her father he can keep back the second instalment of her dowry, since her new family is of lesser nobility; and her arrogance makes the household completely wretched. In 'La Femme-entendue' (*Les Françaises*, II), a foolhardy man marries an ugly, stupid wife simply for her money and status. She spends the income of her dowry on finery and eats into her husband's reserves. They are eventually separated, but his estate is encumbered by her debts for ten years.

Against this plethora of misfortunes, Restif gives one or two instances of marriages which work on a basis of shared responsibility. Madame Lebrun and her husband make the traditional division of labour (he in his business, she steward of the household accounts) and work and save to give all their children equal and substantial dowries, to protect them from exploitation ('La Mère d'une famille nombreuse', *Les Françaises*, IV). A table of the dowries is posted in the dining-room, for the benefit of visitors, and the whole family vets potential suitors and gives support when things go wrong—a strange combination of sentiment and mercantile hard-headedness. There is a similar blend in 'Le Demi-mariage' (*Les Contemporaines*, IX), in which a progressive husband makes up his wife's fortune to equal his own, and promises to exercise his conjugal rights only at her invitation. Restif's need to invent a successful marriage in which the legal bond is replaced by a voluntary one is in itself a sign of the changing times. But it is still noticeable that the husband, while signing away his legal rights, carefully chooses a wife who for other reasons is hardly likely to break the traditional mould: 'She was a young person of the highest birth, more pretty than beautiful, with only twenty thousand francs income for her dowry and a face that had never been spoiled by rouge' (p. 297).

In all these stories, Restif took for granted the indissolubility of marriage. A wife's duty was to suffer and submit, even in the most adverse circumstances. 'L'Epouse du joueur' (*Les Françaises*) has no legal or moral alternative to marriage, and must reform her husband by example, while Restif fulminates against the mere idea of divorce: 'Monster spewed up from hell . . . putting to flight innocence, modesty, marital and paternal affection' (III,112–13). Divorce, however, begins to become more acceptable to Restif as changes in public opinion coincide with his own problems with an unfaithful, calumnious, greedy blue-stocking of a wife (if we are to believe all he says in his novel of 1788, *La Femme infidèle*). Part of the utopian legislation proposed in *Le Thesmographe* (1789) is a divorce law, to improve social morality and ensure the proper transmission of property. The basic subordination of wife to husband stays the same, with the wife essentially part of the husband's property, something 'exclusively his, of which he is lord and master' (p. 81). A man certainly has no right to abuse such a property, 'on pain of being deprived of her'. But divorce remains something invented for man's advantage, with Restif marvelling at the irrationality and unnaturalness of present European marriage laws, which assume that 'a man is made for one single woman' (p. 146). With the help of a five-page appendix (pp. 375–80), he works through a set of detailed provisions. The three grounds of divorce should be sterility, insanity and adultery. Divorced persons should be allowed to remarry (p. 104); Restif here distances himself from the punitive refusals of existing legislation to allow separated spouses to embark on new, legitimate unions. Incompatibility is not suggested as grounds, despite Restif's sentimental assertion that the aim of marriage is to make the couple happy and virtuous. Children are claimed to benefit from divorce, which improves their chances of a sound moral upbringing, and keeps their property intact. Restif envisages parents holding property on trust for their children and paying for their upkeep; failing that, the state must engage to maintain them.

The discussion in *Le Thesmographe* contains much self-interested rhetoric, but mixes this with serious humane and practical considerations. The baroque anecdotes concluding the third volume of *Le Palais-Royal* (1790), 'Le Divorce nécessaire, Prouvé par les faits', cast a different light on the potential Restif sees in the new institution. Ostensibly deploring the criminal tangles into which, he claims, the absence of divorce law is forcing his fellow-citizens, he also rejoices in salacious anticipation of the new sexual freedoms it will bring. Husbands or wives, falling in love with someone else, make arrangements to marry the beloved to an accomplice; the two households then join forces, swapping partners, without the neighbours knowing. A husband deserts an adulterous wife, flees to Paris, and sends home news of his death. He then sets up house with two attractive girl-friends, still unable, unfortunately, to marry more than one. The conclusion is something of a *non sequitur*: 'Allow divorce, believe me! and marriages will be happier and more solid.' Victoire and K . . . n, both mismarried, are finally united only after two deaths, one incarceration in the madhouse, one attempted murder, pretended burials, flights to Belgium and three pregnancies. Divorce, again, could have prevented it all.

In *Le Palais-Royal* the divorce theme, as for many contemporary writers, is really a pretext for melodramatic and entertaining intrigue—though some serious points are made of, for example, the special problems posed for marriage by the upheavals of revolution, compounding, as Restif says, the 'mutability' of the human heart. But for a serious if still somewhat Gothic imaginative account of the trials of marriage, and its real dangers under pre-revolutionary legislation, we have to look elsewhere, to the novel *Ingénue Saxancour*. Written in 1786 and published in 1789, a fictionalisation of the unhappy experiences of Restif's own daughter, this is a useful work to read alongside Roderick Phillips' case-histories of divorces in Rouen, as a *summum* of the powerlessness of women in the married state (*Family Breakdown in Late Eighteenth-Century France*, ch. 3).

Moresquin, Ingénue's husband, had seduced his first wife, extorted substantial gifts from her family in the marriage contract by threatening not to regularise the union, lived on her earnings as a linen-merchant, and finally beaten her to death. He is now engaged in the same process with Ingénue. The narrative, and Ingénue's suffering, is prolonged by the difficulty of finding witnesses to his moral and physical violence in the home; even her father will not side with wife against husband. Neighbours finally see the beatings, and Ingénue leaves with a trunkful of her own belongings. Moresquin accuses her of theft and adultery, and her father of pimping for her. A purported attempt at reconciliation is a pretext for further violence on his part, and for threats to beat her to death or infect her with syphilis. He tries to have her arrested, but Ingénue counter-charges, and the affair goes before the magistrates as a request for separation. The magistrate returns Ingénue to her father, who draws up the formal request for separation, granted on the grounds of Moresquin's threats and his having slandered the moral reputation of the girl and her family.

Two points in Restif's account are particularly striking: firstly, a product of the then legislation, the wife's powerlessness without neighbours' evidence (and especially, evidence of attacks directed not only against her but against her family); and secondly, the ambivalence of Restif's own response. The father-figure in the text recognises the wretchedness of the daughter, but is reluctant to intervene on her behalf at the expense of male authority. The author, perversely, enjoys the subordination of his daughter-figure to a man he portrays graphically as sadist, sodomist, exhibitionist and voyeur. The eighteenth-century *homme moyen sensible* and moralist can organise his fantasies, as later his legislation, to have the best of both worlds. This is, says Ingénue, a moral tale; she was wrong to press to marry against her father's opposition:

> I have only narrated the preceding story to display for the eyes of young people the dreadful consequences of my error, and to show them how dangerous it is not to discover precisely the morals of the man one marries. Alas! it's a master we take on, and not only a master but half our own self; a being with rights over our bodies, souls, modesty, even our chastity, over the happiness and pain of every single moment! (III,72–3).

But there is no way in which Restif could draw the moral to its logical conclusion and argue for legislation within marriage for a more equal relationship. His introduction to *La Femme infidèle* (1786), settling accounts with his own marriage, declares overtly, and with a total lack of self-consciousness, his own vested self-interest. For if women are given anything, then men risk losing everything:

> Ignorance in women is infinitely useful: it keeps them subordinate; it makes them concentrate on the necessary tasks of the household. If you make women more educated, men will be less so, for two reasons: (1) knowledge extended to all classes will become superficial; (2) knowledge will have nothing left to distinguish it; well-disposed young men will no longer be animated by the ardour, the burning fire I felt in my youth, which alone made me devour insurmountable obstacles; their sisters, who used to think them wonderful, will laugh at them. In a word, if you make women clever, you make men silly and stupid . . . this is the moment to apply the maxim of Holy Writ: The folly of men is better than the

wisdom of women. Indeed, we might as well give up everything, and let the women into politics (pp. 7–8).

With Restif's final remark, the discussion enters the realms of the clearly unthinkable. And if we move on now to our account of the developments in marriage law from *ancien régime* to *Civil Code*, what emerges is a parallel disregard for women's rights as individuals and their claims to equal consideration with men. With the exception of one brief moment, the early days of the Revolution, women appear mainly as ciphers in a process of redistribution of property and power which passed through three stages: the *ancien régime* sought to strengthen the family unit and the power of the father; the first phase of the Revolution, up to 1794, saw a democratisation of family structures, a diminishing of marital and paternal authority, and an attempt to redistribute the great family fortunes; the second, up to the promulgation of the *Code* in 1804, retained some of the liberties gained in the first phase but also restored paternal power and reinstated the family unit. According to James Traer, the revolutionary period overall laid the foundations for 'modern' as opposed to 'traditional' marriage, introducing the principle that marriage should be a question of individual happiness (*Marriage and the Family in Eighteenth-Century France*, p. 16). This principle, however, takes its place alongside those already entrenched: post-revolutionary marriage remains as much a question of business and politics as sentiment. And the 'individuals' whose happiness was considered tended not to be of the second sex.

Under the *ancien régime*, the struggle was between monarchy and Church, over whether marriage was a sacrament or a civil contract. From the sixteenth century onwards, marriage and family law came increasingly within the jurisdiction of the secular courts, with the state intervening to reinforce and extend the authority of the male head of the household. Clandestine marriages between minors became far more difficult than under canon law. The royal courts discriminated against women in separation claims, holding female adultery a more serious offence; the Church saw all adultery as equally abhorrent. But Church and state were jointly responsible for the elaboration of institutions which made women in general and wives in particular dependent on and inferior to the male. In marriage, a woman and her property were subordinate to the husband, and a wife was, indeed, part of her husband's property: 'an inferior, a half-slave having alienated to a third party the free disposal of her person and property' (Léon Abensour, *La Femme et le féminisme avant la Révolution*, p. 8). The more barbarous refinements had gone by the eighteenth century, but a husband could still obtain a *lettre de cachet* to imprison an adulterous wife for two years, and then choose whether to take her back or keep her property and leave her in a convent for the rest of her life.

Without her husband's permission, a wife could not enter into contracts or incur debts, unless she was a public merchant in her own right, as was allowed in certain trades (Abensour, *ibid.*, p. 17). Even her power to make a will was restricted, especially in regions of customary law, though she was liable for taxes. Married or not, a woman's inheritance rights varied with regional custom. Under some customs, commoners' children enjoyed equal inheritance rights, but noblewomen were not allowed to inherit a fief. The custom of Normandy allowed fathers to settle a maximum of one-third of their property on unmarried daughters living in the household, but girls had no absolute right to a dowry. Girls whose parents had died fell to the care of their brothers, who needed to provide a dowry only to sisters who had reached the age of twenty without finding a husband, and had kept their chastity.

The nature of the marriage contract varied with the multiplicity of regional codes, but in general two main systems operated, each intended to keep the wife in a subordinate position while protecting her from the economic effects of a husband's negligence, incompetence, or viciousness. The dowry régime prevailed in the South, in the regions of Roman (written) law. The wife's dowry, usually furniture, clothes and jewels, rather than cash, was paid over at marriage, often in instalments. The husband's family had powers of administration over the dowry, but it could not be alienated to them or him, and it was relatively easy to extract undamaged from a dead or indebted husband's estate. In addition, women under the dowry regime had full powers of administration and free disposition over other personal property. In customary law regions, property was held jointly, but was administered solely by the husband. The wife's signature used to be required for the sale of property, but by the eighteenth century, this had fallen into disuse. Her only real right was to recover her share from the estate when the marriage ended, by separation or death. That share would not, as with the dowry, be the original contribution, but devices existed for instances of conspicuous maladministration whereby a widow, renouncing and declaring bankrupt the joint estate, could at least take her half of what was left, unencumbered by debt, and even topped up from the husband's part. Who gained most advantage from the two régimes is a matter of dispute. Philippe Sagnac (1898) believes that the dowry system reinforced paternal power while joint property made for more independence and equality within the family. But Gustave Fagniez (1929) has noted that in areas that enforced joint property the privileges of masculinity and primogeniture were more marked; and he refers to a letter from Etienne Pasquier to President Brisson, arguing that written law provides far better guarantees of individual liberty and equality (p. 136). Restif, as we have seen, was quite convinced that a substantial dowry was harmful to male authority. The debate was to continue throughout the Revolution; but certainly, under the *ancien régime*, neither system was particularly satisfactory for a wife, given the courts' tendency to apply both in the husband's favour. 'Legally,' concluded Abensour, 'woman is an eternal minor' (p. 457). As Restif's Ingénue found out, it was wives, before the Revolution, who were least free of all.

The first phase of the Revolution saw an extension of women's civil rights, to a large extent as an accidental by-product of developments in marriage law. This extension was certainly not a priority for the legislators, who had seen their first task as one of completing the secularisation of marriage, along with the other institutions of the civil state. It was in this context, as part of a general piece of legislation taking over from the Church the registration of vital statistics, that it was established in principle on 3 September 1791 that marriage was a civil contract and a matter of public record. The corresponding law was decreed on 20 September 1792, with the legalisation of divorce as its logical concomitant. There then followed a rationalising exercise. In 1791, the Constituent Assembly decreed that there should be a code of civil laws 'simple, clear, appropriate to the Constitution' and 'common to the whole kingdom' to replace the existing hotchpotch of regional customs. The regulation of marriage was begun by the Legislative Assembly and completed by the Legislative Committee of the National Convention. On 28 January 1793, the Committee split into four sections, of which the first was to regulate civil status, the family and marriage. It submitted its first draft for a *Code* to the Convention on 9 August 1793. Five drafts in all were offered before agreement was reached 21 March 1804—by which time sufficient laws had been promulgated to change radically the condition of marriage.

The laws passed up to 1794 aimed to replace authoritarian rule within the family by greater equality for individual members, not so as to destroy marriage and the family but to maintain unity on a firmer basis of voluntary bonds of affection. In March 1790, as part of a wider piece of legislation abolishing feudal rights, fathers lost the right to control unruly minors with *lettres de cachet*. The law of 16–24 August 1790 vested authority over minors not in the father but in family courts of relatives and friends (*see* Phillips, chapter 1, for a detailed analysis of the family courts of the Revolution). The application of the principle of equality provided considerable opportunity to legislate against the great family fortunes. Primogeniture was abolished (15–28 March 1790); in cases of intestate succession, children—specifically including daughters—were to inherit in equal shares (8–15 April 1791). Cambacérès' first draft for the *Code* pursued the radical line, with proposals for a lower age of consent, removal of the parental veto on marriage for children of full age (and its limitation for minors to a period of one month) and further steps to equalise the inheritance rights of legitimate children and open the closed family circle to the illegitimate and adopted. (Inheritances for illegitimate children were later secured by the law of 2 November 1793; a decree of 6 December 1794 encouraged adoption.) He also suggested limitations on gifts to prevent the concentration of wealth. In an interesting intervention, introducing an unexpected line of argument, Danton opposed the provision restricting gifts between spouses to one-tenth of either one's property, as unfair to a wife who had worked to improve the common fortune and should not see it go to collaterals. However, he was overruled.

Cambacérès' proposed legislation on the marriage contract, encouraging a system of joint property, was deliberately based on the desire to promote family unity on the basis of equality. (Sagnac also points out that it would have the further effect of bringing into circulation the wealth frozen in the dowry.) The dowry regime was not abolished in so many words, but the legislation would remove the safeguard (the 'hypothèque', a form of mortgage) which made it inalienable, a kind of loan to the husband which he could use but not deplete. In the Assembly, Génissieux argued unsuccessfully for its retention:

Your proposals for husband and wife to administer their property jointly and have a kind of reciprocal veto are empty ones, because the husband's influence will nearly always carry the day; and it will be all the stronger when his wife becomes a mother, loses the charms of youth, and is less tempted to apply for divorce, forced to be more circumspect because she will have less to hope for from a change in her situation. It is then that, under the guise of joint administration, the husband often becomes a tyrannical master, tearing signatures from his wife's hand and ruining her with no hope of return; whereas establishing the dowry, with hypothec, will protect her from such mischance (*Le Moniteur universel*, 23 August 1793).

The Convention decided nevertheless that property should be held in common, including the fruits of labour and inheritances received during the marriage, and be handed back equitably on divorce. But furious debate arose on the administration of the common property. The legislative committee wanted joint administration, with the husband requiring the wife's consent to dispose of property. Its reasons were both practical and high-minded:

This innovation may be criticised: the critics have their answer in the principle of equality which is to regulate all the acts of our social organisation, and in our intention to prevent those indiscreet commitments which so often ruin the fortunes of both husband and wife and generate internal discord, grief and unhappiness (*ibid.*).

Danton, Couthon, Camille Desmoulins found the argument persuasive. Desmoulins also thought it politic, and likely to win women to the Revolution. Couthon said that men and women had equal administrative ability, and that if this had not seemed so in the past, it was the fault of the old institutions. Violent opposition came from Lacroix, Merlin de Douai and, with particular force, Thuriot:

This law would be so contrary to basic principles and so dangerous in its effects that foreigners would refuse to engage in business transactions with France as long as it continued in force. This law would enslave and degrade man by making woman his guardian. If a husband were to share administration with a wife because he trusted her, that would do her more honour than any rights she got from the Code.

He asked for an adjournment, and got it. This particular article was not discussed again. The key to female emancipation, this issue was also its major stumbling-block; and Thuriot and Restif joined forces to stop the Revolutionary tide.

One progressive piece of legislation that *was* pushed through success-fully, and the greatest single factor improving women's condition in this period, was that on divorce. The *ancien régime* allowed only judicial separation (*séparation de corps et d'habitation*), where physical danger or slander of moral reputation were involved, and financial separation (*séparation de biens*), where a wife's property was threatened by a husband's depredations or simple maladministration. The separation could be effected before ecclesiastical or civil authorities; the marriage itself was not dissolved. From the middle of the eighteenth century onwards, the *philosophes* had argued for divorce and the right to remarry, in the name of freedom and equity (*see* Traer, ch. 3). In late 1789–90, divorce became a major popular issue, after a substantial pamphlet campaign (described in detail, Traer, pp. 105–17). Despite rearguard religious resistance in the Assembly, the principle was established on 30 August 1792, and the law followed in September. Divorce was allowed by mutual consent, on grounds of incompatibility and on a list of specific grounds (insanity; opprobrious crime; violence and serious injury; noted debauchery; deser-tion for two years; absence without communication for five years; emigration). Depending on the ground invoked, the procedure, before a family court of friends and relatives, could be more or less speedy. Remarriage was allowed, even to a partner in adultery, though a wife had to wait a year to avoid disputes over paternity. Vague provision was made for financial separation and dissolving the joint property; the family courts helped resolve disputes. A wife had no financial rights when the divorce had been obtained against her, except on grounds of insanity. Despite the last invidious provision, the legislation generally benefited substantially the many women suffering unhappy and violent unions, and there were efforts to go further. In his preliminary remarks to the first draft for the *Code*, Cambacérès argued that divorce, like the marriage contracts, should be a question of the will of the parties. The Convention, taking him at his word, threw out his proposal to retain the specific grounds of 1792, and reduced them all to simple incompatibility. Divorce would be a matter of mutual consent or the request of one partner. The procedure before the family court was to be quicker and easier. By the divorce settlement, each partner should recover his or her own property and the joint property be divided equally, with no special provisions being made against a guilty wife. There would be shared liability for debts contracted within the marriage, and provision for a maintenance allowance for the partner caring for the children, to be fixed by the family court. Unfortunately, the draft failed to be passed as a whole, but the separate laws and decrees that did get through (including, for example, the law of 23–28 April 1794 allowing immediate divorce where a partner had been absent without communication for six months)[3] enabled substantial numbers of divorces to take place between 1792 and 1796, mostly in the cities, where women could more easily find employment and alternative accommodation. In Paris the figure was one in every three marriages (Traer, p. 131; see also Phillips, pp. 92–104). The figures are artificially high, since they include ratifications of separations effected before the Revolution and a number of divorces sought by émigrés' wives to recover property seized by the nation. They indicate nevertheless considerable undermining of the monolithic family fortune and the absolute authority of the male head of the household, and an equally considerable, if short-lived, improvement in women's rights.

Philippe Sagnac characterises the second phase of the Revolution, from the time of the Directory, when the jurists and traditionalists regained the upper hand in the Assembly: 'The revolutionaries distrusted fathers; the legislators of the Consulate only distrust children' (p. 363). The tone was caught and accentuated by Napoleon, reared in the custom of a Corsica where women were totally dependent on their husbands (Abensour, p. 22), with marital problems of his own, and unenthusiastic about revolutionary liberties. For him, divorce was punitive, rather than permissive:

> Women in these days require restraint, and this will restrain them. They go where they like; they do what they like. It is not French to give women the upper hand; they have too much of it already.
>
> There are more women who wrong their husbands than men who wrong their wives. We want a bridle for the class of women who commit adultery for gewgaws, for verses, for Apollo and the muses, and all the rest of it (*cit.* Thibaudeau, p. 194).

At the same time, Napoleon's sentimental idealisation of relationships helped check the reactionary swing, so that marriage in the *Code* of 1804 still retained its revolutionary aspect of love and mutual consent, with 'the union of husband and wife the essential point'. But the nature of the union changed substantially. With measures to reduce individual freedom and hard-won equalities, restore paternal power and reinstate the large family fortunes, marriage was 'a matter of business'.

On 2 August 1795, a year after its institution, the law allowing speedy divorce in cases of absence was repealed. In April and August of the same year, laws of 26 October 1793 and 6 January 1794 declaring retroactive the provisions for equal inheritance were abolished. The Directory also abolished the family courts, which had been hearing the predictably large number of suits arising in this connection (28 February 1796). In his third draft for the Code (14 June 1796), Cambacérès sought to prevent minors using mutual consent and incompatibility as grounds of divorce, to restrict the rights of illegitimate children and to allow fathers to advantage particular children with gifts. He also thought it quite impractical to share the administration of the joint property: 'A shared administration would meet constant obstacles and the diversity of opinions on the tiniest details would bring about the dissolution of the marriage.' Jacqueminot's draft of 1800 produced further measures favourable to the accumulation of wealth and making divorce less easy, to put an end to 'the scandal of those continual divorces which have practically made a travesty of marriage, turning it into a kind of self-confessed concubinage'. His preliminary remarks denounced the 'bias' and 'immorality' of the family legislation of the first phase of the Revolution:

> There were too many prejudices in power that had simply replaced the previous ones. The fanaticism of an insanely defined equality reigned supreme, like the fanaticism of the privileged classes before it. The depravity of political thought was at its zenith, and civil legislation was marked by it. The most enlightened and virtuous representatives could not escape completely from the universal infection, nor throw off the yoke weighing on all society.

Portalis, presenting the report of the commission established by Bonaparte, repeated the charge of improper intrusion of political bias into a civil legislation which should strive only to be 'wise' and 'just':

> They overthrew paternal power because children are more welcoming to new institutions. They had no respect for marital authority because it was through the wider liberty granted women that they were able to introduce new forms and a new tone into the fabric of everyday life.

This was what the *Civil Code* of 1804 set out unequivocally to remedy.

> Husband and wife cannot contract out of the rights consequent on the husband's authority over the persons of his wife and children, or belonging to the husband as head of the household (art. 1388).

The father regained his powers of corrective imprisonment on simple request over his children (arts. 376, 377) and the laws of inheritance were changed to allow him to concentrate more of his fortune on a particular child, though this was balanced by the guarantee of a fixed share to every child, with no distinction between the rights of sons and daughters. But it was the freedoms of wives which were most drastically curtailed. In return for his protection, a wife had to obey her husband and follow him wherever he wished to reside (arts. 213, 214); if suing for divorce, she could leave the family home only for a place nominated by the court (art. 268). She could not register a child's birth (except as a midwife), be a member of a family council (unless the mother), or act as a guardian. Outside the marriage, her legal capacity was almost non-existent. In April 1798, she had already been exempted from legal constraint for debt, which diminished her business credit. She could not be a witness to any legal instrument, or institute legal proceedings without her husband's authority, even if she were separated, or a merchant in her own name (art. 215). Except for making her will (art.

226), she needed her husband's consent for all important acts, including mortgaging her own property and accepting an inheritance (arts. 217, 776); in her husband's absence, even if he were in prison, she needed a magistrate's consent (arts. 221, 222). Here, however, there *was* an exception for women engaged in business in their own right (art. 220). The dowry régime was permitted, with the traditional safeguards, but the preferred régime was that of common ownership of property (art. 1393). The husband was sole administrator, entitled to sell, alienate and mortgage the joint property without his wife's consent (art. 1421). He also administered his wife's property, but was unable to dispose of it without her agreement (art. 1428). Her one remedy against a dissolute husband, financial separation, was available only if she could prove her dowry was under threat and her husband's own estate too much in disorder to compensate her (art. 1443). This article explicitly forbade voluntary separation of property. The wife was not the natural heir to the property, but came at the end of a long list of descendants, ascendants, collaterals and illegitimate children (art. 767).

A wife was much worse off than a spinster, and marriage became harder to get out of. Divorce was handed back from family courts to official tribunals (art. 234). The plea of incompatibility was abolished. Mutual consent stayed, since for many families it conveniently veiled scandal; but a more complex mode of procedure was instituted, and its application was restricted. In particular, parents' consent had to be obtained (art. 278). The specific grounds were reduced to three: adultery, cruelty, or opprobrious crime. Judicial separation was reinstated (art. 306). All pretence of equality was set aside in the differential treatment of male and female adultery. A husband could sue for simple adultery by his wife; a wife, only if the husband had kept his concubine in the marital home (arts. 229, 230). An adulterous wife could be imprisoned for a period from three months to two years, and released when her husband agreed to take her back (arts. 308, 309). a guilty husband was just fined (100–2000 francs). The penal code found it inexcusable to murder a husband; not so a wife.

For the *Code*, then, the issue of woman's place was as clear-cut, 'natural' and 'logical' as for Restif. With supreme confidence, harmonising traditional male sensibility and conservative political interests, the post-revolutionary state was able to formulate in 1804 a definition of women as second-class citizens which functioned as one of the foundation stones of the new social edifice.

There is, however, room for a postscript. The languages of Restif and the *Code* join here in a negative addressed to women that seems firm enough; but of its nature, it could hardly be final. For language, which the conservative would like to see as definitive, a limiter of situations, is in fact an articulator and inventor of possibilities. In its own terms, the *Code* of 1804 sought to define and dismiss women; but those terms—the new notion of the 'individual' as citizen, property-owner, exercising certain rights and freedoms on a certain basis of equality—were not inert, and what they generated was the possibility of alternative definitions and applications. Under divine law, there was a logical case for the immutability of social place and given roles, but what had now been seen was the invention of revolutionary law inventing in its turn the new man and the new state—and consequently accessible to reinvention and reinterpretation. The point was certainly grasped by Condorcet, who reached a feminist position through his philosophical meditations on electoral rights and the nature of equality. In his essay of July 1790, *Sur l'admission des femmes au droit de cité*, he stresses the factitiousness of political and civil legislation. In natural law, women are equal with men; only habit prevents men from conceiving the possibility of their having civil rights. It is as reasonable to deny political rights to the non-aristocratic as it is to deny them to women:

> And one cannot adduce here the fact that women are dependent on their husbands, since it would be possible to destroy this tyrannical provision of the civil law at the same time; and one injustice can never be a reason for committing another (*Oeuvres complètes*, X,126).

Not many women, unfortunately, were articulate in their demands for political rights. The voices that spoke loudest belonged to women like Madame de Genlis, novelist, moralist, educationlist and former Orleanist, who supported Napoleon in exchange for a pension and in anticipation of a better régime. Throughout the Revolution and the Restoration, she propagated the traditional masculine image of woman as husband's handmaid, guardian of the household, 'angel of peace', arguing that women's desire for independence had been a major factor in the destructive upheavals of the Revolution.[4] Of the women who joined the revolutionary Clubs, most were satisfied to second whatever the men decided were the immediate priorities, and made no demands for improvements in women's political or social status.[5] The active feminists operated in tiny, isolated groups, with far too narrow a base. Most women ignored them, and they were feared by men and women alike for their radicalism, which led them ultimately to forge links with the enragés. Though the women of the Halles had played a major and enthusiastic part in the *journées* of 1789, there were few protests in October 1793 when the Convention outlawed women's clubs (at the request of a woman) and accepted the recommendations of the Committee of Public Safety that women should not have political rights, take part in government or meet in associations.[6]

But the opportunity for speech had been provided, and the Club of Revolutionary Women showed its skill in handling, for its own purposes, the language that was shortly to generate the *Code*:

> The prejudice has vanished by which women used to be banished to the narrow circle of the home, turning one half of all individuals into passive, isolated

creatures. . . . Revolutionaries' wives must give . . . the example of a society whose
worthy aim is vigilance and education. . . . The Declaration of Rights is common
to both sexes, and the only difference is in our duties: there are public duties and
private ones. . . . The imperious demands of nature can be reconciled with those of
a love of the public weal. . . . Watchful and wakeful citizens, having fulfilled the
sweet duties of wives and mothers and performed their indispensable tasks, still
have time to devote to their fraternal societies, to vigilance and to education (*cit.*
Marc de Villiers, *Histoire des clubs de femmes et des légions d'Amazones*, p. 239).

For the time being, unfortunately, this particular character *had* picked
up the wrong script, and the appropriation of the new language was to be a
long, hard struggle. But the speech is there, probing its own possibilities;
and from now on, marriage was to be a matter of business, sentiment—and
education.

NOTES

1. Unless otherwise stated, all translations are my own. I am grateful to Hazel
Williamson of Lincoln's Inn for help with English legal terminology; any errors are
my own responsibility.
2. See M. Poster, *The Utopian Thought of Restif de la Bretonne* (New York 1971),
esp. pp. 56–60 and 108–10, for an assessment of the nature of Restif's utopias
which, it is argued, look back to the moralist tradition rather than forward to
the economic and political projects of the nineteenth-century socialists. In, for
example, *Monsieur Nicolas*, Restif offers 'communism' as the ideal social form and
inveighs against the 'immorality' of private property; but at the same time, he is
careful to stress that few examples of the ideal do or can exist, and that present
ownership and distribution of property must be scrupulously respected (vol. VI.
45–50, 257–8, 309 25).
3. Somewhat bewilderingly, the wives of men at the front and functionaries on
public service were allowed to make use of this provision (Traer, p. 123, is a
misreading of the law); however, their request for divorce had to be registered
before the public official at their last common domicile, or at the husband's present
home, and the husband on return was entitled to challenge any dispositions they
had made of the property.
4. See for example 'Le Philosophe pris au mot ou le mari corrupteur' in *L'Epouse
impertinente par air* (1804) and the *Dictionnaire critique et raisonné des éti-
quettes de la cour et des usages du monde* (1818), arts. 'Divorce', 'Famille', 'Femmes',
'Mariage'.
5. See Henriette Perrin, 'Les Clubs de femmes de Besançon', *Annales révolutionnaires*, 9 (1917), 629–53; 10 (1918), 37–63, 505–32, 645–72.
6. See the excellent account by Jane Abry, 'Feminism in the French Revolution',
American Historical Review 80, no. 1 (Feb. 1975), 43–62.

BIBLIOGRAPHY

A. Restif de la Bretonne

Works (referred to in text)
*Le Pornographe, ou Idées d'un honnête-homme sur un projet de règlement pour les
    prostituées* (Londres—La Haye 1769)

Les Contemporaines (Leipsick—Paris 1780–6), 42 vols
Les Françaises (Neufchâtel—Paris 1786), 4 vols
La Femme infidèle, 2nd edn (La Haye 1788), 4 vols. (1st edn Neufchâtel—Paris
    1786)
Ingénue Saxancour, ou La Femme séparée (Liège—Paris 1789), 3 vols
Le Thesmographe, ou Idées d'un honnête-homme, sur un projet de règlement,
    proposé à toutes les nations de l'Europe, pour opérer une réforme générale des
    loix (La Haye—Paris 1789)
Le Palais-Royal (Paris 1790), 3 vols
Monsieur Nicolas, ou Le Coeur humain dévoilé (Paris 1959, eds. Pauvert), 6 vols.
    (1st edn Paris 1794–7, 16 vols.)
L'Anti-Justine, ou Les Délices de l'amour (Paris 1798)
(*Ingénue Saxancour* is readily available in the Collection 10:18, Union générale
    d'éditions (Paris 1978). A selection of Restif's work is also available ed.
    H. Bachelin, *L'Oeuvre de Restif de la Bretonne* (Paris 1930–2), 9 vols.)

Secondary sources
    E. Le Roy Ladurie, 'Du social au mental: une analyse ethnographique', in
    Histoire de la France rurale (eds. G. Duby and A. Wallon), vol. 2 (Paris 1975)
    M. Poster, *The Utopian Thought of Restif de la Bretonne* (New York 1971)

B.   General

L. Abensour, *La Femme et le féminisme avant la Révolution* (Paris 1923)
J. Abry, 'Feminism in the French Revolution', *American Historical Review* 80, no. 1
    (Feb. 1975), 43–62
Code civil des français (Paris 1804)
M. J. A. N. C. Condorcet, 'Sur l'admission des femmes au droit de cité' (1790) in
    Oeuvres complètes (Paris 1847–9), vol. 10
J.-B. Duvergier, *Collection complète des lois, décrets, ordonnances, règlements et avis*
    du Conseil d'état etc. de 1788–1857 (Paris 1834–58)
G. Fagniez, *La Femme et la société française dans la première moitié du 17ᵉ siècle,*
    1598–1648 (Paris 1929)
P.-A. Fenet, *Recueil complet des travaux préparatoires du code civil* (Paris 1927–8)
J. Godechot, *Les Institutions de France sous la Révolution et l'Empire*, 2nd edn rev.
    & aug. (Paris 1968)
Le Moniteur universel
H. Perrin, 'Les Clubs de femmes de Besançon', *Annales révolutionnaires*, 9 (1917),
    629–53; 10 (1918), 37–63, 505–32, 645–72
R. Phillips, *Family Breakdown in Late Eighteenth-Century France: Divorces in*
    Rouen 1792–1803 (Oxford 1980)
Ph. Sagnac, *La Législation civile de la Révolution française, 1789–1804* (Paris 1898)
A. C. Thibaudeau, *Bonaparte and the Consulate* (tr. G. K. Fortescue) (London
    1908)
J. F. Traer, *Marriage and the Family in Eighteenth-Century France* (Ithaca and
    London 1980)
M. de Villiers, *Histoire des clubs de femmes et des légions d'Amazones* (Paris 1910)

IX

Marriage and Law Reform in Nineteenth-Century America

Patricia Lucie

Department of Public Law, University of Glasgow

There was not one American way of marriage but many, reflecting a strikingly diverse society. Rich and poor, black and white, native and immigrant, believer and unbeliever, built marriages on different foundations and with different prospects. The law touched all their unions, but not as a common denominator, transcending differences. It reflected the interests of those who made it—men, particularly men of property. The law had one face for men and one for women, one for rich and one for poor, one for white and one for black.

The American federal system multiplied variations on these themes by the number of states in the Union. Each state jealously guarded its autonomy in matters relating to marriage, divorce and property law. Sometimes the differences between states were gross. Those most obviously distinct were the eight states (Arizona, California, Idaho, Louisiana, Nevada, New Mexico, Texas and Washington) which adopted community property systems based on the civil law idea of marriage as a partnership. In these states, property acquired separately by husband and wife before or during the marriage remained separate, while everything acquired by mutual effort was owned jointly, though under the control and management of the husband. Even within this group of states there were differences. Louisiana inherited its civil code primarily from the French Code Napoleon while the states of the Southwest which adopted community property systems retained their Spanish character, intermingling elements of the common law.

Most states had common law systems. But they, too, were far from uniform. The environment worked as many changed between neighbours in the New World as it had between the New World and the Old. Differences of colonial background, religious history and subsequent social, political and economic development made the laws of New England, the mid Atlantic states, the South and West quite distinctive. Even within regions, no two states had quite the same laws.

To the difficulties in the way of discovering 'the law' which federal history and geography impose must be added the dimension of time. Two developments were particularly momentous. First, it became easier both to get married and divorced. By the last quarter of the nineteenth century, this apparent laxity worried many Americans bent on the improvement of public and private standards or simply on the rationalisation of a very messy branch of law. The rising divorce rate was a particular source of alarm to those who feared that marriage and family life were decaying. Most states responded by tinkering with their laws of marriage and divorce. Some reformers asked for more, and lobbied—in vain—for a national, uniform law either by constitutional amendment or by voluntary agreement among the states.

The second development, which forms the main theme of this chapter, was the 'emancipation' of women from disabilities which the law imposed on their ownership and management of property when they married. While the divorce question aroused public passions on both sides, property reforms proceeded quietly. By 1900, lawyers eulogised married women's property law reform as one of the great achievements of the age. Women, it seemed to them, had travelled quite a distance from 'civil death', their legal identity submerged in that of their husbands', to a position where they enjoyed all the rights they could need or legitimately want.

While the new married women's property laws brought reform, they did not bring rationalisation. Individual states varied markedly in how far and how fast they proceeded. The women's movement offered the only challenge to the autonomy of the states in the matter of women's status and civil rights by pleading the relevance of the Fourteenth Amendment's standards of national citizenship, designed in the wake of the Civil War primarily to protect the life, liberty and property of newly freed Negro slaves. But their arguments cut even less political ice than the movement for a national presence in the law of marriage and divorce. It remained exclusively state business.

1 Marriage and Divorce

Nineteenth-century Americans placed a high value on individual choice and style, and the law placed few burdens on entering matrimony. The law required that the parties intended to marry and that they consented without duress, fraud or error. States varied in their procedural requirements in such matters as the proclamation of banns, the registration of marriages and the forms of religious and civil ceremonies. Everywhere, by the middle of the nineteenth century, the formalities had been relaxed. Even where there were statutory requirements about publication, parental consent and so on, the flouting of them would at worst lead to the imposition of a penalty but not to the invalidation of the marriage.

Courts it seemed made every allowance in favour of recognising marriage, no matter how irregularly contracted. The colonists' rejection of the Anglican clergy's monopoly of marriage combined with frontier circumstances to necessitate the validation of unsolemnised marriages, despite the well recognised hazards of bigamy and illegitimacy. Most states recognised these so-called common law marriages, though it has been erroneously claimed that they were 'probably an American innovation' (Friedman, p. 179). It is no coincidence that Joel Bishop, writing on marriage and divorce law in 1852, peppered his chapters on irregular marriage with Scottish examples. He acknowledged the special relevance of Scots law 'because its common origin and substantial ancient identity with ours, in that particular department which concerns the subject of these volumes, and its growth in a protestant country under like influences seemed to render such illustrations pecularly appropriate' (*Commentaries*, Preface).

In the South, however, slaves did not benefit from the law's informality. Their irregular unions were not recognised, and their offspring had no legitimacy. Slavery and marriage, it seems, were inconsistent. A husband could not promise to support his wife when he had no right to earn money or own property. He could not protect her or retaliate against an owner's violence. Only an owner could exercise a right to decide on domicile. A wife could not offer her husband the domestic services which belonged to another master, and which often had to include sexual services as well. Ultimately an owner could terminate slave family life by the separate sale of its members. It was not until after the emancipation of the slaves during the Civil War that the Southern states found the body of law which had evolved to sanction irregular white marriage was a necessary practical tool to make sense of the complex informalities of family life in the period of transition from slavery to freedom.

For free Americans there were of course some legal impediments to their choice of partner. Insanity, want of age, and prior marriage were among the civil impediments which invalidated marriage. Others, derived from canonical law, such as consanguinity, affinity and impotence, did not necessarily invalidate the union but made it potentially voidable by the courts. The different practices of the states, however, blurred distinctions between void and voidable contracts and were a source of irritation and confusion. State laws differed with respect to age of consent, prohibited degrees of consanguinity and affinity, and on such matters as whether the 'guilty' party in a divorce suit was eligible to remarry.

When a couple moved from one state's jurisdiction to another's, the question might in theory arise whether the marriage would be recognised by the laws of their new home, in that laws sanctioning marriage had no extra-territorial force, and whether a person was regarded as married or single was determined by the law of his or her present domicile. In practice, however, natural law and the law of nations were summoned to support the idea that a marriage which was valid under the laws of the place where it was contracted was good anywhere. Marriages which were forbidden by the law of nature, such as incestuous ones, were of course good nowhere. Some authorities also held that marriages which were contracted elsewhere for the sole purpose of avoiding the law of a couple's home state should not be recognised when the couple returned home. Such cases included marriages celebrated out of state to circumvent laws forbidding interracial unions or the remarriage of divorced persons (Bishop, ch. VII).

The state's interest in acknowledging valid marriage contracts was different from its interest in ongoing marriage. Once a state recognised a couple as husband and wife, it had the right to impose upon that relationship a wide range of laws about support and services, inheritance, contracts, torts, and so on. Marriage was not a contract in the usual sense in that its duties were not derived from mutually agreed terms but from the law of the state. Divorce was thus not 'an action upon contract, but a proceeding *sui generis*, founded on the violation of duties enjoined by law' (Bishop, p. 19). The state which created the obligations was an intrinsic third party to every divorce suit. The trouble was that the American states interpreted their interest in very different ways, and conflicts of law between them abounded.

Judicial divorces had replaced legislative divorce in almost all the states by the middle of the nineteenth century. There were great differences between states, however, both in the range of grounds which they allowed and the residence requirements they demanded. As to grounds, South Carolina had none and New York granted divorce only for adultery, but at the other end of the spectrum, Connecticut and Maine in the 1850s had moved towards the modern idea of irretrievable breakdown. Maine's 1850 law had a discretionary clause allowing courts to terminate a marriage on 'facts tending to show that the divorce would be reasonable and proper, conducive to domestic harmony, for the good of the parties, and consistent with the peace and harmony of society' (Bishop, Section 542).

Adultery, desertion and cruelty were grounds which were common to most states, and as the century progressed the list lengthened to include such matters as habitual drunkenness and gross neglect of duty. Critics blamed the rising divorce rate on the liberalisation of the law but shortening the list of grounds only led to a greater concentration on those which remained, to greater elasticity in the interpretation of 'cruelty', or perhaps more collusion in 'adultery'. Where there was a will there was a way.

What seems to have dictated the choice of those who sought out of state divorces was not the menu of grounds but the length of their residence requirements. Ohio, Illinois and Indiana acquired reputations as easy divorce states and the divorce rate was higher in the counties of these states which were most accessible to migrants. Indiana, with its one-year residence requirement was a particular target for criticism after a well publicised dispute between Horace Greeley and Robert Owen in the columns of the *New York Tribune* in 1860. In the 1870s and 1880s, however, the migratory divorce business moved west, where California, Nevada, Dakota, Idaho and Montana granted divorces after a period of residence measured in months rather than years (Blake, *The Road to Reno*, ch. 9).

The availability of 'quickie' divorces did not cause divorce any more than the proliferation of grounds. Although in 1909 Commissioner of

Labor Statistics, Carroll D. Wright linked permissive laws with the rising divorce rate, he concluded that the migration shown by the divorce tables was not as great as that of the population at large. Only 20 per cent of divorces were granted in states other than where the marriage had taken place. The historian, George Howard, estimated that after due allowance was made for normal population movement, only about 10 per cent of the plaintiffs migrated for the express purpose of obtaining a divorce (vol. 3, 1904, p. 206).

There was no guarantee that a divorce granted in one state would be good in another. While states in general bent over backwards to recognise marriage, they did not accord divorce the same privilege. It was not, like marriage, a 'natural' right. It raised many complex issues of state interest in property, the economic survival of the family and the nebulous field of 'social stability'. Divorces which plaintiffs acquired out of state often left unsatisfied defendants at home, perhaps without adequate notice of the proceedings, and with families and property to be reconciled to an unsought status. Once again, states reacted in very different ways to one another's laws. New York, Pennsylvania, North Carolina and South Carolina did not recognise divorces unless both parties were domiciled in the divorcing state or had at least appeared in the proceedings. The others recognised divorces where the defendant had been served notice, not necessarily in person, and the plaintiff had acquired *bona fide* residence in the state in which divorce was sought. Differences in residence and notice requirements provided fuel for conflict. Although the United States Constitution bade the states give 'full faith and credit' to one another's laws and judicial proceedings, the Supreme Court and lower federal courts failed to evolve a satisfactory or consistent formula to resolve conflicts of divorce laws (Blake, ch. 12).

After the Civil War, more and more Americans confessed their fear that marriage was in danger. In the 1870s, there was a 'growing belief that marriage was too vital a social institution to be left to the partners to that contract' (Morton Keller, *Affairs of State*, p. 468). The states responded by imposing more social control. The age of consent was raised. New laws imposed mental and physical health standards and forbade certain kinds of union, including polygamy. Irregular marriages met disapproval and six states forbade them by statute (Howard, vol. 3, p. 183).

Divorce laws were tightened up. In 1873, Indiana's residence requirement was extended from one year to two, the pressures were brought to bear on western states so that by 1908, only Texas, Nebraska, Idaho and Nevada had six-month residence periods. Permissive laws on grounds were also a target for criticism, and Connecticut's 'general misconduct' clause was repealed in 1878 after a campaign led by Theodore Woolsey, who became President of the New England Divorce Reform League founded in 1881. In 1884, two constitutional amendments were introduced empowering Congress to regulate marriage and divorce. Theodore Roosevelt lent public support to the idea of a nationwide law in 1905, but all the proposals died for lack of serious political interest (Blake, ch. 10). Divorce remained a federal quagmire.

There were two sides to the divorce debate. Joel Bishop and George Howard were prominent among advocates of law reform along very different lines from Woolsey. They believed that the stability and happiness of family life was best served by liberal divorce laws and perceived that the rising divorce rate was not a symptom of moral decay but of less sinister social and economic changes which the law could not stem. The divorce rate kept rising.

The rise reflected the changing status of women, their expectations of marriage, and growing possibilities of economic independence outside marriage. Women's movement leaders Susan Anthony and Elizabeth Stanton regarded liberal divorce laws as closely related to women's emancipation. Whereas Wendell Phillips had argued in 1860 that divorce was not an appropriate matter on the agenda of a women's rights convention because the law affected both sexes equally, they saw marriage as 'Man Marriage' and divorce from it a woman's right and a necessary escape clause. 'The states that have more liberal divorce laws', wrote Mrs. Stanton, ' are for women today what Canada was for the fugitive in the old days of slavery' (in Blake, p. 151). Between 1867 and 1886, 112,540 divorces were granted to husbands, 216,176 were granted to wives.

For women these were times of change in every way. Their hard uphill battles for educational and economic opportunities and political rights are documented elsewhere. The reform of married women's property law was relatively undramatic. Women petitioned and campaigned for it. Men initiated it, controlled it, and conceded—how much? The evidence suggested that it was an unfinished evolution rather than a bloodless revolution.

2   Property Law for a Changing World—a Father's Tale?

The common law affected the rights and duties of both husband and wife, but not equally. William Blackstone's eloquent description of coverture has often been used to demonstrate how complete a woman's subjection was:

> By marriage, the husband and wife are one person in law, that is, the very being or legal existence of the woman is suspended during the marriage, or at least is incorporated and consolidated into that of the husband; under whose wing, protection and cover, she performs everything (*Commentaries on the Laws of England*, p. 430).

In fact, the concept of the unity of the spouses was of only limited usefulness in describing the complex legal relation of husband and wife, especially with respect to property. It was a more accurate description of what happened to a woman's personal property, than her real property such as land. When they married, a husband became the absolute owner of any moveable or personal property which his wife brought to the marriage or subsequently acquired. He was free to do what he liked with it, and it could be attached by his creditors. This *jus mariti* extended to her earnings, and to her *choses in action*, such as bonds and promissory notes which he might realise during the marriage. His rights over her real property were of a different character. He could not alienate or sell her land. His *jus administrationis*, however, allowed him to use and keep its rents and profits without having to account to anyone for them. A wife's legal title or *seisin* was not extinguished, however, and her separate legal interest continued to be recognised in the requirement that she be joined with her husband in suits concerning her property. For that reason, Pollock and Maitland's description of the husband's 'profitable guardianship' is more apt than the idea of legal unity (Glanvill Williams 1947).

Marriage imposed burdens as well as rights on a husband. He was obliged to support his wife; in return he had a legal right to her services and her *consortium*, or companionship. He was restricted in selling or alienating his own land by his wife's right to *dower* when he died, usually a life interest in one-third of his estate; for his part, he had a right to *curtesy* in her lands, a life interest in the whole, usually on the condition of a live child born to the marriage. Although he derived substantial benefits from his wife's property, he was liable for her debts and her torts. He was also responsible in law for some of her crimes where the law presumed his coercion, especially if he was present. Even here, however, the law departed from the idea of unity of the spouses and made her personally responsible for more serious crimes. Some other aspects of the law were clearly influenced by the logic of unity; a married couple could not steal from each other, or conspire together; or commit torts against each other.

The laws governing the reciprocal rights and duties of husband and wife gave each a status relative to the other, but the wife alone acquired an absolute status, that of married woman. The difference is described by R. H. Graveson:

> The wife has a legal status . . . in relation to her husband, the husband having a correlative status towards her. Neither can exist without the other. In this sense, therefore, such status as those of husband and wife, guardian and ward, adopter and adopted child may be described as relative, while status such as those of the soldier, infant, married woman, slave, alien, convict, and bankrupt, which alike concern all persons dealing with them, may be conveniently termed as absolute (*Status in Common Law*, p. 135).

A married woman acquired, as wife, considerable legal handicaps. She could not make contracts, beyond acting as her husband's agent in limited purchases of household necessities for which he was held liable. She could not sue and be sued unless her husband joined her in the suit. Only her husband could recover for torts against her. Only her husband could recover her earnings from her employer. She could not make a will, or convey or dispose of her property on her own initiative. She could not appoint a guardian for her children.

It would be a matter of time until the tide of individualism and humanitarianism found these relics of a distant social order unjust, and the world found them as much a nuisance in its daily dealings with women as women found them in dealing with the world.

The absolute status of married women was not, like the slave's, impregnable. Stanley Elkins (1959) offered an interesting if controversial explanation of why reformers were unable to treat Negro slavery as like any other institution, open to 'adjustment'. His observations may have some relevance to the position of women. He argued that Americans had either cast aside or weakened institutions in their New World. In the absence of an established church, or organised bar, cohesive political parties or structured financial institutions, society had no shared channels for absorbing guilt and dealing with what he calls 'sin situations'. In the void, the individual had to shoulder the full burden of guilt, and had no alternative but to demand the annihilation rather than the adjustment of slavery.

Marriage, on the other hand, had not been a casualty of this anti-institutional society. Far from being a peculiar institution, an anachronism and an embarrassment to the political philosophy of the new nation, marriage was a universal and extremely popular institution. Its American genre was not only acceptable to the world, but appeared humane and liberal sometimes to the point of laxity in the eyes of European observers. It was the only surviving institution which was accustomed to submerging crude individualism in broader social values. Any challenge to its existence, to those laws which reflected God's natural order, was unthinkable, or if contemplated, fiercely resisted. But where society could perceive the difference between these rules, and the artificial ones which had evolved to protect material interests, particularly property, it had been 'adjusting' them for a very long time, in the Old World as in the New.

By 1800, change was well under way. To describe marriage then in terms of strict common law rules is to offer a faded black and white photograph as a poor substitute for movement and variety. Although the early colonists borrowed the common law, they transformed it in its new home. Land was plentiful and market forces quickly began to work against encumbering it with feudal obligations. Women were in short supply and in a position to make more favourable marriage settlements. Economic necessity and absent husbands often demanded that women run businesses, administer estates, execute wills and find ways around their contractual incapacity. Lawyers were relatively thin on the ground and the lax application of the common law facilitated the development of local customs favourable to the property rights of married women. As a result women made significant gains in private law in the eighteenth century.

Equity had an important part to play in these early advances. Especially after the abolition of primogeniture and entail more and more women became property owners. As Englishmen had appreciated since the sixteenth century, women with property had to be protected against improvident husbands and their creditors. To this end the Court of Chancery evolved a number of equitable remedies to supplement or correct the common law, most commonly by honouring prenuptial agreements which would have been void at law, and by the creation of trusts from which a married woman derived the benefit of her estate. American fathers, brothers and other benefactors also found these remedies a necessary adjustment to the common law. Through them, *some* women came to exercise *some* control over their property. Indeed the historian Mary Beard (1946, ch. VI) argued that so many women reaped such substantial benefits that it was nonsense to describe their legal position in terms of subjection.

Although no account of eighteenth or nineteenth-century practice could ignore the impact of equity, its availability was limited to wealthier, substantially propertied women in states which offered equitable remedies—and not all did. Nor did equity always benefit women. The fertile imagination of conveyancers had also been applied to the task of designing trusts which would enable husbands to avoid honouring their wives' claim to dower, and thus free them to market their land without the encumbrance of life uses. Despite these efforts dower survived, especially in the South, and outlived a husband's right of curtesy in his wife's estate, a right which was disappearing by the mid nineteenth century. Economic reality caught up with inheritance law, however, and in the last quarter of the century legislation showed an increasing trend towards abolishing life uses in favour of outright shares to survivors.

Equity was an inadequate tool for reconciling the needs of families to those of the market place. In 1848, New York and Pennsylvania passed the first important Married Women's Property Acts. To add that other states followed their example is to distort the way things happened. Although as Lawrence Friedman claimed (1973, p. 186) some seventeen states had laws allowing women some legal capacity by the 1850s, changes were timid at first, and stretched out over half a century of seemingly almost annual revision and amendment. The early laws gave women protection of their property, the later ones gave them the right to protect it themselves, to convey and transfer it, sue and be sued, and contract as though they were unmarried, to make wills, set up businesses, and recover their own earnings. Each state proceeded in its own way, and at its own pace. Mostly they began by codifying equity rules with all their limitations, but generated a process which went further and finally drove a wedge through the legal unity of the spouses.

The Married Women's Property Acts must be seen as part of a more general phase of legal creativity which aimed to make land more marketable 'by transforming it into an ordinary item of commerce' (Rabkin 1981, p. 11). The business community, land speculators, and creditors all stood to gain from the greater certainty and generality of legislation which located ownership in the same person who had a right to convey, transfer, dispose of it, and make contracts on the strength of it. Equity had not offered so much and indeed creditors who had attempted to do business with women on the basis of their rudimentary contractual capacity had run a high risk of finding the road to recovery of their debts blocked by narrow judicial constructions of a married woman's liability. Understandably the pressure of the market worked consistently in favour of reform.

The interests of families were more complex and not always best served by exposing property to the vagaries of the market place. Nevertheless the deficiencies of equity left fathers no choice if they wanted to protect their daughters' assets from their husbands' creditors. Fathers who had commercial wealth to pass on had a particular interest in legislation, since equity had never extended the same protection to personal wealth, including stocks and bonds, as it had to land. Their numbers were growing all the time.

Landed fathers also had reason to seek firmer protection for their daughters' estates. In New York, codification of property law in the 1830s had created a gap in the protection of married women's property and the abolition of the Court of Chancery there in 1846 deprived them of equity. Hence the gap was filled by legislation in 1848. Elsewhere, codification and the merging of law and equity may have prompted similar responses. If legislation was in part a paternal reaction to a period of uncertainty it helps to explain why the early laws were little more than the codification of equity rules and why they were acceptable to legislators who would not have countenanced more radical changes in the legal relations between the sexes. Fathers may have wanted to protect their daughters from their husbands creditors, but they also feared their daughters' injudicious use of property which they hoped to transfer safely to their grandchildren. Thus legislation, like equity, was legal emancipation with brakes on. Courts helped to apply the brakes by using equity as a guide to construction hence delaying women's progress in such matters as contracts and liability for debts.

Husbands have been considered as the common enemy whose improvidence equity was designed to counteract (Dicey, pp. 376, 389). But although trusts reflected parental fears of bad matches and conflicts of interest between a son-in-law and the family of the bride, many marriages would have shared economic goals. Indeed equity courts had to keep a watchful eye to ensure that trusts had been set up in good faith and not for the benefit of husbands. Mary Beard noted:

> In particular it had to be watchful lest the husband entered into collusion in this respect for the purposes of defrauding his or her creditors (p. 140).

Deviousness and collusion need not have been behind the benefits a married couple derived from securing a wife's assets from her husband's creditors by legislation. There were also many circumstances where it could have benefited a family to make her separate estate more readily marketable. Often a wife's property was caught up quite legitimately in a family's dealing with creditors, banks, and employers, and it is not surprising that studies of the judicial enforcement of the Married Women's Property Acts uncover more cases where husband and wife were on the same side of a suit, engaged in a common legal struggle, than cases where they were adversaries (Rabkin, chs. 12 and 13).

Husbands, however, were slow to relinquish their control over married women's property. The new laws contained much evidence of this in clauses which qualified a woman's freedom of action by requiring her husband's consent to some transactions, or his joinder to suits in others.

The Married Women's Property Acts were the meeting ground between new economic and social forces and old family values. Quite how these forces interacted in legislative chambers and roll calls has not yet been fully explained. There is no possible method of separating the interests of fathers, creditors, husbands, businessmen and land speculators. They could all be facets of one man. The tensions between their roles could not be resolved by creating a half way house where women exercised incomplete rights and liabilities. The reservations of fathers and later still the lingering rights of husbands had to give way to the eventual legal emancipation of women—still in progress.

3   The Married Women's Property Laws and 'Emancipation'—the Wife's Tale

Women did not get much credit for contributing to the reforms or, indeed, even for understanding the legal issues. Mary Beard accused the women's movement in the nineteenth century of exaggerating women's historic subjection. They mistook Blackstone for the law as it really was, ignored equity developments, and even after the passage of the first Married Women's property law in New York, the 1848 Seneca Falls Declaration described the legal effect of marriage in the inappropriately extreme language of 'civil death'. They 'adopted a myth and made a frontal assault on that' (p. 115).

The relationship of the women's movement to the reforms stands in need of reconsideration. The fact that the laws were framed by men need not relegate women to the role of passive beneficiaries. Richard Rapaport has suggested this connection between the strength of the women's movement and the historical geography of reform:

Both the comprehensiveness and liberality of the reform legislation of the states where the women were most active far surpass the laws of states outside the movement's direct influence. In particular, the legislators of New York, Ohio, New Jersey, Massachusetts, Pennsylvania, Indiana, Wisconsin and Kansas, were pressed to go further towards genuine reform more quickly than their counterparts in other states. . . . Another group of states . . . where feminist activity was minimal . . . including Connecticut, Delaware, Maryland, New Hampshire,

Vermont, and West Virginia . . . did not alter the common law until after 1865. Finally, south of the Mason-Dixon line . . . where women's rights activities only started during reconstruction . . . reform in married women's property law did not come, except for Mississippi, until the 1870's, 80's, and 90's (*in* Babcock, Freedman, Norton and Ross (eds.), *Sex Discrimination and The Law*, p. 594).

His argument awaits documentation and may be as impossible to establish as the origins of the hen and the egg, since differing social, economic and legal climates among states may have determined the extent to which they nurtured the women's movement in the first place.

Leaders of the women's movement certainly felt that women deserved some credit for changes in the law. Their own account, the *History of Women's Suffrage* records many collective and individual contributions. From Massachusetts, where the movement was strong, came the boast of 'great changes in legislation for the women of Massachusetts as the result of their own labors' (*H.W.S.*III.293). Individual efforts, by Ernestone Rose and Elizabeth Stanton for the 1848 New York law, and Isabella Hooker in Connecticut for the 1877 reforms were of course honoured, along with lesser known battles by women like Mrs. Connelly of New Jersey and Mrs. McCulloch of Illinois for equal guardianship laws in their states.

The women's movement also recorded its indebtedness to others, occasionally to the press, and to men of goodwill, notably Robert Owen for his work in liberalising the laws of Indiana (*H.W.S.*IV.619). But judges, lawyers and state governors make fleeting appearances on the pages of *H.W.S.*, and their relationship to the women's movement was never adequately explained. Thus Isabella Hooker wrote to 'that eminent conservative lawyer' Governor Hubbard of Connecticut to congratulate him for his effort to secure reform of married women's laws there in the 1870s. He replied, 'Thank *yourself*, and such as you for what there is of progress in respect of women's rights among us' (*H.W.S.*III.326–7). In the circumstances of the correspondence, a little allowance may be made for courteous exaggeration. Accounts by women of their role in the events are stronger on anecdotes than on political analysis.

The Married Women's Property Acts had more effect on women than *vice versa*. Peggy Rabkin describes how they benefited the women's movement:

> These acts had a profound impact on the status of women. In addition, they gave impetus to the women's movement by providing a focus for presuffrage demands. Moreover the polemics that could be used in feminist activities were secure from any serious opposition as long as they related to the removal of common-law disabilities. Almost everyone realised that these disabilities were feudal and out of place in an increasingly commercial America. Yet once married women's property rights were won, it was a logical next step to demand the suffrage—the recognised instrument for the protection of property (p. 10).

For men it was 'sensible' to argue for law reform. But women argued an end to their legal disabilities for reasons which were different, which stressed natural right and individual dignity above economic and social realism. Their argument took them to the boundary of what was popularly described as 'Woman's Sphere'.

The idea that women had different (not inferior) abilities and virtues, but only four walls within which to find appropriate outlets for them, was a potentially stifling rationale for excluding women from the 'different' (more important) affairs of men. But it did offer a woman the opportunity to establish her autonomy within that sphere. Women in nineteenth-century America began to assert more control over their own bodies, to regulate how many children they would have, either by primitive birth control methods or even abortion; they set sexual 'standards' within the conjugal relationship; and they played an increasingly important part in the discipline and raising of the children. The four walls expanded to include many activities outside the home, but which resembled home in that they called upon a woman's 'special' interests and virtues. A wide range of philanthropic and religious causes and, of course, the temperance movement shared these characteristics and drew women in increasing numbers. The antislavery cause attracted women whose heightened moral sensitivities were horrified by an institution which denied marriage and family ties to millions. All this was socially acceptable—until these same moral sensitivities were alerted to the similarities between slavery and their own marital bondage, and they demanded the right to say so!

Their activities outside the home nourished a sense of sisterhood among white, middle-class women, and in many cases stirred longings to cross the boundaries from 'Women's Sphere' to equality. For a woman who was provoked by its limitations to go further, suffrage was indeed a radical demand. It was the one demand she made for herself, as an individual, and not in her relationship to the family. It spoke of interests in a world outside her allotted sphere. It raised the spectre of a husband and wife's divided voice in that world, with all the threat that seemed to imply for the stability of the family (Degler, ch. XIV).

Between 'women's sphere' and the suffrage, there was a middle ground where the battle for legal emancipation took place. Designed as it was by men, in a curious blend of self interest and social justice, law reform could be seen within the context of 'women's sphere' as reinforcing her growing autonomy within the family by giving her more control of her property to use for the benefit of the family. But where the laws gave women full contractual capacity and real control of their property, they also gave women a possible base for looking outwards from the family to set up and carry on a business, or simply earn a living. Law reform *could* loosen the 'bonds of womanhood'.

Women themselves had a more sophisticated understanding of the issues than they have been credited with. The editors of volume IV of *H.W.S.* set about the task of collecting and presenting a digest of information on legal changes affecting women from all forty-nine states. It was a formidable task and the state reports are only as good as individual reporters, and whatever help they had from the attorney generals and other advisers from whom the editors requested information. Men were responsible for many of their deficiencies. The reports varied widely in accuracy and perception, and the editors willingly acknowledged their limitations in keeping abrest with a complex field of law which was subject to almost daily revision somewhere in the Union.

Despite this, and the added handicap of belonging to a sex which had been denied the opportunity to acquire formal legal skills, the editors made some perceptive comments about the limitations of the married women's property laws. In particular, they pointed to the fact that however far the reforms went to protect a woman's separate property, they did nothing to give a woman a right to a share in joint property and earnings. Many women had no opportunity to acquire property of their own. What constituted a husband's 'separate' estate was often what he had been able to acquire because his wife's domestic services freed him to earn. She had no claim to that property and earnings during his life, and inheritance laws in the common law states treated joint property as the husband's separate property. If she died first, it belonged to her husband, and she could not secure a share of it for her children, her parents, or other kin. If he died first, she could claim only a third of it, and had no control over the disposition of the remainder. The eight states which adopted community property systems (*see* p. 138) had fairer inheritance laws which gave each spouse an equal share in the joint property of the marriage. Nevertheless, during the lifetime of the couple, the husband had complete control over the community property, including his wife's earnings.

Feminist critics rejected the argument that such legal inequality could be justified because the husband had to shoulder the burden of supporting his family. Not all the states compelled a husband to support his wife, and in those which did, the laws imposed minimal penalties or were unenforceable because in effect it was left to the husband to decide what were 'necessities'. Besides, this duty was more than offset by a husband's right to his wife's services, a lifetime's unpaid labour in the home. The married women's property laws in most states also eased his sole burden by making a woman's separate property liable for the support of the family where her husband failed or was unable to support it.

The leaders of the women's movement in 1900 shared with other participants in their emancipation the sense that many useful and important changes had been made over the century. More than others, however, they realised how much was still to be done, and how fragile their newly won rights were when they came to court. Where doubts of construction arose, it seemed to them that the courts fell back on the common law 'which in all cases is unjust to women' (*H.W.S.*IV.454).

Beyond specific criticism of the law, some women perceived that there were deeper questions to raise about marriage. Elizabeth Stanton wrote that 'the right idea of marriage is at the foundation of all reforms' (quoted in Blake, p. 88). But the women's movement did not offer a radical philosophical critique of marriage. By and large they accepted its traditional form and revered motherhood. They did not challenge the function of the law to protect private property. Instead, they sought to equalise it sufficiently to reflect their own rights and interests. They were women of their class, the property-owing class.

Fredrick Engels' critique of marriage and private property went much further and deeper into questions of economics and social organisation, and the nature of exploitation. Engels saw property laws, reformed or otherwise, as having little relevance to sexual equality and still less to the lives of working people. 'The law costs money', he wrote, 'and, on account of the worker's poverty, it has no validity for his relation to his wife.' Essentially, the laws of marriage were made by bourgeois man for the selfish perpetuation of private property, the purpose for which monogamy was established and male supremacy perpetuated.

There were 3,230,642 women wage earners by 1900, for whom it is argued, 'The ballot, legal rights, and other reform issues seemed irrelevant or secondary compared to the more pressing problems of daily life' (Gordon and Buhle, in *Liberating Women's History*, p. 291). Of course, it will not do to lump together a great variety of women's experiences in the nineteenth century without recognising that women had other ways of identifying themselves than by their sex. Working women no doubt shared a common sense of economic struggle with their husbands and families before they felt a sisterhood with women's rights leaders like Miss Anthony and Mrs. Stanton.

But the removal of common law disabilities and other reforms were not irrelevant to their lives. Especially in the West, working women could not have been indifferent to laws which aimed to secure homestead rights for widows. Nowhere were the laws giving women equal guardianship of their children irrelevant. Above all, working women had a real interest in the right to give married women the right to their own earnings.

It was a long, uphill battle and the outcome remained uncertain long after it became clear that middle-class women were well on the way to winning control over their separate property. New York was again among the first to reform its law, in 1860, and again, it is worth making the point that scholarly concentration on that state distorts the chronology of change by suggesting that it happened nearer the middle of the century than the end. It is equally misleading to say that the new laws gave married women control over their own earnings. Although the reforms generally established a woman's right to recover and keep her earnings where she worked for an employer outside the home, it was a very different matter where she worked in her husband's business or looked after boarders in her own home. No state abolished a husband's legal right to his wife's services and not all states allowed spouses to contract with each other. Courts were inconsistent in disentangling the areas of employment where a wife's right to her earnings and a husband's right to her services overlapped. In the community property states, a wife's earnings continued to be community property, under the control of her husband. Elsewhere, progress by 1900 was uneven and incomplete (Warren 1925).

4   From Slavery to Marriage—Black Women and Property Laws

The fascinating story of the relevance of the married women's property laws to the lives of the propertyless has yet to be told, however. Until 1865, slave women were property, like their menfolk. They were the important subject of prenuptial contracts and trusts. Their babies were the profits and increase of a white married woman's property during coverture. When their owner died, the lives of slaves were caught up in dower and curtesy, life uses, wills and inheritances, and the claims of creditors. When the law was reformed, as in the 1839 Married Women's Property Act in Mississippi, any benefit white women secured was not shared by their slave property.

Often slaves lost the chance of freedom because of laws governing their owners' marital property. Rachel Magruder manumitted her slaves before she married, but the deed of manumission was not confirmed by the county court at the time of her wedding. She further complicated the case by dying, but the court held that, by marrying, she lost the power to free her slaves (Catterall, *Judicial Cases*, vol. 1, p. 161). To avoid such situations, it was not uncommon for female owners to make prenuptial agreements reserving their rights on such matters. Sometimes more drastic methods had to be employed to avoid the consequence of matrimony, as this tale of panic suggests:

> On the day of her marriage and before its solemnisation, she made a bill of sale to her mother of the negroes . . . without the knowledge . . . of her intended husband (*Johnston* v. *Hamblet*, 1815, Catterall, vol. 2, p. 27).

Black families were literally divided by the property conflicts of white marriages, and even trusts would not always prevent it. Thus, although a trust had been set up for Elizabeth Ann Haw, reserving for her sole use Negroes Sophia and Anthony, nevertheless her husband 'became entitled to whatever issues or profits accrued, and were actually received by his wife during the coverture . . . Negroes Mary and John, as children of Sophia, are issues of the trust property' *Townshend* v. *Matthews* 1956, Catterall, vol. 4, p. 130). Some courts, however, did try to prevent family breakups in such cases, acknowledging that 'a difference had been adopted between slaves and other property, founded upon motives of humanity and having regard to the moral as well as legal relations between master and slave' (*Herndon* v. *Herndon* 1858, Catterall, vol. 5, p. 202).

After 1865 and the ratification of the Thirteenth Amendment, slaves ceased to be property and as free persons became entitled for the first time to marry. Despite the laws which until then denied them the status of husband and wife, slaves had indeed always married. Herbert Gutman's

1976 study of the black family in slavery establishes beyond doubt its capacity for survival against the odds. Although slave marriages were often encouraged by owners in order to exploit family loyalties for disciplinary purposes, the marriages were not just weak imitations of white institutions. Slave family life produced its own rich customs and values which were transmitted from one generation to the next, and also responded to changes in the same way that all societies build upon their inheritance. These values were far from the licentiousness portrayed by white observers. Nor did slave marriage differ from white marriage by being matriarchal and emasculating. Despite all the external pressures to deny a man his traditional place, the black family kept it an honoured and important one.

Of what possible consequence could married women's property laws be to the women who attempted to carry these shaky family ties from slavery to freedom? Frederick Douglass, black leader and feminist sympathiser, attempted to put it into perspective in 1859:

> Other women suffer certain wrongs, but the wrongs peculiar to women out of slavery, great and terrible as they are, are endured as well by the slave woman, who has also to bear the ten thousand wrongs of slavery in addition to those common wrongs of woman. It is hard to be underpaid for labor faithfully performed. It is harder still not to be paid for labor at all. . . . It is hard for the widow only to receive the third part of the property of her deceased husband; it is harder still to be a chattel person to all intents and purposes. It is hard to enjoy a qualified right to one's children; but it is harder still for a woman to have no rights which white men are bound to respect (*in* Philip Foner (ed.), *Frederick Douglass on Women's Rights*, p. 76).

Women's rights leader Pauline W. Davis, was just as concerned about the rights that a black husband was bound to respect and, in 1869, voiced the fear that newly freed men would be hard masters:

> The coloured women of the South say they do not want to get married to the negro, as their husbands can take their children away from them, and also appropriate their earnings. The black women are more intelligent than the men, because they have learned something from their mistresses (*in* Foner, p. 89).

How wrong she was. Freed black women immediately joined their men in a remarkable drive to legitimise old unions or establish new ones. The records of the Union army and the Freedmen's Bureau confirm the strength of slave marriages. Those of Tennessee, Mississippi and Louisiana suggest that between 6 per cent and 20 per cent of those recorded were unbroken from slave days, and that by far the largest proportion of 'broken' marriages were broken by death, or separations enforced by masters (Blassingame 1972, pp. 90–1). Sales of slaves caused numerous problems of potential bigamy for reunited spouses, besides a proportion who made different marital choices when freedom presented them with the opportunity. After the Civil War, the state authorities coped with these problems in various ways, sometimes requiring registration of marriages, sometimes simply recognising them. The law in America had long experience of legitimising irregular unions. But it was remarkable how many poor and illiterate people found the money to secure a licence, and showed an extremely strong desire to 'do things right'. For them marriage had nothing to do with the perpetuation of private property. It was about the right to make and maintain family ties. It was hardly surprising that those who had known what it was like to have no security of home and family should want the benefit of the rules which kept these things sacred for whites.

And so black slave women, like their husbands, enjoyed the civil status of marriage for the first time. They also became 'femmes couvertes', subject to a new set of legal handicaps. Like white wage earning women, they did not find these disabilities so unsupportable that they would have put the rights of their sex before the rights of their race. They agreed, it seems, with one of the few black women in the women's rights movement, who said 'that when it was a question of race, she let the lesser question of sex go' (*in* Foner, p. 90). Strong, tough women themselves, they conspired to return their men's manhood to them. As Eugene Genovese (1975) noted, 'A remarkable number of women did everything possible to strengthen their self-esteem and to defer to their leadership' (p. 500).

But ex-slave Sojourner Truth, over eighty and an old campaigner for two causes, was not a woman to forget her rights:

> There is a great stir about colored men getting their rights, but not a word about the colored women, and if colored men get their rights, and not colored women theirs, you see the colored men will be masters over the women, and it will be just as bad as before (quoted in Gerda Lerner, *Black Women in White America*, p. 569).

Although slavery had disinherited them and deprived them of the kind of property worries which were the subject of the married women's property laws, nevertheless white men's ways prevailed. This was the court's decision in a Florida dispute between an old black man and his wife:

Ocala, Florida
May 12th 1814

Be it known throughout all christendom that the husband is the head of the wife, and whatever is hers is his'n, and come weal or woe, peace or war, the right of all property is vested in the husband, and the wife must not take anything away. The ox belongs to Uncle Ben, and he must keep it and the other things, and if the old woman quits she must go empty-handed. Know all that this is so by the order of the Judge of Probate.

(Signed) Wm. R. Hillyer

(H.W.S.III.829)

5 Equality before the Law

The American Civil War was the occasion for much thought and discussion about a status which white Americans had taken for granted—citizenship. To protect newly freed Negroes in the exercise of their civil rights in hostile state environments the Republicans fashioned constitutional change which for the first time made the nation responsible for guaranteeing the individual the equal protection of the laws. New civil rights laws and constitutional amendments spoke neutrally of persons and citizens, and women could be forgiven for thinking that they were included.

The 1866 Civil Rights Act promised that 'all persons born in the United States' would have 'the same right ... to make and enforce contracts, to sue, be parties and give evidence, to inherit, purchase, lease, sell, hold and convey real and personal property'. The text to this point would have revolutionised many state laws relating to married women, as they stood in 1866. But the act went on to qualify a right of 'full and equal benefit of all laws and proceedings for the security of person and property' with the words 'as is enjoyed by white citizens'.

James Wilson, one of the act's framers, explained the inclusion of the phrase, 'the same rights as white citizens' as necessary because 'unless these qualifying words were incorporated in the bill, those rights might be extended to all citizens, whether male or *female*, majors or minors' (*Cong. Globe*, 29th Cong. 1 Sess., App. p. 157, 1866). The act introduced new black citizens to the same rights as white citizens of the same sex, or age group. A black woman's freedom was to be as different from her husband's as a white woman's from hers.

During the course of Congressional debates on civil rights measures after the war, it is fascinating to observe how often objections were raised to a particular draft on the grounds that it might alter the status of women, or deprive states of their previous prerogative in the field of married women's property law. Women were not to be the unintended beneficiaries of the extension of civil rights to black men (*see* Patricia Lucie 1978). The women's movement protested that the constitutional revolution in citizenship had passed them by and left their liberties to the states, where they had always been 'the football of legislative caprice' (*H.W.S.*III.33). Mrs. Elizabeth Stanton charged, 'You did not trust the Southern freedmen to the arbitrary will of courts and States!' She went on, 'Why send your mothers, wives, and daughters to the unwashed, unlettered, unthinking masses that carry popular elections?' (*H.W.S.*III.88).

In the long run, she was wrong about the difference between the claims of blacks and women on the nation's protection. Blacks, too, were disappointed and remanded to the states after Supreme Court decisions of the 1870s and 1880s interpreted the life out of the Fourteenth Amendment and other civil rights laws. In the case of the status and capacities of married women, state interests ran too deep for too long to tolerate the nation's 'interference' in the absence of political pressure to do so. It was not until the 1970s that the Supreme Court invoked the Fourteenth Amendment against sex discrimination and the remaining disabilities of married women. Until then, outside the women's movement, the language of equality and individual right seemed inappropriate, even indelicate to apply to marriage, with all its 'special' obligations and sacrifices. It is not difficult to compile a list, as Mary Beard did, of impossible domestic situations where property interests cannot apparently be resolved by counting and dividing (Beard, pp. 166–9). But if there is more to marriage than equality, there is also more to equality before the law than arithmetic.

BIBLIOGRAPHY

The English background
William Blackstone, *Commentaries on the Laws of England* (London 1765)
C. S. Kenny, *The Effects of Marriage on Property* (London 1879)
A. V. Dicey, *Lectures on the Relations Between Law and Public Opinion in England During the Nineteenth Century* (London 1905)
William Holdsworth, *A History of English Law*, 17 vols. (London 1903–72)
Glanville Williams, 'The Legal Unity of Husband and Wife', *Modern Law Review* (10 1947)
R. H. Graveson, *Status in Common Law* (London 1953)

The law in America
Joseph Story, *Commentaries on Equity Jurisprudence as Administered in England and America* (Boston 1836)
Joseph Story, *Commentaries on the Conflict of Laws* (London 1841 edn)
Joel P. Bishop, *Commentaries on the Law of Marriage and Divorce* (London 1852 edn)
Theodore Woolsey, *Divorce and Divorce Legislation* (N.Y. 2nd edn, 1882)
Joseph Warren, 'Husband's Rights to Wife's Services', *Harvard Law Review* 38 (1925)
Richard B. Morris, *Studies on the History of American Law* (N.Y. 1930)
Nelson M. Blake, *The Road to Reno* (Greenwood 1977, reprint; originally published 1964)
William O'Neill, *Divorce in the Progressive Era* (N.Y. 1973, reprint of 1967 edn)
Lawrence Friedman, *A History of American Law* (N.Y. 1973)
Morton J. Horwitz, *The Transformation of American Law, 1780–1860* (Cambridge 1977)

Women and the law
Frederick Engels, *The Origin of the Family Private Property and the State* (N.Y. 1902, transl. of 1st edn, Zurich 1884)
Elizabeth Stanton, Susan Anthony and Matilda Gage, *History of Woman Suffrage*, 6 vols. (Rochester 1881–1922)
Mary Beard, *Woman as Force in History* (N.Y. 1946)
Leo Kanowitz, *Women and the Law. The Unfinished Revolution* (Albuquerque 1969)
John D. Johnston, 'Sex and Property: The Common Law Tradition, the Law School Curriculum and Developments Towards Equality' *N.Y.U.L. Rev.* 47 (1972)

Barbara Babcock (ed.), *Sex Discrimination and the Law: Causes and Remedies* (Boston 1975)

Bernice Carroll, *Liberating Women's History* (Chicago 1976)

Nancy F. Cott, *The Bonds of Womanhood* (New Haven 1977)

Keith Melder, *Beginnings of Sisterhood: The American Women's Rights Movement, 1800–1850* (N.Y. 1977)

Patricia Lucie, 'On Being a Free Person and a Citizen by Constitutional Amendment', *Journal of American Studies* 12 (1978)

A. Sachs and J. Wilson, *Sexism and The Law* (Oxford 1978)

Carol Du Bois, *Feminism and Suffrage, 1948–1869* (Cornell 1978)

Peggy A. Rabkin, *Fathers to Daughters: The Legal Foundation of Female Emancipation* (Westport 1980)

Histories of marriage and the family

George E. Howard, *History of Matrimonial Institutions*, 3 vols. (Chicago 1904)

A. W. Calhoun, *Social History of the American Family*, 3 vols. (N.Y. 1945, originally published 1917–19)

Willystine Goodsell, *A History of Marriage and The Family* (N.Y. 1935)

Joseph K. Folsom, *The Family and Democratic Society* (N.Y. 1943)

Sidney Ditzion, *Marriage, Morals and Sex in America* (N.Y. 1953)

Carl Degler, *At Odds: Women and the Family in America from the Revolution to the Present* (N.Y. 1980)

Race

Helen Catterall (ed.) *Judicial Cases Concerning American Slavery and the Negro* (Washington 1926–37)

Stanley Elkins, *Slavery* (Chicago 1959)

John Blassinghame, *The Slave Community* (N.Y. 1972)

Gerda Lerner, *Black Women in White America* (N.Y. 1972)

Eugene Genovese, *Roll Jordan Roll, The World The Slaves Made* (London 1975)

Herbert Gutman, *The Black Family in Slavery and Freedom* (Oxford 1976)

Philip Foner (ed.), *Frederick Douglass on Women's Rights* (Westport 1976)

Civil war and reconstruction

Harold Hyman, *A More Perfect Union* (N.Y. 1973)

Morton Keller, *Affairs of State* (Cambridge 1977)

X

Woman and Marriage in Victorian Society

Phillip Mallett

Department of English, University of St. Andrews

> What should a woman do with her life? . . . Fall in love, marry the man, have
> two children, and live happy ever afterwards.
> Anthony Trollope, Can You Forgive Her?

The most cherished theme of Victorian literature at every level was the
sanctity and dignity of marriage and the family. No one in Victorian
England who attended at church or chapel, read a newspaper or a
periodical, or whiled away the evenings with a novel from the circulating
libraries—and most middle class Victorians did most of these things—
could miss hearing of the family as the vital moral centre of English life. At
the highest level, it was an article of faith for the Christian believer that the
family had been divinely ordained for the welfare and education of
mankind. Family relationships, wrote Charles Kingsley, were 'given to us
to teach us their divine antitypes': 'Fully to understand the meaning of "a
Father in Heaven", we must be fathers ourselves; to know how Christ loved
the Church, we must have wives to love, and love them.'[1] On the political
level, the family was hailed as 'the unit upon which a constitutional
Government has been raised which is the admiration and envy of
mankind', and it was a commonplace that the secret of national greatness
was to be found in those virtues—truthfulness, obedience, subordination
of self to the needs of others—which were first learned and practised within
the family.[2] Only a little less grandly, it was the family portrait, whether in
words or pictures, which revealed the Victorians to themselves as they
wished to be seen. In Dean Stanley's *Life of Dr Arnold*, for example, the
discussion of Arnold's religious and political convictions is rounded out
with an account of 'the almost awful happiness of his domestic life'—
walking quietly beside his wife's pony, holding a mock siege with his
children in a nearby clay-pit, gathering the family together at the end of the
day for prayers and readings from the scriptures. Arnold's dream, records
Stanley, was of 'the blessing . . . of a whole house transplanted entire from
earth to heaven, without one failure'; the 'very idea of a family life' was
invested in his eyes with a 'peculiar sense of solemnity'.[3] In such sentiments,
Arnold and his biographer were unquestionably at one with their age.

At the still centre of the Victorian home was the wife and mother, and much of what was written in praise of marriage and family life was addressed directly to her, expounding her duties to husband, children, and nation. The best known of such texts, and also the most eloquent, is John Ruskin's lecture 'Of Queens' Gardens', delivered in Manchester in 1864 and published the following year in *Sesame and Lilies*.[4] The task Ruskin set himself was to resolve a question 'quite vital to all social happiness': that of 'the relations of the womanly to the manly nature' in a wisely ordered society. He began by clearing the ground. To insist on woman's inferiority, seeing her as merely 'the shadow and attendant image of her lord', was 'the most foolish of all errors'; woman was made to be 'the helpmate of man', and a man could not be helped 'effectively by a shadow, or worthily by a slave'. But it was also an error to suppose that the 'mission' and the 'rights' of women could be established without reference to the mission and the rights of men: men and women were not to be regarded as 'creatures of independent kind, and of irreconcilable claim'. The truth lay between these extremes. Firstly, the powers and capacities of men and women were inherently and designedly different: 'Each has what the other has not: each completes the other, and is completed by the other: they are in nothing alike, and the happiness and perfection of both depends on each asking and receiving from the other what the other only can give'. Secondly, these differences were properly reflected in the existing division of functions within society. The man's 'power' was 'active, progressive, defensive'; he was 'the doer, the creator, the discoverer', equipped by his nature to perform 'rough work in open world'. The woman's power was not inferior to his, but complementary: 'for rule, not for battle, . . . not for invention or creation, but for sweet ordering, arrangement, and decision.' Her nature, more tender and less assertive than the man's, was framed for domestic duties and a life of service within the home.

To describe the world reserved for men in honorific terms, as the arena of invention and discovery, was to do what custom and good manners required. But if Ruskin was to persuade the women in his audience that they should look for fulfilment only within the home, he had to change his ground. The world of masculine activity was not good, but brutal and corrupting; in his daily traffic with it the man would often be 'wounded or subdued; often misled; and *always* hardened'. By contrast, the home was 'a sacred place', a refuge from the 'terror, doubt, and division' of an 'inconsistently-minded, unknown, unloved, or hostile society'. Here, and only here, the woman could find protection from the cares and dangers which her husband faced on her account in the outer world. Her husband's house, therefore, was her proper sphere, both preserving her and preserved by her: 'Within his house, as ruled by her, . . . need enter no danger, no temptation, no cause of error or offence.' It was her duty to renounce any ambition or desire which might lead her away from the home, since she alone could maintain it as 'the place of Peace' in an embattled world; it was her reward to learn that 'a true wife, in her husband's house, is his servant', but 'in his heart . . . she is queen'. Trained from birth in the principles of self-sacrifice, and untouched by the evil of the world, she could attain to a spiritual authority which her husband was bound to venerate; through her influence over him she could determine the moral character of an entire society. This was the central claim of Ruskin's lecture: that in a 'true wifely subjection' lay the seed of an all but unlimited power, 'purer than the air of heaven, and stronger than the seas of earth', transcending all disputes about 'the rights of women'.[5]

Ruskin's fervour was evidently gratifying to his audience, and the lecture was a considerable success. But it was only the fervour that was new: the argument itself had been anticipated in the 1830s and 1840s in a host of manuals and handbooks, many of them written by women, setting forth in detail the duties of the mothers, wives, and daughters of England. Mrs. Ellis, Mrs. Lewis, and Mrs. Sandford were, however, addressing readers who hardly aspired to be Queens, but who were deeply anxious to be recognised as Ladies, and wished to know what rules they ought to follow. For their benefit, the doctrine of 'separate spheres' was elaborated into a code regulating virtually every aspect of a woman's life. For Mrs. Ellis, as for Ruskin, men belonged to the world of 'action', where they wielded 'power', and women to the world of 'feeling', where they exercised 'influence'. Caught up in the 'fierce conflict of worldly interests', men were occasionally 'compelled to stifle their best feelings' in order to succeed, and it was therefore the woman's task to maintain the home as an emblem on earth of the divine peace and order, where her husband could recover those 'best feelings':[6] for her to leave the home to undertake paid work on her own account would be to betray this sacred trust. Hardly less important, however, it would also be to lose caste for herself and her husband: 'So soon as a woman begins to receive money', warned Mrs. Ellis, she is 'trans-formed into a tradeswoman, and must find her place in society as such.'[7] Her proper work—the work she could perform with propriety—was within the home, and Mrs. Ellis exhorted her readers to value housework as an antidote to the feminine vices of vanity, idleness, and frivolity. But if paid work was demeaning, good works were not: indeed, the degree of a woman's involvement in local charities was one measure of her status within the community. Lucy Aikin noted in 1841 that visiting the sick and poor had become 'a fashion and a rage' among ladies of the middle class: so too did almost every task associated with Victorian philanthropy, from raising funds at a bazaar to sitting on the management committee of a charitable society.[8] Such work provided an outlet for energies which might otherwise have been left to fust unused, and was exempt from the prejudices associated with women in paid employment.[9] The 'whole law of woman's life', as Mrs. Ellis put it, was 'a law of love': it was only fitting that she should be allowed to exhibit in the wider community the capacity for service and self-sacrifice she had first learned to practise within the home.[10]

Mrs. Ellis's books were undoubtedly successful—*The Women of England* went through thirteen editions within a year of its publication in 1838—but they make dispiriting reading today. According to Mrs. Ellis, the 'first thing of importance' for a woman was to acknowledge the superiority of her husband 'simply as a man': 'You may have more talent, with higher attainments, . . . but this has nothing whatever to do with your position as a woman, which is, and must be, inferior to his as a man.'[11] In this view Mrs. Ellis was following a long line of Christian moralists who had argued that the dependence of women upon men was enjoined both by the scriptures and by the laws of nature. Even more than their relative physical weakness, the greater moral frailty of women required that they be subject at all times to male guidance or restraint, and the one irrefragable claim of every woman on her society was that she be passed safely from the custody of her father into that of her husband. On the whole, however, this view was in decline during the nineteenth century. There were those, such as John Burgon, the Dean of Chichester, who continued to insist that the 'primaeval decree' concerning the inferiority of women had never been cancelled,[12] but they were fighting a rearguard action, and from the mid-century onwards eloquent tributes to the healing and redemptive powers of Victorian womanhood were the order of the day. It was the privilege of the woman, wrote J. G. Phillimore, 'to form those by whom laws are made . . . to inspire those principles, to inculcate those doctrines, to animate those sentiments, which generations yet unborn, and nations yet uncivilised, shall learn to bless'.[13] To Charles Kingsley, the woman was 'the natural, and therefore divine, guide, purifier, inspirer, of the man'; and to the elderly Thomas Carlyle, as to John Ruskin, the dutiful wife and mother was 'in a soft, beautiful, and almost sacred way, the Queen of the World'.[14]

There were, however, some women who refused to be disarmed by the rhetoric: 'This has ever been the flattering language of man', warned a pioneering American feminist, 'since he laid aside the whip as a means to keep woman in subjection.'[15] These misgivings gained strength from the way assumptions about the essentially different natures of men and women were used to justify their unequal position before the law, which was much closer in spirit to Mrs. Ellis and John Burgon than to Ruskin or Kingsley. In effect, a woman surrendered her legal existence on marriage: by virtue of a legal fiction supposing the absolute coincidence of interests between man and wife, she and her husband were merged into a single legal identity. 'By marriage,' as Sir William Blackstone explained in his *Commentaries on the Laws of England*, 'the husband and wife are one person in law: that is, the very being or legal existence of the woman is suspended during the marriage, or at least is incorporated or consolidated into that of her husband, under whose wing, protection, and *cover*, she performs everything.'[16] The consequences of this system of coverture were far-reaching. A single woman had control over her property and earnings, but on her marriage they passed under the common law to her husband, unless she had previously been protected by a settlement in equity. The children of the marriage were similarly held to be the property of the husband, and the mother might at any time be denied access to them; even after the Custody of Infants Act of 1886, according to which the welfare of the children was to determine all questions of custody, the father remained during his lifetime their sole legal guardian.[17] As with her children, so too with her own person: in theory at least a married woman's body belonged to her husband. If she left his house, he could enforce this right by a writ of *habeas corpus*; he could claim damages against his wife's alleged lover, for 'trespass . . . in his marital property';[18] and until 1891 the Courts would uphold his right to keep his wife as a prisoner in his house.[19] There was justice as well as indignation in William Thompson's protest in 1825 that on these terms the home was not 'the abode of calm bliss' it was claimed to be, but 'the eternal prison-house of the wife. . . . The house is *his* house, with everything in it; and of all fixtures the most abjectly his is his breeding machine, the wife.'[20]

By the middle of the century the laws relating to women had a number of critics, but these were for the most part more concerned to find remedies for particular injustices than to estimate the effect of less tangible harms, such as the indignity of being denied a legal existence. This pragmatic approach perhaps helps to explain why so little attention was given to what amounted to a denial of women's sexual existence, despite the fact that the underlying assumption was in each case the same: that women were to be regarded as existing only contingently. 'In men,' claimed W. R. Greg in 1850, 'the sexual desire is inherent and spontaneous. . . . In the other sex, the desire is dormant, if not non-existent, till excited; always till excited by undue familiarities; almost always till excited by actual intercourse.'[21] This view was given medical support by William Acton, who published in 1857 his study of *The Functions and Disorders of the Reproductive Organs*. It was Acton's belief that 'a modest woman' desired no sexual gratification for herself, and submitted to her husband 'only to please him': 'The best wives, mothers, and managers of households, know little or nothing of sexual indulgences. Love of home, children, and domestic duties, are the only passions they feel.'[22] The point Mrs. Ellis had made in general terms, that 'the love of woman appears to have been created solely to minister; that of man, to be ministered unto', was to be applied in the bedroom no less than elsewhere in the Victorian home.[23] Neither Greig nor Acton saw any injustice in these arguments; on the contrary, they congratulated women on what Greg described as the 'kind decision of nature' to spare them from the torments of sexual desire, much as Blackstone had earlier congratulated them on the kindness of the English law in relieving them of the burdens of legal and political responsibility. However, their fortunate exemption from sexual feeling did bring with it corresponding duties. Once again, it was their task to save men from themselves: to inspire them to purity outside marriage, and to moderation within it. In doing so they would lessen the strains imposed on men by their coarser natures, and at the same time help to preserve the good order of society. Greg spelled out the danger: if the passions of women were as strong and spontaneous as those of men 'sexual irregularities' would quickly 'reach a height, of which, at present, we have happily no conception', causing profound damage to the moral and physical health of the entire community.[24] On this view, a woman who made sexual demands on her husband, stimulating instead of restraining the coarser elements in his nature, was failing in her responsibilities both as a wife and as a member of society, just as surely as the woman who took paid work outside the home; she was to be classed with the 'loose, or at least, low and vulgar women' who threatened society, and not with those 'best mothers, wives, and managers of households' who sustained it.[25]

The question obviously arises of the relation between the wifely ideal set out in the literature, and the social reality of the marriages actually made by Victorian men and women. It is in the area of sexuality that this question is hardest to answer. In part, the problem has to do with the nature of the evidence: writers of memoirs and autobiographies were generally reticent about their sexual lives, and in the absence of direct personal testimony arguments about the sexual experience of our great-grandparents are bound to be speculative. But the difficulty is compounded by the temptation for the modern historian to assume the tone and manner of 'one who has come through' when writing of Victorian sexuality.[26] This is unwarranted. The availability in the twentieth century of sex clinics, manuals, and therapists may reflect a more open attitude to sexual life, but it does not indicate more widespread sexual happiness; nor can it be taken as read that the Victorian code of chivalry towards women was necessarily incompatible with a real concern for their sexual satisfaction within marriage, despite the unfortunate examples of Ruskin and Carlyle. Moreover, there were a number of Victorian doctors who rejected Acton's views: notably George Drysdale, who argued in *The Elements of Social Science* (1854) that 'ignorance of the necessity of sexual intercourse to the health and virtue of both man and woman, is the most fundamental error in medical and moral philosophy'.[27] Drysdale's book clearly answered a need, since it was still in print fifty years later, in its thirty-fifth edition, but reaction in the medical press was hostile. Not only did Drysdale advocate 'free love' rather than marriage (which he condemned as the chief instrument used for the degradation of women), he also broke ranks in order to explain various methods of birth control, a subject which remained taboo until well into the twentieth century. But here it seems public opinion may have run in advance of the medical profession. Works giving advice on contraception sold in large numbers, and declining family size among sections of the middle class suggests that some of those who would not tolerate the public discussion of birth control were beginning to practise it from about the late 1860s.[28] The reduced risk of pregnancy, and of such attendant dangers as puerperal fever, must have enhanced the quality of sexual life for at any rate some women; and presumably the use of such contraceptive methods as the vaginal sponge (which Drysdale recommended) worked against the level of innocence, or ignorance, taken for granted by Acton.

But it seems clear nonetheless that the medical profession was generally unsympathetic to the idea that middle-class married women might

naturally desire sexual satisfaction. The *Lancet* in particular provided a
forum for some remarkable arguments, as when an opponent of the use of
anaesthesia in childbirth pointed out that etherisation occasionally stimulated feelings of sexual pleasure, and concluded that 'to the women of this
country the bare possibility of having feelings of such a kind excited . . .
would be more shocking even to anticipate, than the endurance of the last
extremity of physical pain'.[29]No doubt this was the view of a minority, and
few doctors can have been quite happy to propose 'death before dishonour'
to the women under their care; but like the spate of clitoridectomies in the
1870s, and the increasing tendency to regard all specifically female
functions as pathological, it does suggest how prevalent was the sense that
sexuality was dangerous, or, more precisely, that female sexuality was
dangerous to men.[30] In an age which saw what has been described as 'the
medicalisation of sex', the views of so confident a profession carried a good
deal of weight, and the current revision of the received picture of Victorian
sexuality is not likely to change that picture's essential outlines.[31] Most
middle-class men and women were willing to accept the model of female
sexuality offered to them by Greg and Acton, and endorsed and underlined
in countless poems and novels of the mid-century.[32]

   The question of how far the domestic role prescribed for Victorian
women corresponded with actuality can be answered with more certainty:
most women had little choice but to subscribe to the ideal of the 'angel-
wife', familiar to the modern reader from the novels of Dickens and
Thackeray in particular. Indeed, so pervasive was this ideal that it comes as
no surprise to find instances of life seeming to imitate art. The relationship
between Blanche Smith, a cousin of Florence Nightingale, and her eventual
husband, the poet Arthur Hugh Clough, affords a notable example. In 1848
Clough had resigned his Fellowship in Oxford because he was unwilling to
commit himself to the Thirty-Nine Articles, and in his letters to Blanche
before their marriage he revealed himself similarly mistrustful of romantic
commitments, the 'everlasting unions, and ties that no change can modify'
of so much Victorian fiction: 'Do not dream of them . . . it is no evidence for
them that the exacting hearts of girls would fain believe in them, and make
their lovers (mostly) pretend to do so.'[33] Blanche was understandably hurt
by these letters, and further disturbed by the frank sexuality she found in
Clough's poetry: 'I don't mean to blame, but I don't like it. I don't like men
in general; I like women—why was not the world made all women— . . . I
did hardly know that good men were so rough and coarse.' Clough yielded
to the reproach. In 1848 he had disdained the advice of the Provost of his
college in Oxford, but to this deeply conventional woman he was ready to
confess to a moral and spiritual 'perplexity' for which he besought her aid
and counsel; and, eventually, the gratified Blanche was able to congratulate
herself on having guided him, as Agnes had guided David Copperfield, and
as both Helen and Laura had guided Arthur Pendennis, towards 'a higher
idea of what things ought to be'. In later years, Blanche was to write a
memoir of her husband: 'After his marriage there was nothing of [the

previous] enforced and painful communing with self alone . . . the new experience which he was daily gathering at home made many perplexed questions, both social and religious, clear and simple to his mind.' This is a picture of domestic fulfilment which might have graced the pages of any one of a thousand novels, but its complacency is not necessarily an argument against its sincerity, and, such as it is, it lends support to Laurence Lerner's contention in *Love and Marriage* that 'Victorian women as well as men accepted the domestic ideal and defined themselves in relation to their role: not to believe this is not to be interested in evidence'.[34]

But by the middle of the century there were already a number of women beginning to chafe at the restrictions imposed upon them by the domestic ideology. Florence Nightingale was one such woman, and in 1852 she set down her thoughts on the coercive power of the Victorian ideal of womanhood, demanding to know why women had been given 'passion, intellect, moral activity . . . and a place in society where no one of the three can be exercised'.[35] Women, she complained, were compelled to 'act the farce of hypocrisy, the lie that they are without passion', with even the passionate communion they looked for in marriage denied them by husbands anxious not to trouble the presumed innocence of their wives. The 'conventional frivolities' known as the 'duties' of women required that their intellectual activities be regarded as 'merely selfish amusement', to be laid aside at the whim of 'every trifler more selfish than themselves'. Even the moral energies which might have found an outlet in philanthropic work were thwarted by the official wisdom that women had no need to understand the society in which this work was to be carried out. Women were expected to find their life's Mission ('with a grand M') within the family, but the family was 'too narrow a field for the development of an immortal spirit', and married women too often found that 'the sacred hearth' was in reality sacred only 'to their husband's sleep, their sons' absence in the body and their daughters' in mind'. The truth was that there was 'no longer unity between the woman as inwardly developed, and as outwardly manifested', and if women were not to perish inwardly, the outer conditions of their lives must be changed. The domestic ideal was no longer enough: women must be allowed to give up their domestic roles in exchange for the chance to seek work outside the home.

Florence Nightingale described herself in 'Cassandra' as one 'wandering alone in the bitterness of life', but to a large extent her frustrations were in keeping with the spirit of the age. Like their male counterparts, middle-class women wanted to share in the benefits of an expanding economy and, much more importantly, they wanted to contribute to it. Both the Protestant and the liberal traditions provided good grounds for arguing that the helpless dependence of women was not feminine and adorable, but degrading. The Protestant faith had been founded on the conviction that it was the duty of each individual to work out his or her own salvation, and this led naturally to the claim that each person, man or woman, was bound to contribute to the work that needed to be done in the world; to many feminists, and especially to those who had to face the opposition of family or friends, this belief was to prove an indispensable source of comfort and inspiration. At the same time, the Protestant emphasis on individual responsibility accorded closely with one of the main principles of nineteenth-century liberalism: the principle, as John Stuart Mill explained it, 'that conduct, and conduct alone, entitles to respect: that not what men are, but what they do, constitutes their claim to deference'.[36] This principle was easily applied to the position of women: if a claim to respect could not be inherited at birth, then it could not be acquired by marriage; only work successfully accomplished could confer status, and, that being so, it was clearly unjust to deny women the chance to undertake such work. Barbara Leigh Smith's *Women and Work* (1856) was typical of much feminist writing of the mid-century in drawing freely on both traditions: 'To do God's work in the world is the duty of all, rich and poor, of all nations, of both sexes. . . . Adult women must not be supported by men if they are to stand as dignified, rational beings before God. . . . Women must have work if they are to form equal unions.'[37]

Other forces were also at work to cast doubt on the adequacy of the domestic ideal, of which the most immediate was the increasing percentage of women over men during the nineteenth century evident in the census returns of 1851. Yet the domestic ideal offered no place to the single woman who wished or needed to be self-supporting; she had either to exist on the margins of society—for example, as a governess or a lady's companion—or sink out of it altogether into those trades allowed to 'women' but prohibited to 'ladies'. The problem attracted a good deal of attention, much of it unsympathetic: men were urged to be more charitable, and to marry earlier; women who could not find husbands at home were advised to set out *en masse* for the colonies, where they might hope to be more successful.[38] These proposals did not, for the most part, recommend themselves to the women in question, who argued instead that the real solution was two-fold: to provide more and better paid work for women, and to remove the stigma of social and sexual failure attaching to those who remained single. As Frances Power Cobbe put it in 1862, the imbalance of the sexes made nonsense of the 'the old assumption that marriage was the sole destiny of woman', since an increasing number of women would now require 'the standing-ground of a happy and independent celibacy'.[39] Clearly, the domestic ideal could no longer be supposed to answer every need of every woman.

By the end of the 1850s, enough like-minded women had banded together to make it possible to speak of a 'feminist movement' in England, and by 1869, with the publication of John Stuart Mill's essay on *The Subjection of Women*, the movement had unquestionably come of age. Twenty years earlier, Mill had written that 'the ideas and institutions by which the accident of sex is made the groundwork of an inequality of legal rights, and a forced dissimilarity of social functions, must ere long be recognised as the greatest hindrance to moral, social, and even intellectual improvement'.[40] In *The Subjection of Women* he set himself to make good these claims: to challenge the core of the doctrine of 'separate spheres', that the different positions in society of men and women rested on an inherent difference in their natures, and to establish that the disabilities of women, far from ensuring the moral health of the community, were in fact a barrier to human advancement.

To make the first point required only the application of a little Benthamite reasoning. According to Mill, the triumph of the nineteenth century was to have created an open society, where all were 'free to employ their faculties . . . to achieve the lot which may appear to them most desirable'. The exclusion of women from this freedom stood out as 'the single relic of an old world of thought and feeling exploded in everything else', an anomaly which passed unrecognised because the subordination of women to men was held to be 'natural'. This was a familiar argument: absolutist monarchs had maintained that absolutism was the 'natural' form of government; slave-owners in the American South had defended the institution of slavery as one sanctioned 'by nature'. But in all these cases, replied Mill, the same desire to retain a position of privilege had issued in the same fundamental error: the confusion of the 'natural' with the merely 'customary'. What was now called 'the nature of women' was in truth 'an eminently artificial thing—the result of forced repression in some directions, unnatural stimulation in others'. It was indeed possible to say what women *had* become under the existing order of society; but given only imperfect knowledge of the influences which form character, it was not possible to predict what women *might* become in a differently ordered society. Assumptions about the nature of women could not, therefore, be used to justify withholding from them the rights and opportunities afforded to men.

Mill's second point was that the changes he proposed in the customs and institutions of society would be generally beneficial. First, however, he had to show that the 'free direction and disposal of their faculties' really was a desirable goal for women. Clearly, it was open to his opponents to contend that a Mrs. Ellis, for example, might prefer to forgo the uncertainties attaching to a life of freedom, in return for the security afforded by continuing dependence upon Mr. Ellis. To this objection Mill could only reply with the principle he had urged throughout his essay *On Liberty* (1859): that freedom is not only a means to happiness, but a necessary constituent element of it, and that this is so far true that the quality of happiness to be gained from a life of rational freedom will always outweigh the lesser pleasures to be derived from a life of subjection, no matter how easy the terms of service might appear. It is not easy to see how this principle can be made to square with Mill's general position as a Utilitarian, but rather than pursue the point further Mill appealed to the test of experience which, he claimed, showed that once the primary necessities of food and raiment had been provided, freedom was in fact 'the first and strongest want of human nature'. Individuals, no less than nations, had always preferred freedom to dependence: women too, if allowed to do so, would choose freedom.[41]

Mill offered two main sets of reasons for supposing that it would be to the general good to bring to an end the subjection of women. First, the community as a whole would benefit from the resulting increase in the number of its useful citizens. As things stood, half of the moral and intellectual resources of the nation were left undeveloped; to place women on an equal footing with men would be to double 'the mass of mental faculties available for the higher service of humanity'. Second, marriage itself, as the one place in Victorian society where men and women could come together, could only be strengthened by the changes Mill wished to see introduced. The existing inequalities between men and women were hurtful to married life, reducing it in many cases merely to a 'school of despotism', in which men learned to be selfish, and women to be cunning. Marriage between equals, on the other hand, would be a school of mutual improvement: 'The moral regeneration of mankind will only really commence, when the most fundamental of the social relations is placed under the rule of equal justice, and when human beings learn to cultivate their strongest sympathy with an equal in rights and in cultivation.' Mill is evidently thinking—somewhat priggishly—of his own married life with Harriet Taylor, but the idea of marriage as a means of 'moral regeneration' is in keeping with the rest of the essay. Mill hoped to see changes in the laws governing marriage, and in the way it was generally experienced, but he was far from wanting to undermine the institution itself, or to derogate from the seriousness with which it was regarded by his conservative opponents.

More than a century of debate has done remarkably little to impair the status of Mill's essay, and it is easy to underestimate the extent to which it was a work both of and for its age. Two points seem to need particular attention. First, Mill's feminism is closely related to his individualism. Mill considered his to be an age of mediocrity, in which only a small minority had the courage to question the ideas and values approved by society at large; women especially, trained from childhood to a life of submission, were too often ready to surrender to public opinion, and to drag down their husbands to the same level of timid conformity. But Mill held that challenge and diversity were the preconditions of moral and intellectual progress; the liberation of women was necessary because it would enable them to contribute to this diversity, to undertake new and potentially fruitful 'experiments in living', and so bring nearer the goal of a society in which there would be 'as many possible independent centres of improvement as there are individuals'.[42] This aspect of Mill's argument has found only occasional echoes in subsequent feminist writing. Indeed, much modern feminism, in emphasising a 'shared sisterhood' or 'feminine consciousness', has come close to adopting for its own purposes the doctrine of 'separate spheres': the difference being that the nineteenth century conservative thought that women could and should redeem the male world, and therefore celebrated their role by the domestic hearth, whereas the radical feminist has rejected it as beyond redemption, and offered in its stead the women's commune. *The Subjection of Women* does not stand in this line. Mill's feminism was intended to liberate the greatest variety of individuality, and not to bring about a sense of collective identity. It was, precisely, feminism for a liberal society.[43]

The second point too easily lost sight of has to do with the psychology underpinning Mill's essay, which is that of an age in many respects more confident than our own. Like the first, it reflects Mill's indifference to the question of a specifically feminine nature, and in this instance Harriet Taylor Mill, writing in the days when she was still Mrs. Taylor, perhaps showed more insight than her future husband. Mrs. Taylor accepted the view that 'all men with the exception of a few lofty minded, are sensualists more or less', while 'women on the contrary are quite exempt from this trait', but she was undecided as to whether this was the result of education, or genuinely a fact of nature. However, she had no doubt that sexual life would be different in the future:

> As certain as it is that there is equality in nothing now—all the pleasures such as they are being the man's and all the disagreeables and pains being women's, as that every pleasure would be infinitely heightened both in kind and degree by the perfect equality of the sexes.[44]

The suggestion here seems to be that the advance towards equality of the sexes might bring with it, *pari passu*, the awakening of women's sexual identity, and with that the intensification of sexual pleasure for men. In Mill's essay there is no room for such speculations. The omission might have been tactical, since he also avoided committing himself on divorce and birth control, but it seems more likely that Mill, one of the 'lofty minded', simply allowed almost nothing to the urgencies of sexual feeling. He certainly allowed less than most feminists of the twentieth century, and would have found quite alien Dora Russell's belief that 'the most important task of modern feminism is to accept and proclaim sex', or Germaine Greer's insistence that the denial of female sexuality has been 'the chief instrument in the deflection and perversion of female energy'.[45] Mill, in this a true child of the Enlightenment, did not recognise anything in human nature (except what education would soon overcome) which might inhibit the re-shaping of 'the most fundamental of the social relations' according to the light of reason. The modern reader, exposed to the arguments of Freud and Nietzsche, as well as to those of the radical feminists, is unlikely to share Mill's confidence.

Mill's essay is important both in its own right, and because it fairly represents the feminism of the mid-century—liberal, middle class, and, above all else, moderate in its approach and ambitions. Confident that an age which had freed the slaves and extended the franchise must eventually yield to the force of argument, the feminists of the 1850s and 1860s sought to modify the effects in practice of the domestic ideology. The position of women in society was to be transformed by the development of new opportunities in higher education, and the consequent opening up of areas of employment previously reserved for men. The legal position of married women was to be improved, especially with regard to their property rights under the common law. And, more problematically, attitudes towards sexuality were to be changed, as protests against the double standard of sexual morality led on to a crusade against the laws regulating prostitution. Taken collectively, these campaigns amounted to an assault on the principle of male supremacy, and opposition to them was bitter and passionate. But for all their vigour, these early feminists did not think of themselves as demanding a revolution. Like Mill, they looked only for the more equitable treatment of women within the existing framework of society; and, again like Mill, they seem to have assumed throughout that personal life, in and out of marriage, would somehow adjust itself spontaneously to the changes they hoped to introduce. They were, undoubtedly, too optimistic; but one of the remarkable features of the social history of Victorian England is the extent to which marriage was still seen, even at the end of the period, as the ideal way of life—the goal of a man's labours, and the summit of a woman's expectations.

The campaign to improve the level of women's education illustrates the gradualist approach favoured by mid-Victorian feminists. To claim that women could study classics or medicine with as much profit as men was necessarily to cast doubt on the idea of their 'separate' natures, with all that that idea implied of women's special vocation in the family, but wherever possible this more radical question was kept out of the campaign. Thus, Maria Grey argued that 'marriage should not be the first object of a woman's life, any more than of a man's', but she disowned 'the wild theory of feminine independence': 'Only in the union of man and woman is human life perfect and complete.'[46] Similarly, Frances Power Cobbe defended celibacy, and herself remained unmarried, while continuing to insist that marriage was 'manifestly the Creator's plan for humanity'; the need to defend the sanctity of marriage was in itself sufficient reason for increasing the alternatives open to women, since 'when we have made it *less* women's interest to marry, we shall indeed have . . . fewer interested marriages'.[47] And when Millicent Fawcett daringly remarked that educated women might be able to assist their husbands in their business or profession, she refrained from adding, and perhaps even from thinking, that educated women might in fact prefer to compete in business with men who were not their husbands.[48] In short, the common theme was that the changes sought with such determination would hardly change anything at all: fathers and husbands would still be able to rely on the support of their helpmeets; household management and the nurture of children would continue to be 'good true womanly work'. 'No one', explained Emily Faithfull, 'wants to take women from homes where there are home duties to perform.'[49]

The moderation with which the feminists argued their case was largely ignored by their opponents, who called on the authority of science to prove from first principles that any movement towards sexual equality would be attended by dangerous consequences. There must be, wrote James Allan MacGrigor, 'radical, natural, permanent distinctions in the mental and moral conformation, corresponding with those in the physical organisation of the sexes'.[50] Predictably these distinctions, as they were uncovered by 'scientific inquiry', matched point by point those assumed by Ruskin and other advocates of the doctrine of 'separate spheres'. George Romanes, for example, taking his cue from Darwin's discussion of secondary sexual characteristics such as the plumage of birds and the horns of mammals, sought to classify 'the secondary sexual characteristics of a mental kind' which distinguished men and women.[51] Men, it appeared, excelled in creativity, self-control, and tenacity of purpose: women in refinement, self-denial, and patience under pain or disappointment. Men were intellectually superior, and more often capable of the heroic or civic virtues: religious feeling, sympathy, and the 'gentler or domestic' virtues were 'the natural heritage of women in all but the lowest grades of culture'. But despite the revealing slip between 'natural' and 'cultural', it was Romanes' case that these differences were not (pace Mill) the result of education but of the process of evolution and, in the last analysis, of the smaller size and lesser efficiency of women's brains: even under the most favourable conditions it would require 'many centuries for heredity to produce the missing five ounces of brain'. But, as other theorists had already shown, the distinction between male and female brains was in fact seen to increase rather than diminish with the progress of civilisation, so much so that one of the main factors separating the primitive from the developed races was the more marked differentiation by sex of both character and social function in the latter.[52] The *Saturday Review* was quick to point out the moral, that to assimilate the work of women to that of men would be 'a direct retrogression': 'If perfection is to be the aim of our efforts, it will be best advanced by further divergence of male and female characteristics.'[53] The laws of evolution had bestowed their seal of approval on the doctrine of separate spheres, and the women's campaign neither could nor should be allowed to succeed.

The argument that caused the feminists most concern was that put forward by Dr. Henry Maudsley in an article on 'Sex in Mind and Education' (*Fortnightly Review* 1874), that higher education would be damaging to women's health.[54] Maudsley derived his case from the principle of the conservation of energy, which he supposed (incorrectly) to apply to the human body. In women, and especially in young women, the demands made on the body's store of energy by menstruation were so great, argued Maudsley, as to leave no surplus for serious study: 'When nature spends in one direction, she must economise in another direction.'

Women were the prisoners of their biology, and any attempt to 'rebel . . . against the tyranny of their organisation'—for example, by studying for a university degree—would be likely to leave them permanently weakened, and possibly incapable of motherhood; at best, they must expect to become the mothers of 'a puny, enfeebled, and sickly race'. And this was not merely a prediction: it had already been confirmed by observations made in America by Dr. Edward Clarke. Mill had only been able to write his essay on *The Subjection of Women* because he had ignored the simplest laws of physiology: the fact was, concluded Maudsley, that 'the main reason of woman's position lies in her nature'.

The next issue of the *Fortnightly* carried a reply to Maudsley from Elizabeth Garrett Anderson, arguing strongly that women were more likely to suffer from 'the depressing influence of dulness' at home than from such well-conducted schemes of education as were beginning to be available.[55] More significantly, however, she rejected Maudsley's account of women's nature. Maudsley had argued that menstruation left women 'for a quarter of each month during the best years of life . . . more or less sick and unfit'. But, replied Mrs. Garrett Anderson, women knew this to be untrue: healthy women were as a rule able to disregard their menstrual periods almost completely. Domestic servants, for example, continued to work as usual without detriment to their health, and were expected to do so; and with regard to 'mental work', it was 'within the experience of many women' that menstruation was less an occasion of weakness than 'an aid, the nervous and mental powers being in many cases greater at those times'.

Two points stand out in this argument. Firstly, women were naturally healthy and not, as Maudsley had suggested, naturally sick. The idea of female invalidism had been gaining ground for more than a century, but during the 1870s and 1880s it was vigorously opposed not only by the feminists, but also by the advocates of callisthenics, bicycling, and rational dress, all in their own way committed to the belief that women were naturally strong in body; this was a point that needed to be made, for until it was admitted it was too easy to sneer at the 'strong-minded woman' as a sport in nature.[56] Secondly, and more importantly, it was for women, and not for the men of science, to determine what was or was not women's 'nature': 'the experience of many women' was its own authority, not to be brushed aside by the assumptions of the medical establishment, almost exclusively male as that was. Moreover, there was in this claim what could be seen as an invitation to women to examine their own physical experience, and even to be ready to cite it where necessary in the debate about women's role in society. The convention of silence was beginning to break, and it was only a small step from the dispute between Dr. Maudsley and Mrs. Garrett Anderson in the *Fortnightly Review*, to the more self-conscious exploration of women's physical and sexual nature to be found, for example, in Olive Schreiner's letters to Havelock Ellis, in Emma Frances Brooke's novel, *A Superfluous Woman* (1894), or in Ménie Muriel Dowie's *Gallia* (1895).

The campaign to win higher education for women had taken the feminists farther than they could have anticipated in the 1850s. By the end of the century, the educated woman was still likely to think of marriage as the most desirable goal open to her, but she entered it with more confidence in her own knowledge of herself—with, according to one self-styled 'woman of the day', a new 'realisation of her nature's complexity', and a new 'prescience that no one man will ever learn it thoroughly'.[57] The transparent simplicity of Dickens' Agnes Copperfield, or of the 'fair young English girl' so beloved of the anti-feminist Eliza Lynn Linton, could not long survive a public debate about what was possible to women's physical nature. By the 1890s, Agnes Copperfield had to make room for Hardy's Sue Bridehead, and the 'fair young English girl' for such overtly radical 'New Women' as Mona Caird and Mary Chavelita Dunne ('George Egerton').[58]

The campaigns to improve the legal position of married women found the feminists less embarrassed at the implications of their own arguments. It was clearly an affront that a married woman should be classed together with criminals, lunatics, and minors, as legally incompetent and irresponsible; and the existing laws did in fact give rise to cases of real hardship, some of which attracted considerable publicity. At the centre of the debate were the laws relating to women's property rights.[59] On her marriage, the control of and income from a woman's *real property* (that is, her property in freehold land) passed under the common law to her husband. However, he could not dispose of it without her formal consent, and if he predeceased her it returned to her possession; while if she predeceased him, it was divided among her children or other legal heirs, subject to his retaining a life interest in it where a child had been born of the marriage. Her *personal property* (that is, all other forms of property, including leasehold land, money from earnings or investments, and personal belongings such as jewellery), passed absolutely into her husband's control and disposal. He could, if he wished, make a will devising all his personal property, including whatever he had received from her on their marriage, away from her and her children; if he died intestate, she never recovered more than half, with the remainder going to his children or other near relatives or, if he had none, to the Crown. A married woman, however, could bequeath her personal property only with her husband's consent, which he could revoke at any time before probate; if she died intestate, her personal property continued in his possession.

A woman who wanted to evade these provisions could do so by means of a settlement drawn up before her marriage according to the principles of equity, by which her property could be secured to her by a trust, and thereby removed from her husband's common law rights of control. But while a married woman with an estate settled to her separate use enjoyed virtually the same property rights as a single woman, this situation was unsatisfactory for several reasons. First, it created obvious anomalies. Under the common law, a husband had a number of responsibilities. He was required to support his wife and children at least to the extent that they should not become a burden on the parish; and, since his wife had no legal existence apart from his, and could not therefore either sue or be sued, he also became liable for her debts and contracts, and for any torts committed by her before or during marriage: these common law responsibilities remained with her husband even where a marriage settlement had provided his wife with an estate settled to her separate use. Second, and more important, marriage settlements were too costly to be generally available. There was, in effect, equity law for the rich, and common law for the poor.

In 1854 Barbara Leigh Smith's *Brief Summary of the Laws of England Concerning Women* prompted the Law Amendment Society to take up the cause of reform, and in 1857 Sir Thomas Erskine Perry introduced in Parliament a Married Women's Property Bill, intended to place single and married women on the same footing by means of a general law based on the principles of equity. The Bill safely passed its second reading, but at this point what eventually became the Divorce and Matrimonial Causes Act (1857) was handed down from the House of Lords. Added to this measure, after bitter debate, had been various clauses protecting the property of women estranged from their husbands: in particular, the husband was deprived of his right to the earnings of his deserted wife, and a woman who had been granted either a divorce or a judicial separation recovered the property rights of a single woman. These provisions were used to defeat Perry's proposals. Now that the injured wife was to be protected, ran the argument, there was no need to risk legislation which would invade further into the sacred precincts of the family.

Despite this setback the campaign for reform continued, and in 1870 the Commons gave a second reading to a bill similar in outline to that proposed by Perry in 1857, only to have it sent back from the House of Lords in sadly mutilated condition. The Married Women's Property Act (1870), as re-written by the Lords, allowed a married woman to retain earnings or property acquired *after* her marriage, but all that she owned on marriage was to pass as before into her husband's ownership and control. Even in this form the Act represented a substantial gain, in that the earnings of about three-quarters of a million working wives were now to be protected, but continual pressure led to the passage twelve years later of a further Act, allowing women to keep possession of what they owned at the time of their marriage. The Married Women's Property Act of 1882 in effect extended to all women the benefits of a settlement in equity: married women were at last to have the same property rights, and roughly the same responsibilities, as those who stayed single. In one major area, the legal fiction of the non-existence of married women was at an end.

The importance of these Acts was considerable. That every woman now had the right to own property separately from her husband marked a step forward on the road to full political equality; after 1882, the argument that the enfranchisement of women would merely provide a second vote for every married man began to look less convincing. But it is likely that the psychological effect of the Acts was of still greater consequence, as the commentators remarked with alarm. Henry Raikes, for example, opposed the 1870 Act because it would create 'a factitious, an artificial, and an unnatural equality between man and woman', changing for ever the relations between husband and wife.[60] Ralph Thicknesse, reflecting in 1883 on the new legislation, also feared its probable 'deteriorating effect on domestic manners'. Not only might a wife with independent property develop independent views, and even a taste for independent society, but she might also leave her husband and children, and use her property to set up, not an independent, but *a rival household*.[61] Even the reviewer in *Chamber's Journal*, tentatively welcoming the Act of 1882, went on to raise the question of whether women would avail themselves of the protection of the law if that meant taking legal proceedings against their husbands, and concluded that in most cases they would. The 'spaniel-like submission' of the legally non-existent woman was a thing of the past; the woman of the future would exhibit 'a more pronounced individuality of character' than men had been used to encounter.[62] On this point, it seems, both the supporters and the opponents of the Acts were agreed: the new legislation would bring into being a new kind of woman.

The women who campaigned for access to higher education and for the reform of the property laws were for the most part able to fight on ground of their own choosing, but this was not to be the case with their challenge to the double standard of sexual morality. The issue here was forced upon them when the double standard was formally embodied in English law by the Divorce and Matrimonial Causes Act of 1857, and while they could hardly help but recognise the injustice of the sexual attitudes tolerated in their society, most of those who came forward to oppose these attitudes did so with extreme reluctance. The ensuing debates divided the feminist movement: more importantly, they helped to bring about a new and radical analysis of marriage and the family in Victorian England.

Since the Restoration marriages in England had been nominally indissoluble, but it was possible for a man with enough money and influence to secure a divorce by following an established but cumbersome procedure: first, to prove the adultery of the wife by suing her alleged lover in the civil courts for 'criminal conversation'; next, to obtain from the ecclesiastical courts a divorce *a mensa et thoro* (a form of separation permitting neither party to re-marry); and, finally, to obtain a private Act of Parliament granting a divorce *a vinculo matrimonii*, which allowed re-marriage. The wife's adultery was in effect both the sole and the sufficient grounds for divorce: in only four out of some two hundred cases had a woman succeeded in divorcing her husband. The Act of 1857 brought all these processes before a single matrimonial court, cutting the cost of divorce, and thus making available to the merely well-to-do a privilege hitherto enjoyed only by the very rich.[63] However, it remained much easier for a man to divorce his wife than for a woman to divorce her husband: a man could seek a divorce on the simple grounds of his wife's adultery, whereas a woman had to prove adultery aggravated by desertion (for a period of two years), or by cruelty, rape, incest, sodomy, or bestiality. The husband lost his right to bring an action for 'criminal conversation', but it was still possible for the courts to award him damages against his wife's lover: no such award could be made to the wife divorcing her husband. In short, the purpose of the Act was to tidy up the procedures by which men were permitted to divorce their wives, and not to introduce into the law any new principle of equality between men and women; the *in*equalities, glaring as they were, were not removed until 1923, when the grounds for divorce were made the same for both parties.[64]

Contemporary discussion of the bill concentrated on two main issues. The more urgent was the question of whether or not divorce had been sanctioned by the scriptures, and, if it had not, whether it was allowable for the laws of England to contradict the laws of God. In the event, the scriptures proved to be ambiguous, and not even the eloquence of Gladstone was enough to persuade the House to reject as contrary to religion a bill which commanded the votes of eleven bishops. Even so, the earnestness of the arguments provides further evidence of how deeply held was the belief that the moral health of the nation depended on the institution of marriage: where the family was in question, 'the moral face of Britain still lived in the Christian past'.[65]

The other issue to trouble opponents of the bill was that of the double standard itself: the rule of chastity for women, but licence for men. Gladstone argued both in and out of Parliament that the law should not admit a principle of inequality between men and women where there could be no inequality in the sight of God; Henry Drummond observed caustically that in this matter a male House of Commons was 'very much in the position of Turks legislating for the inhabitants of the seraglio'.[66] But theirs was a lost cause. Supporters of the bill replied that laws had to reflect the needs of society, and while the chastity of women was essential for the safe transmission of property, that of men was not: as Lord Cranworth explained, 'The adultery of the wife might be the means of palming spurious offspring upon the husband, while the adultery of the husband could have no such effect with regard to the wife.'[67] However, this argument took no account of the fact that an unfaithful wife was not held to be any less guilty even when there was no question of 'spurious' issue, and it was clearly not the only reason for clinging to the double standard. Some of the other arguments put forward in its defence were coarser and more revealing. Men's sexuality, it was argued, was such that they, unlike their wives, could not be required to forgo adultery: sexual licence among men was, and had always been, universal. Moreover, while a sensible woman did not trouble herself unduly about her husband's infidelity, it was not possible for a man to forgive a similar lapse by his wife: 'The infidelity of the wife inflicts upon the husband so much larger an amount of suffering than . . . the infidelity of the husband inflicts upon the wife.'[68] Behind such arguments, Keith Thomas has suggested, lies 'the desire of men for absolute property in women, a desire which cannot be satisfied if . . . the

woman has once been possessed by another man'; if this is correct, men's
desire for 'property in women' reached its apogee in Victorian England
(without, of course, being peculiar to it), and by the end of the 1850s every
woman who gave any thought to the moral and political questions of the
day must have been aware that it was now a desire endorsed by the law of
the land.[69]

The passage of the Divorce and Matrimonial Causes Act did not close
the debate about the double standard. From the beginning of the century
there had been widespread concern about the effects of prostitution,
leading to calls for state intervention along continental lines: that is, a
system of regulation which would accept prostitution as a necessary and
permanent fact of society, and provide for the regular medical inspection of
the women involved, in order to protect the health of their male clients. In
the 1860s demands for regulation were stepped up, following reports that
as many as a quarter of the men in the home forces were suffering from
venereal diseases, and in 1864 the first Contagious Diseases Act passed
quietly into English law, to be revised and extended in 1866, and again in
1869. In their final form, these Acts provided that where either a registered
doctor, or a member of the newly-formed *police des moeurs*, suspected that
a woman was a 'common prostitute' plying her trade within a ten-mile
radius of one of eighteen naval and garrison towns, he was to lay this
information before a Justice of the Peace, who could then summon her to
attend for medical examination at one of the hospitals set up for this
purpose under the Acts; provided he was satisfied as to the truth of the
information laid before him, he could order these examinations to be
repeated fortnightly for a year. If at any time the woman was found to be
diseased, she could be detained for up to nine months for treatment; refusal
to attend the hospital could be answered by forcible examination, or by
imprisonment. Although a clause added in 1866 made provision for
religious instruction for women undergoing treatment, the aim of the Acts
was not to stamp out prostitution (which was not in itself a crime), but to
ensure that the women who serviced the armed forces were clean and
healthy: a fact which was clearly recognised by those women who attended
voluntarily for inspection, and presented themselves to their clients as
officially licensed 'Queen's women'.[70]

On 1 January 1870 the feminists launched their challenge to the Acts with
the publication in the *Daily News* of the 'Women's Protest', signed by 124
women, including Josephine Butler, Harriet Martineau, and Florence
Nightingale. They listed eight objections: of these only the seventh
attempted to meet the regulationist case head-on, by denying that sexual
diseases could be controlled while only the one sex was subject to
examination. The remaining points all took the high ground of principle.
Two were concerned with the danger to civil liberties represented by
legislation which had been passed with the minimum of discussion, and so
loosely framed that a key term ('common prostitute') had been left
undefined; two others complained that the state was facilitating the path to

evil, by declaring prostitution to be necessary, and by seeking to alleviate the consequences of vice instead of attending to its causes. The second, fourth, and sixth points, however, all indicated an overtly feminist concern with the position of fellow-women: the Contagious Diseases Acts deprived women of personal security by putting 'their reputation, their freedom, and their persons absolutely in the power of the police'; they unjustly punished the women who were 'the victims of the vice', and left unpunished the men who were 'the main cause'; and in practice they degraded women, 'violating' and 'brutalising' all those who came under their action.

The Women's Protest marked the beginning of a long and bitter campaign, in which women continued to play a prominent part. Within a few months the Ladies' National Association had formed branches in every major city, all pledged to resist the state regulation of prostitution, and by 1886, when the Acts were finally repealed, women campaigners had between them presented 17,000 petitions containing 2.5 million signatures; staged more than 900 public meetings (at one of which the barn where Josephine Butler was speaking was set on fire by her opponents); and even engineered the defeat at a by-election of Sir Henry Storks, the government candidate and a well-known regulationist. Throughout this campaign, the directly feminist issues were kept well to the fore. Mrs. Butler went before a Royal Commission set up to investigate the working of the Acts to denounce them as 'an outrageous piece of sex legislation', 'a regulating of vice for the facilitating of its practice'; and in the *Shield*, the journal of the repeal movement, she quoted a woman who had suffered under them:

> It is *men, men, only men*, from the first to the last, that we have to do with! To please a man I did wrong at first, then I was flung about from man to man. Men police lay hands on us. By men we are examined, handled, doctored, and messed on with. In the hospital it is a man again who makes prayers and reads the Bible for us. We are had up before magistrates who are men, and we never get out of the hands of men till we die![71]

At the same time, the pro-regulation lobby frequently set itself up as an easy target for feminist attacks. Sir Henry Storks wanted to see soldiers' wives as well as suspected prostitutes made subject to examination, and this despite the fact that the army had already abolished the routine inspection of enlisted men on the grounds that it was damaging to morale; while the Royal Commission of 1870–1 blandly dismissed feminist opposition to the unequal provisions of the Acts: 'There is no comparison to be made between prostitutes and the men who consort with them. With the one sex the offence is committed as a matter of gain; with the other it is an irregular indulgence of a natural impulse.'[72] The insouciance of such arguments infuriated Mrs. Butler and her colleagues in the repeal movement, and increasingly, as she had foreseen it must, the campaign against the Acts took on the more general character of a 'revolt and rebellion . . . against men'.[73]

The prospect of such a development brought alarm and dismay to many feminists. Some women could not bring themselves even to consider the issues involved, let alone to enter a public debate about the efficacy of mercury in the treatment of venereal diseases, or the use of the speculum on unwilling women as a form of 'instrumental rape'. Others, including Emily Davies and Millicent Fawcett, were privately sympathetic to repeal, but chose to remain aloof in public for the sake of other causes with which they were associated. But for a minority of women, the effect of the repeal campaign, and perhaps still more of the hostility it aroused, was to push them towards a new and more searching examination of marriage and society in Victorian England.

What that examination uncovered was described by Mona Caird as the 'twin-system of marriage and prostitution', where one idea, 'the purchase of womanhood', ruled 'from base to summit of the social body'.[74] Point by point the details of this system were spelled out. Society pretended to frown on mercenary marriages, but for most women there was no reasonable alternative except to surrender to the highest bidder: 'common respectable marriage' was in truth merely 'the worst, because the most hypocritical, form of woman-purchase.' Even those more fortunate women whose marriages were founded on love were nonetheless required to submit to a contract drawn up without regard for their wishes, and framed in terms of their role as potential vehicles for the transmission of property: so much was clear from the laws concerning divorce, the custody of children, and, at least until 1882, the property rights of married women. As for the other side of this 'twin-system': with chastity the rule for middle-class women, and licence the norm for middle-class men, the laws of supply and demand ensured the steady recruitment into prostitution of women from the working class. As age or disease forced some women out of the market, others came forward to replace them: that was provided for by the low wages and long hours endured by the majority of working women. The function of the Contagious Diseases Acts was to see that any women who might infect their male clients were detained in hospital until they could be cleaned up and returned to the streets—a process which had the incidental advantage of professionalising those driven into casual prostitution by unemployment or by fluctuations in the seasonal trades. In short, the laws regulating marriage and the laws regulating vice pointed towards the same harsh fact: the sacrifice of the rights of women to the interests and even the appetites of men.

The emergence of this analysis marks a watershed in the history of the women's movement in England. The feminists of the 1850s and 1860s had been pragmatic and reformist, rather than systematic and radical: prepared to challenge the ideal of an exclusively family vocation for all women, but not to call into question the sanctity and dignity of marriage itself. During the 1880s, however, the 'Marriage Question' was being raised on all sides. 'What is to be the future of marriage?', asked Elizabeth Chapman in the *Westminster Review*: 'Will the deliberate verdict of the future be given in favour of marriage-rejection or of marriage-reform?'[75] She cast her own

vote in favour of reform, with a rider against divorce, but there were
already advocates for this and every other alternative, including celibacy
and polygamy. Inevitably the debate reflected sharply divided views of
human nature. According to Karl Pearson, there were those who held that
men's sexual instincts had been 'so abnormally developed as to have
become a disease', while there were others, such as James Hinton, who
looked forward to a re-awakening of human sexuality as a means to
overcome 'the selfishness of monogamy and the home, the cruelty of virtue,
the rigidity of arbitrary rules and feelings'.[76] Elsewhere it was argued that
the sexual instinct was actually in decline, at least among the higher classes
of society, and the human race in danger of sinking back into barbarism, or
dying out altogether; Pearson himself took this danger seriously, and
criticised the feminists for their 'complete disregard of the sexualogical
difficulties'.[77] Diverse as they were, these theories bear witness to a growing
recognition that the movement for the freedom of women had precipitated
a challenge on sexual issues which could no longer be evaded: in the last two
decades of the nineteenth century the social and sexual conventions used to
safeguard marriage came under scrutiny as never before.

The Contagious Diseases Acts and the subsequent agitation had a
profound effect on attitudes to marriage and sexuality within the women's
movement. Revulsion at male sexual licence was intensified by disclosures
about the extent of child prostitution, in particular by W. T. Stead's articles
in 1885 on 'The Maiden Tribute of Modern Babylon', and contributed
significantly to the militancy of Edwardian suffragists—hence Christabel
Pankhurst's pamphlet on *The Great Scourge*, with its claim that three in
every four men were sexually diseased, and the slogan 'Votes for Women
and Chastity for Men'; and, as Judith Walkowitz has pointed out, the
violent activities of the Women's Social and Political Union can be seen as
'part of a real sex war, whose explicit political precedent may be traced to
the campaign against the C.D. Acts'.[78] Yet this was not enough to erode
economic and social confidence in marriage. The tone was more urgent in
the 1900s, but the message was the same as it had been in the 1850s:
marriage and family life were 'the very foundation of society', 'the bedrock
of all well organised states', inseparable from 'the very first ideas of social
order'.[79] If there was 'a real sex war', Victorian society felt able to contain
it, or at least to keep it at the level of a series of local skirmishes. This
requires some explanation.
 Part of the reason lies in the uncertainty among the feminists themselves,
even at their most radical, as to what was to follow the rejection of
marriage. The socialist movement claimed to offer an alternative. Marriage
as a social institution would give way to a 'contract . . . of a purely private
nature without the intervention of any public functionary'. At the same
time, housework and child care would be taken out of the private domain
to become a public responsibility. The result would be an end to the

economic dependence of women upon men, and their liberation from the mesh of property relationships in which they could be bought and sold, legally as in marriage, or extra-legally as in prostitution.[80] On the face of it, there was much to be said for this: if the existing system was sustained by the desire of men for 'property in women', then it might be appropriate to attack the principle of property itself. However, the socialists were divided in their response to feminism. Belfort Bax disliked women, and regarded feminist aspirations with contempt; H. M. Hyndman was indifferent, seeing the activities of the women's movement as a diversion from the real tasks of socialism; William Morris was sympathetic, but puzzled as to the way forward: 'It is a ticklish subject, but one day or another we must face it.'[81] Furthermore, where socialism became entangled with eugenics, as it did for Karl Pearson and some of the Fabians (Bernard Shaw, H. G. Wells, the Webbs), it was a moot point whether the overthrow of capitalism would represent a net gain for women. In common with most socialists, Pearson argued for 'complete freedom in the sex-relationship', but he added to this a defence of 'state interference where necessary in the matter of child-bearing'. This interference promised to be extensive. Not only might the less fit members of society be denied the right to reproduce themselves, but the more fit, including 'the best women', might have parenthood required of them as a 'duty', even at the expense of their own personal development: 'If child-bearing women must be intellectually handicapped, then the penalty to be paid for race predominance is the subjection of women.'[82] The nineteenth-century feminist could be forgiven for wondering whether the new-style socialist state might not resemble the old-style patriarch writ very large indeed.

But not all feminists were drawn to socialism, and for those who were there remained the problem of how to live in the interim, while working for the transformation of society. Some 'New Women', including Mona Caird and Olive Schreiner, moved towards an ideal of 'free unions' (carefully defined so as to exclude promiscuity), and, more tentatively, towards the rehabilitation of female sexuality, considered as a good in itself, without reference to the domestic or maternal 'instincts': 'Sex intercourse', wrote Olive Schreiner, 'is the great sacrament of life . . . it may be the most beautiful sacrament between two souls without any thought of children.'[83] For other women the answer seemed to lie in the opposite direction, in complete sexual abstinence: both Kathlyn Oliver and Christabel Pankhurst rejected men and marriage as inimical to their position within the feminist movement. But each of these possibilities presented hazards of its own. The relationship of Edward Aveling and Eleanor Marx was painful evidence that a woman could be treated as ungenerously within a 'free union' as within a conventional marriage; and while the role of a celibate was not necessarily unfulfilling, it was not easy to sustain, even as a political act, in a society inclined to submerge 'womanhood' into 'motherhood'. 'What chatter it is to talk of being free, or of getting free!' exclaims the heroine of Ménie Muriel Dowie's *Gallia*: 'As if we ever could!' Even in their fiction, the 'New Women' showed little faith in their ability to resist the pressures driving them towards marriage.

While those who questioned marriage were uncertain, those who offered to defend it did so with increasing vigour, as the sexual radicalism of the 1880s and 1890s came up against a strong current of moral conservatism. To some extent this was part of an attack on feminism, but it was also, and more importantly, a tendency within feminism itself. Even among those friendly to the women's movement, there had always been a majority who saw much to value in the received idea of womanhood, and who feared what might be lost if it were to be abandoned outright. George Eliot, for example, although prepared to live with G. H. Lewes in clear defiance of the marriage convention, still took every opportunity to insist on the need for continuity in an era of change:

> There lies just that kernel of truth in the vulgar alarm of men lest women should be 'unsexed'. We can no more afford to part with that exquisite type of gentleness, tenderness, possible maternity suffusing a woman's being with affectionateness, which makes what we mean by the feminine character, than we can afford to part with the human love, the mutual subjection of soul between man and woman— which is also a growth and revelation beginning before all history.[84]

This more cautious feminism had its own account of the C.D. Acts and the campaign against them: in their efforts to deal with the evil in the world, men had been led to compromise with sin; their error had been redeemed by the essential goodness of women. On this view, the important questions were moral rather than political, to be discussed in terms of profligacy and the rescue of the fallen, not in terms of the economic disabilities of women, and the 'twin-system of marriage and prostitution'. What the C.D. controversies pointed to was the need for a new and more urgent crusade against vice, and not the existence of an undeclared war between the sexes.[85]

The result of such arguments was the formation of a large number of groups to campaign for 'social purity'.[86] These moral reformers saw it as their first task to protect the sanctity of marriage and the family, and with the emphasis on family life and values came the customary insistence on the woman's role as the supreme guardian of those values. The effect, inevitably, was to reinforce conservative attitudes. However, the cult of domesticity could also be given a feminist edge and purpose. Women had secured the purity of that little corner of the world called Home: might they not also, given the means, bring order and decency into the world at large? Society was harsh, and lacking in compassion: what was needed was 'the infusion of the home spirit and the setting free of feminine powers and influence' in order to 'humanise' its institutions. It was time for women to extend their domestic role into the public arena and take up their position, in Millicent Fawcett's revealing phrase, 'as the mothers of the race'.[87] In such phrases the feminists saw a way to advance their case without disturbing the pieties of the age. The claim for legal and political equality, which John Stuart Mill had treated as an argument about 'women's rights', based on the essential similarities between men and women, could be re-fashioned as an argument about 'women's duties', and grafted on to an account of womanhood which stressed the differences between the sexes—and especially those 'special' moral qualities which constituted 'what we mean by the feminine character'. There was no need, therefore, to follow the lead given by the feminist 'left' in questioning the primacy of marriage: it would in fact be counter-productive to do so.[88]

Even at the end of the century, then, the majority of feminists were still seeking to accommodate their case to the dominant beliefs and values of their society. The task facing the radically-minded feminist, who could not be persuaded to acknowledge these values, was to assimilate into her personality a new vision of herself, and of her relation to others, in a society generally inclined to look on her efforts with suspicion or hostility. As Olive Schreiner recognised, it was not a task to be undertaken lightly, or in hope of easy answers: 'When one breaks away from all old moorings, and shapes a higher path of morality for oneself, and perhaps for others who shall follow one, it cannot be done without suffering.'[89] From the first, the struggles of those women who sought to initiate new codes of behaviour laid hold of the literary imagination, and through Ibsen's Nora, Hardy's Sue Bridehead, Wells' Ann Veronica, or Lawrence's Brangwen sisters, they hold it still. The literary evidence is invaluable: perhaps nothing else records so fully the felt experience of change—its anticipations, confusions, disappointments. But the pioneers for a new way were a minority, and while it might be that the future was with them, in the 1880s and 1890s they had little reason to think so. Despite the emergence of the 'Marriage Question', and the dramatic arrival of the 'New Woman', these were decades which saw the re-grouping of conservative forces, rather than decades of revolution. For most women in 1900, as for most women fifty years earlier, it was still the case that the true dignity and special mission of women lay in their power to influence the minds and actions of the men to whom they belonged; and the most fulfilling way to do so was as a wife and mother.

NOTES

Bibliographical Note. The most helpful essays are O. R. McGregor's 'The Social Position of Women in England, 1850–1914: A Bibliography', *British Journal of Sociology* VI (1955), 48–60, and a two-part essay by Barbara Kanner on 'The Women of England in a Century of Social Change, 1815–1914', of which the first part is in *Suffer and Be Still* (Bloomington 1972), and the second in *A Widening Sphere* (Bloomington 1977), both edited by Martha Vicinus. Also useful are the bibliographies in Carol Bauer and Lawrence Ritt, editors, *Free and Ennobled: Source Readings in the Development of Victorian Feminism* (Oxford 1979), and Olive Banks, *Faces of Feminism* (Oxford 1981).

1. *Charles Kingsley. His Letters and Memories of his Life* ed. Fanny Kingsley, 2 vols. (London 1879), I. 166, 222.

2. W. Cooke-Taylor, quoted without reference in H. L. Beales, 'The Victorian Family', in *Ideas and Beliefs of the Victorians*, paperback edn (New York 1966), p. 348.

3. Arthur Penrhyn Stanley, *The Life and Correspondence of Thomas Arnold, D.D.*, 9th edn, 2 vols. (London 1875), I. 189, 191.

4. References to Ruskin are to two lectures: 'Of Queens' Gardens' (*Sesame and Lilies* 1865), and 'War' (*The Crown of Wild Olive* 1866). Both are quoted from *The Works of John Ruskin* (ed. E. T. Cook and Alexander Wedderburn), 39 vols. (London 1903–12), XVIII. 109–44, 489–93.

5. The argument that women's goodness consists in their selflessness is discussed by Janet Radcliffe Richards in her *The Sceptical Feminist*, paperback edn (Harmondsworth 1982), pp. 212–15.

6. Sarah Ellis, *The Daughters of England* (London 1845), pp. 22–3.

7. Sarah Ellis, *Education of the Heart: woman's best work* (London 1869), p. 14.

8. *Correspondence of W. E. Channing and Lucy Aikin*, quoted from Ian Bradley, *The Call to Seriousness* (London 1976), p. 124.

9. See F. K. Prochaska, *Women and Philanthropy in Nineteenth-Century England* (Oxford 1980), especially the Introduction and Part One.

10. *The Daughters of England*, p. 23.

11. Sarah Ellis, *The Wives of England* (London 1843), ch. 1.

12. John William Burgon, B.D., *A Sermon Preached before the University of Oxford, June 8, 1884* (Oxford 1884), p. 17.

13. J. G. Phillimore, 'Women's Rights and Duties', *Blackwood's Magazine* LIV (1843), 373–97.

14. Charles Kingsley, *op. cit.* II. 330; Thomas Carlyle, in a letter of 9 February 1871, quoted from Marlene Springer, 'Angels and Other Women in Victorian Literature', in Marlene Springer (ed.), *What Manner of Woman* (Oxford 1978), pp. 129–30.

15. Sarah Grimke, *Letters on the Equality of the Sexes* (1838), quoted from Alice S. Rossi (ed), *The Feminist Papers* (New York 1973), p. 308.

16. William Blackstone, *Commentaries on the Laws of England* (Oxford 1765–9); see vol. I, ch. 15, 'Of Husband and Wife'.

17. From 1839 an innocent wife could be granted the temporary custody of her children under seven years of age, and from 1873 of her children under sixteen years.

18. S. B. Kitchin, *A History of Divorce* (London 1912), p. 181.

19. See the case of *R. v. Jackson*, 1.Q.B.671, summarised in Ray Strachey, *The Cause*, paperback edn (London 1978), p. 223.

20. William Thompson, *Appeal of One Half of the Human Race, Women, against the Pretensions of the Other Half, Men, to Retain Them in Political, and Thence in Civil and Domestic Slavery* (London 1825), pp. 79 and 85. Thompson's italics.

21. W. R. Greg, 'Prostitution', *Westminster Review* LIII (1850), 448–506: the passage quoted is on p. 457.

22. William Acton, quoted from Steven Marcus, *The Other Victorians* (London 1966), pp. 31–2.

23. Sarah Ellis, *The Wives of England*, ch. 3.

24. W. R. Greg, *op. cit.* p. 457.

25. William Acton, quoted in Marcus, *op. cit.* p. 31.

26. This is a weakness in Marcus' *The Other Victorians*, and more conspicuously so in otherwise useful studies such as Fraser Harrison's *The Dark Angel* (New York

1977), and Ronald Pearsall's *The Worm in the Bud* (Harmondsworth 1969). Eric Trudgill, in *Madonnas and Magdalens* (London 1976), is more fair-minded.

27. George Drysdale, *The Elements of Social Science: or Physical, Sexual and Natural Religion*, 3rd edn (London 1860), p. 345. Drysdale put this sentence in italics, but he did not put his name on the title page.

28. The best study is Angus McLaren, *Birth Control in Nineteenth-Century England* (London 1978). O. R. McGregor writes that 'the lifting of the crushing, debilitating burden of too frequent pregnancies was the most important single factor affecting the social position of married middle-class women' (*see* his *Divorce in England* (London 1957), pp. 84–5).

29. Tyler Smith, 'On the Utility and Safety of the Inhalation of Ether in Obstetric Practice', *Lancet* I (1847), pp. 321–3: quoted from A. J. Youngson, *The Scientific Revolution in Victorian Medicine* (London 1979), p. 97.

30. On clitoridectomy and ovariotomy in the nineteenth century, see Lorna Duffin, 'The Conspicuous Consumptive: Woman as Invalid', in Sara Delamont and Lorna Duffin (eds), *The Nineteenth-Century Woman* (London 1978), pp. 42–4.

31. On the 'medicalisation of sex', see Michel Foucault, *The History of Sexuality. Volume One: an Introduction*, paperback edn (Harmondsworth 1981), pp. 30, 54–7. For attempts to question received ideas about Victorian sexuality, see F. Barry Smith, 'Sexuality in Britain, 1800–1900: Some Suggested Revisions', in *A Widening Sphere*, and Jill Roe's review article, 'Modernisation and Sexism: Recent Writings on Victorian Women', *Victorian Studies* XX (1977), 179–92.

32. Mrs. Craik, in *A Woman's Thoughts about Women* (London 1858), explains that women are 'mercifully constituted with less temptation to sin than men': a notable instance of the way the Victorian idealisation of women contradicted the older, Pauline teaching about their inherent sinfulness. See Françoise Basch, *Relative Creatures* (London 1974), pp. 3–4 and *passim*.

33. Quotations from Clough and Blanche are from chapter X of Robindra Kumar Biswas, *Arthur Hugh Clough* (Oxford 1972).

34. Laurence Lerner, *Love and Marriage: Literature and its Social Context* (London 1979), p. 153.

35. Florence Nightingale's 'Cassandra' was published in full for the first time in Ray Strachey's *The Cause: A Short History of the Women's Movement in Great Britain* (1928). Quotations here are from the paperback edn (London 1978), pp. 395–418.

36. John Stuart Mill, *The Subjection of Women*. Unless otherwise indicated, quotations from Mill are from this essay: text from *John Stuart Mill: Three Essays*, edited and with an introduction by Richard Wollheim (London and Oxford 1975).

37. Quoted from Patricia Hollis, *Women in Public, 1850–1900: Documents of the Victorian Women's Movement* (London 1979), p. 9.

38. See W. R. Greg, 'Why are Women Redundant?' in his *Literary and Social Judgements* (London 1868), and originally in the *National Review* (April 1862).

39. See her two articles, 'Celibacy v. Marriage' and 'What Shall We Do with Our Old Maids?' in *Fraser's Magazine* LXV (1862), 228–35, and LXVI (1862), 594–610. The passage quoted is on p. 597 of the second article.

40. John Stuart Mill, *Principles of Political Economy* (1848), paperback edn (Harmondsworth 1970), p. 125.

41. For the relationship between 'freedom' and 'utility', see ch. 5 of C. L. Ten, *Mill On Liberty* (Oxford 1980).

42. *On Liberty*, in *John Stuart Mill: Three Essays*, p. 87.

43. Gertrude Himmelfarb, in *On Liberty and Liberalism* (New York 1974) and

Susan Moller Okin, in *Women in Western Political Thought* (London 1980), both discuss the relationship between *The Subjection of Women* and *On Liberty*. Mill's feminism is generally taken as a special application of his liberalism: Himmelfarb argues that Mill's sympathy with feminism led him to what she considers an extreme and untenable form of liberalism.
44. Alice S. Rossi (ed.), *Essays on Sex Equality. John Stuart Mill and Harriet Taylor Mill* (London 1970), pp. 84–5. The passage is commented upon by Derek Gill in his *Illegitimacy, Sexuality and the Status of Women* (Oxford 1977), p. 167.
45. See Dora Russell, *Hypatia* (London 1925), pp. 23–5; Germaine Greer, *The Female Eunuch*, paperback edn (London 1971), p. 67.
46. Maria Grey, *On the Special Requirements for Improving the Education of Girls* (London 1872): quoted from Bauer and Ritt, *op. cit.* p. 119.
47. 'Celibacy v. Marriage', p. 234, and 'What Shall We Do with Our Old Maids?' p. 596.
48. Millicent Garret Fawcett, 'The Education of Women of the Middle and Upper Classes', *Macmillan's Magazine* XVII (1868), pp. 511–17. Feminists of a later generation found this an especially unpalatable argument.
49. Emily Faithfull, 'The Unfit Employments in which Women are Engaged', in the *Victoria Magazine* (November 1863): quoted from J.A. and Olive Banks' invaluable *Feminism and Family Planning in Victorian England* (Liverpool 1964), p. 41.
50. James Allan MacGrigor, 'On the Real Differences in the Minds of Men and Women', *Anthropological Review* 7 (1869), cxcvi.
51. George J. Romanes, 'Mental Differences Between Men and Women', *Nineteenth Century* XXI (1887), 654–72.
52. See, for example, W. L. Distant, 'On the Mental Differences Between the Sexes', *Journal of the Royal Anthropological Institute* IV (1874), 78–87. *See* Jill Conway, 'Stereotypes of Femininity in a Theory of Evolution', in *Suffer and Be Still*, for discussion of similar arguments in the work of Patrick Geddes and J. Arthur Thomson.
53. 'The Probable Retrogression of Women', *Saturday Review* 32 (1871), 11.
54. *Fortnightly Review* XXI (1874), 446–83. Maudsley seems to have been following Herbert Spencer, whose *Education, Intellectual, Moral and Physical* appeared in 1861.
55. 'Sex in Mind and Education: A Reply', *Fortnightly Review* XXI (1874), 582–94.
56. For callisthenics, see Paul Atkinson, 'Fitness, Feminism and Schooling', in Delamont and Duffin, *op. cit.*; for bicycling, see David Rubinstein, 'Cycling in the 1890s', *Victorian Studies* XXI (1977), 47–71; for dress reform, see Stella Mary Newton, *Health, Art and Reason* (London 1974).
57. The *Saturday Review* ran a series of articles under the title 'Dies Dominae' in May and June 1895, by 'A Woman of the Day', with rejoinders by Lady Jeune. The quotation is from *S.R.* 79 (1895), 688.
58. See E. Lynn Linton, *The Girl of the Period and Other Social Essays*, 2 vols. (London 1883): most of these essays were reprinted from periodicals such as the *Saturday Review*.
59. For fuller treatment of the property laws, see Lee Holcombe, 'Victorian Wives and Property: Reform of the Married Women's Property Law, 1857–82', in *A Widening Sphere*. A full-length study by the same author has been announced for 1983.
60. *Hansard*, 18 May 1870: quoted from Patricia Hollis, *op. cit.* pp. 195–6.
61. Ralph Thicknesse, 'The New Legal Position of Married Women', *Blackwood's*

Magazine CXXXIII (1883), 207–20: the passage quoted is on p. 218 (italics added).

62. 'The Married Women's Property Act (1882)', *Chamber's Journal* XIX (1882), 819–21.

63. Even under the 1857 Act, divorce remained too expensive for most people. Following the Matrimonial Causes Act of 1878, and various later amendments, English law had in effect two sets of procedures: for the affluent, divorce from a centralised divorce court; for the less well off, a system of separation and maintenance orders granted by the magistrates' courts. This continued until it was possible to seek legal aid after the Second World War.

64. For a fuller account of English divorce law, *see* O. R. McGregor, *Divorce in England* (London 1957).

65. Owen Chadwick, *The Victorian Church*, 2 vols. (London 1966), I. 482.

66. Quoted from S. B. Kitchin, *A History of Divorce*, p. 194.

67. Quoted from Fraser Harrison, *The Dark Angel*, p. 10.

68. See the article on 'The Marriage and Divorce Bill', *North British Review* XXVII (1857), 162–93: the passage quoted appears on p. 173.

69. Keith Thomas, 'The Double Standard', *Journal of the History of Ideas* 20 (1959), 195–216: the quotation is from p. 216.

70. See Judith R. Walkowitz, *Prostitution and Victorian Society*, paperback edn (Cambridge 1982), p. 187; and Paul McHugh, *Prostitution and Victorian Social Reform* (London 1980), p. 147.

71. Paul McHugh, *op. cit.* pp. 64, 167–8.

72. Report of the Royal Commission, quoted from Millicent Fawcett and E. M. Turner, *Josephine Butler* (London 1927), p. 68.

73. Josephine Butler's diary, September 1869, quoted by Michael Pearson, *The Age of Consent* (Newton Abbott 1972), p. 58.

74. Mona Caird, 'Marriage' and 'Ideal Marriage', *Westminster Review* CXXX (1888), 186–201 and 617–36: the passages quoted appear on pp. 635 and 195. See also her *The Morality of Marriage and Other Essays on the Status and Destiny of Women* (London 1897).

75. Elizabeth Rachel Chapman, 'Marriage Rejection and Marriage Reform', *Westminster Review* CXXX (1888), 358–77.

76. Karl Pearson, *The Ethic of Freethought* (London 1888), p. 389. (This volume includes two papers by Pearson first printed separately, on 'The Woman's Question' and on 'Socialism and Sex': both attracted much attention in feminist circles.) Hinton's views were summarised by Havelock Ellis in two articles, 'James Hinton as Religious Thinker', *The Modern Review* (October 1881), and 'Hinton's Later Thought', *Mind* (July 1884): the quotation is from the second article.

77. Karl Pearson, *op. cit.* p. 371; see also Grant Allen, 'Plain Words on the Woman Question', *Fortnightly Review* LII (1889), 448–58.

78. Judith Walkowitz, *op. cit.* p. 255.

79. The first two quotations are from 'How Shall We Solve the Divorce Problem?' *Nash's Magazine* 5 (1912), 677, and the third from Frederic Harrison, 'The Emancipation of Women', *Fortnightly Review* LVI (1891), 448.

80. Eleanor Marx and Edward Aveling, 'The Woman Question: From a Socialist Point of View', *Westminster Review* CXXV (1886), 207–22, for the argument and quotation.

81. See Jeffrey Weeks, *Sex, Politics and Society* (London 1981), ch. 9, on 'Feminism and Socialism'. E. P. Thompson quotes Morris' letter to Charles Faulkner, 16 October 1886, giving Morris' views on marriage under socialism, in *William Morris: Romantic to Revolutionary*, rev. edn (London 1977), pp. 707–9.

82. Karl Pearson, *op. cit.* pp. 445 and 389. For the context of Pearson's views, see Jeffrey Weeks, *op. cit.* ch. 7, on 'The Population Question in the Early Twentieth Century'.
83. In a letter of 1911 to Havelock Ellis, quoted in Ruth First and Ann Scott, *Olive Schreiner* (London 1980), p. 291.
84. *The George Eliot Letters* (ed. by Gordon S. Haight), 7 vols. (New Haven 1954–5), IV. 468.
85. See F. K. Prochaska, *op. cit.* ch. 6, 'In Streets and "Dens of Vice"'.
86. These included the Social Purity Alliance (1873), the Moral Reform Union (1881), and the National Vigilance Association (1885): many of them were run mainly or largely by women. See Edward J. Bristow, *Vice and Vigilance. Purity Movements in Britain since 1700* (Dublin 1977).
87. *Josephine Butler*, pp. 27–8.
88. Richard Evans points out that moderate middle-class feminists were defending the interests of their class in advancing the status of the family: an orderly family life was seen as an inducement to the working man to remain sober and industrious. See Richard J. Evans, *The Feminists* (London 1977), pp. 35–6.
89. Olive Schreiner, quoted by Lloyd Fernando, *'New Women' in the Late Victorian Novel* (Pennsylvania 1977), p. 20.

Index